IF GONDOLAS COULD TALK

JOHN HEMMING-CLARK

101 SUPERLATIVE SHORT SKI STORIES FROM THE SNOWY SLOPES AND BEYOND

© Searchline Publishing 2022
First edition 2022

ISBN: 978 1 897864 68 5

British Library Cataloguing in Publication Data available.

Published by Searchline Publishing, Searchline House
Holbrook Lane, Chislehurst, Kent, BR7 6PE, UK

Tel: +44 (0)20 8468 7945

www.johnhemmingclark.com

All rights reserved

No part of this publication may be reproduced, or stored in a retrieval system, or transmitted, in any form or by any means, mechanical, electronic, photocopying, recording or otherwise, without the permission of Searchline Publishing.

Printed in England by www.catfordprint.co.uk

If Gondolas Could Talk is mostly based on actual events. Some individuals' names, business names and place names have been changed.

Written, compiled and edited from contributions, by John Hemming-Clark.

Pixie Lott photo acknowledgement: Paul Robertson
Long ski photo acknowledgement: Ali Couper

Front cover and drawings by John Hemming-Clark

Dedicated to Eva Nilsson who taught me to ski and thus saved me from a second year of thinking I didn't need lessons.

Thanks to Joelle, Billy, Willy, Michael, Steve and Linda, Joey, Steve and Annie, Jo, Debs, Debra, Jack, Dan, Katie, Louise and Neil, Guy, Martin, Gary, Tom, Jimmy, Mark, Phillip, Paul, Webbo, Connor, Jackie, Bev, Jane, Lynne, Peter, Neil, Michelle, Tony and Sue, Simon, David, Ali, Matt, Charles and Zoë and everyone else I have ever skied with, crashed into, shared a flugel or two with, or just chatted to about skiing experiences. Special thanks to Susie whose ski hood incident remains in my top five. Some of our experiences are quite simply unbelievable and that's why I've included them.

Acknowledgements to so many other contributors. All of them wanted, perfectly understandably, to remain anonymous.

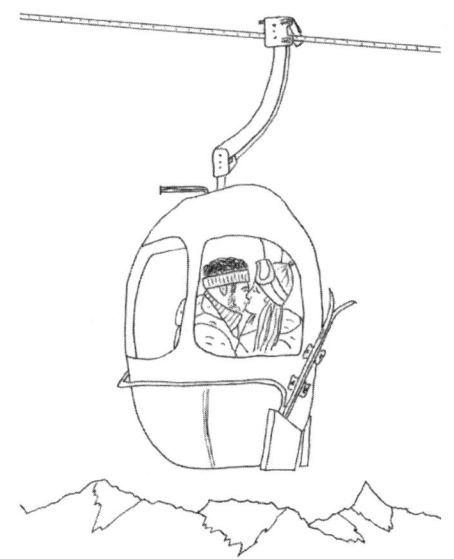

Contents...page

Alpe d'Huez...1
Les Arcs...6
Aspen...10
Avoriaz...14
Banff...17
Beaver Creek...22
Bourg-en-Bresse...26
Bourg-Saint-Maurice...30
Brides-les-Bains...32
Calais...36
Cervinia...43
Chalet Girl Shorts...45
Chamonix...53
Courchevel...60
Davos...63
Les Deux Alpes...66
England...68
Flaine...72
Le Fornet...75
Geneva...78
Les Gets...83
Gstaad...88
Heathrow...92
Les Houches...95
Ischgl...98
Lenk...101

Le Lioran...109
Mayrhofen...112
Méribel...127
Méribel Les Allues...130
Morillon...135
Obergurgl...138
On the Motorway...141
Passo Tonale...143
Le Péage...147
La Rivière Enverse...150
La Rosière...155
Saint-Dizier...157
Saint-Dizier outskirts...162
Sainte Foy...168
Sestriere...175
Shorts...179
Le Snow Train...220
Swiss Alps...225
Tignes...231
Troyes...233
Val d'Isère...237
Vercland...246
Wengen...250
Zell am See...254
Zermatt...263
Zürs...266

Introduction

I was sitting on the terrace of La Rosée Blanche at the bottom of the ski slopes in La Daille, part of Val d'Isère's vast Espace Killy ski area, sipping on a large, cold *pression*. It was late afternoon on a beautiful early March day. My wife, friends and I had just bypassed La Folie Douce, a crazy open air bar at the top of the several runs that we could now see in front of us, and descended OK Coupe du Monde that runs all the way down from the top of Bellevarde. We decided on this more genteel après ski venue as it's an almost obligatory stop after tackling the challenging red slope that is used for the women's World Cup.

I was watching several games of human skittles taking place on the other red, as dozens of hopelessly out of control (mostly) English skiers, fuelled by afternoon excesses, attempted to get down to the valley floor as quickly as possible, not necessarily particularly skilfully. Some were succeeding rather too well. I turned to Will. "That reminds me. Have I ever told you about the time I played skittles in a bar in Austria?" Will sighed; he had heard that story a dozen times before. However the couple sitting next to us hadn't. "Tell us," they said and in return they told us a couple of theirs. "Everyone seems to have a ski story," Will pondered aloud. "You have quite a few Johnnie, you should write them down." So I did and, along with those from various other contributors, both young and old, the best are now in this book. They're mostly an Alpine A to Z, from Alpe d'Huez to Zürs with a few other resorts from further afield plus related ferry, airport, motorway, snow train, over-night stops and a section of ultra-short "Chalet Girl Shorts" and "Shorts" stories thrown in for good measure.

I hope that you enjoy them as much as my family, friends, complete strangers and I enjoyed experiencing them!
John Hemming-Clark

Alpe d'Huez

Sharing a shower with a snowboard, disappearing into a snow hollow, snow chain snag and a vanishing hotel. Not bad for one trip.

One of my friends had purchased, some years ago, an apartment in a soulless concrete block in Alpe d'Huez, however itself a fantastic resort for sun and skiing. Not for nothing is it called, "The island in the sun." It has La Sarenne, a black run that is the longest in Europe if not the world.

Six of us stayed in this tiny but homely apartment. It had two double bunk beds in the corridor and a sitting room with sofa bed, and a sort of kitchen in the wall. There was a toilet and a bathroom with small bath plus shower hose, and a sink. You could open the door of the apartment, climb onto one bunk bed then jump onto the next and from there leap onto the sofa and another leap onto the balcony without once touching the floor. But it did for us, well most of us. Five of us were all skiers but Michael was a snowboarder* which was fine until he found that the ski locker on the lower ground floor was so tiny that he couldn't fit his macho snowboard in without leaving the door open which would somehow defeat the object. He had to find somewhere else to store it. As a result this was the one and only ski holiday I have ever taken where I've had to have a shower every evening with a snowboard instead of, as has happened once or twice in my time, a snowboarder - albeit of the female variety.

To get from the airport to the resort we had hired a minibus. When we went to pick it up we found that it was a brand spanking new Mercedes Sprinter. "Look after it," said the young lady on reception. I asked her if she had any snow chains and she handed me a set. "You won't be needing them," she advised me with a smile. "There's not much snow around in the forecast for a while."

One of our number, Simon, only lasted one night in the apartment before going off in a huff first thing in the morning with all his stuff and a dreadful hangover but no directional ability to check into a hotel, having made a full complaint to the rest of us centred around claustrophobia, night noises and bad smells. He had a point. He tried several places before he eventually found one that had availability and had paid up front for the week to get the best rate that was still eye-wateringly high. We met back up at the Alpauris chair lift an hour later to go over to Auris. We reckoned this part of the mountain would be quieter than the more immediate pistes due to the ski schools not venturing too far from the main centre at the beginning of the week. Auris has some great and varied skiing but this scare-chair chair lift is fun enough in its own right. It appears to go nowhere more exciting than on the level underneath the altiport runway however it then drops steeply down to the bottom of the Sarenne gorge before suddenly ascending up the other side. For anyone that's been on Val d'Isère's own scare chair, the Leissières Express, also known as the "Up and oh-ver," that takes you over the top of the valley wall, Alpauris comes a close second going down and up rather than up and down. (I've been on the Leissières Express a number of times. Once I found some *pisteurs* perched on the ridge with their shovels freeing up some of the snow to ensure a smooth passage for the riders who would otherwise experience a sort of mechanised powder off-piste for a few metres. On another occasion I watched four women on the chair lift in front of me lift up the restraining bar just before the ridge and jump off - a very risky manoeuvre for one would have about a two second window before the jump would result in a fall of some considerable distance. By the time that we reached the ridge and gone over the women were already halfway down to Le Fornet, skiing and not tumbling fortunately.)

Despite the vehicle hire lady assuring us that snow was not in the air, once we had arrived at our apartment it started to snow and continued to snow throughout the night. It was everywhere! Snow can come down the size of cotton wool balls. Not just on the immaculately groomed pistes but off the pistes, on the roads, on the pavements, truly a winter wonderland. From the top Michael decided to take his Lynx Africaed snowboard slightly off piste but then disappeared. I have heard of and seen static skiers disappearing under moving avalanches but never vice-versa. There was a huge snow hollow to one side of the piste that was full of recently fallen snow. Michael had tried to snowboard it but had encountered a gap in the snow drift, a bit like very soft falls of snow around tree trunks, and literally all but disappeared. We found him soon enough, we just sniffed. He rejoined us with the comment, "If you want to get the taste of powder, first you have to eat it." "Looking at the state of you I reckon you've just had a five course meal," Simon replied.

After skiing the blues and reds we headed back to the scare chair that one can join from the bottom of the valley, having gone into the excellent La Combe Haute restaurant for a rather long lunch. Back in Alpe d'Huez we slid down a few of the easy blues before deciding to have an early après ski. We staggered out of Smithy's several hours later and made our way back to our apartment. It's not the easiest resort to find one's way around initially, especially as we were staying out on one of its extremities but we knew we were behind a car skid circuit so when we found that we could get our bearings. It was only once we were inside our flat and beginning to take it in turns reacquainting ourselves with Michael's snowboard that Simon suddenly realised that he was no longer staying in this apartment but was now in a hotel. We arranged to meet back in Smithy's for an aperitif in an hour's time and sent him on his way. When Simon eventually turned up still in his ski gear it was to inform us that he had yet to have a shower as he couldn't remember which hotel he had booked into. Poor old Simon! We arrived on the Saturday, he had checked in, out and in on Sunday and he still hadn't found his hotel by Wednesday. By that time not only he but all of his clothes he was wearing smelt of Lynx Africa. At least he had a bunk bed to sleep in but no night clothes and his day clothes were drying every evening. That Wednesday evening he finally went out and bought a new ski bag, jeans, tops, underwear, wash kit, thermals and pyjamas.

During the week I had to drive some of the party back to the airport for them to return home. As I drove down the steep mountain road that regularly forms, with its twenty-one hairpin bends, part of the Tour de France cycle race, it began to snow again. By the time we were on the main road to Grenoble it was pouring with rain. We reached the airport with stacks of time but something wasn't right. The lights were out. The airport was closed. No, Grenoble airport does not stay open all night; it shuts its doors and turns off the lights. Mark checked the tickets. "Silly me, we're flying back from Lyon." We made it, but only just.

As I climbed back up the twenty-one hairpin road and the rain turned to heavy snow I knew that I was going to have to put the snow chains on at some point. On a straight but steep stretch I stopped and got them out. If there's one thing I always do now before driving to the Alps it's have a dry run with the snow chains although it wouldn't have helped me much on this particular occasion as I had been given the completely wrong size of chain. They may have fitted a Mini but that was about it. I tried my best but after just a few meters they became mangled round the back axle and I ground to a halt. I jumped out, locked the minibus and began to walk. I managed to get hold of Simon on my mobile and he sent a cab down the mountain to pick me up. In the morning when I returned with the cab driver I found all the snow cleared apart from under the minibus. It was in its own little snowdrift. I failed to extract the snow chains completely so left them partially wrapped round the back wheels and drove back up the mountain. You can only imagine what I was thinking when I eventually returned the minibus to the hire place with the chains still *in situ* having rattled all the way along the wet motorway for an hour and a bit. I said to the lady at the hire desk when she asked where the snow chains were, "They're sort of on the two back wheels." Her reply was, "You're only supposed to put snow chains on when it's been snowing sir." I didn't reply, I just sighed.

Simon never did find his hotel.

*An alpine (downhill) skier is one who thinks that Nordic (cross-country) skiing isn't dangerous enough. A snowboarder is someone who feels that alpine skiing isn't lethal enough.

Les Arcs

Never mess with chalet staff's night off.

Four Arc villages come together to provide mile after mile of intermediate cruising in this snow-sure purpose-built resort that's accessible from the TGV / Eurostar station at Bourg-St-Maurice.

I was there with my wife and three other couples. We had rented a very attractive chalet near the slopes that came with its own staff of two: one was the chef, the other the waitress and maid, that sort of thing.

We were on half board which meant a cooked breakfast and dinner. The standard of the food was very high and so evenings were mostly spent in the chalet, lingering over our meal. We were allowed half a bottle of wine each per evening meal so used to get the equivalent of four bottles every evening. We could always get a top-up if we paid but after après ski we found that our free ration was usually more than enough.

On the Tuesday evening, Mary, our waitress etc., told us that the staff day off was Wednesday and, although breakfast would be left out, we would have to fend for ourselves at dinner time. Ordinarily this would mean going out somewhere to eat but we decided that we always did that when we went skiing and so, to ring the changes, we would eat in. The only problem with this was that a catered chalet set-up isn't designed around the guests taking over the kitchen for the evening. The fridge and freezer were full of the chef's food for us, the cupboards had the tins that he needed plus herbs and spices and other culinary delights.

We didn't care. They hadn't told us we couldn't eat in so we decided that that was what we were going to do.

After après ski the following day we came home, had a shower and then went to the Sherpa supermarket which was always well stocked with everything we would ever need, whatever resort we were in. Once back at the chalet, after fighting our way through something of a blizzard, we set to work on preparing a fairly basic but appetising meal, making full use of the chef's oils and other staples and condiments. We were getting close to having the meal ready and on the point of serving when one of my friends remarked, "We don't have any wine!" This had the potential of being a catastrophe. No one had thought to buy any alcohol as it had always been provided on the previous days. Remembering the saying, attributed to basically everyone, "A meal without wine is like a day without sunshine," there was no argument when I suggested that we had to have wine; where there was some disagreement was in the discussion on where we were going to source it. Unfortunately the supermarket was a five minute walk away without the blizzard and no one was particularly keen on doing the trek. "I have an idea," said Derek, and that's where it all started to go horribly wrong.

Derek was a locksmith and another of our group, Tony, was a carpenter which was possibly the reason for Derek formulating a practical solution that didn't involve going back out into the snow. "I know where Mary keeps the wine," he said as if none of the rest of us knew. "It's in the cupboard under the stairs in the hallway. She keeps it in huge five gallon drums from which she fills the bottles up. I'm sure we can just help ourselves. She didn't say we couldn't," he added as if not saying something was prohibited meant that it was okay. This was a bit of perverse logic but we had had a few drinks already and so a measure of rational thinking had already gone out of the window.

Derek and Tony went off in search of a five gallon drum of wine but, sadly, came back empty-handed. "It's unbelievable!" Derek announced. "The door's locked!" "There's your answer then," I said. "It's prohibited." "It may be prohibited but this is an emergency; I'm sure we can justify breaking in," said Derek. "We don't need to break in," said Tony. "All we have to do is remove the lock." And that is what they did. Between the two of them they unscrewed the catch that the padlock was on. This took a bit of time because the screws were very long and two of them were quite difficult to get at because the padlock was in the way which is probably the point. Then they were told that dinner was ready but they were now on a roll to get to the wine. "What happens if Mary walks in now?" was not the right question to ask this intrepid pair although both were no doubt thinking it themselves.

They finally removed the padlock and opened the hasp but the door didn't open because there was also a lock built into the body of the thick door. Derek said that he could get it opened and he did, but it took him long enough. Still, we learnt a few tricks along the way on how to get locked doors open. Derek managed to pick the lock and finally we could open the door. Our excitement didn't last very long because we then found another door inside the first one! But Derek reckoned that he could open this one also. He succeeded after about ten minutes and received a round of applause for his trouble. With padlocks, brackets, hasps, screws and the improvised tools of Derek's trade littering the ground he turned the handle. It opened! There was no light so I went and fetched a torch. Dinner was over-ready and all we needed was a few decanted bottles of red. I gave my powerful torch to Derek and he pointed it into the cupboard. Then he screamed. He actually, physically screamed. The wine had gone. He went and found a more powerful torch and shone the light all over the vast cupboard. There was definitely nothing resembling alcohol, just a load of tinned food, and we had plenty of that, all getting cold.

By the time that the pair of them had unscrewed the outer door, unpicked the inner door lock, replaced the padlock and brackets and hasp and not relocked the inner door because, as Derek explained, "...unlocking is easy, but locking a door without a key is almost impossible," we had been waiting around forty minutes for our wine. "It would have been quicker twice over going down to the supermarket and buying a few bottles," was not the right thing for me to say given the circumstances we found ourselves in. Strangely, mysteriously, the wine was back in the cupboard in its drums the following evening. No one dared asked Mary how she performed her disappearing wine trick; if the truth be told, we probably all knew.

Aspen

An unexpected birthday celebration gift that wasn't.

I had been looking forward to my ski trip to Aspen for months. With its top-notch hotels and great skiing it's not for nothing known as one of the top resorts in the world. The only downside was that I had left the booking of the hotel to my husband Martin's cheapskate mate Nick and he did himself proud as usual. Whereas the other couple in our threecouplesome, Patrick and Penny, had booked one of the best hotels in the resort - that they had been to once before, I was left to slum it with my husband and Nick and Val in a hotel that had no indoor swimming pool and only two restaurants. Patrick and Penny, on the other hand, had three restaurants and a café and an indoor pool as well as an outdoor one. I was not at all impressed and told Nick so. He tried to tell me that the other hotel was fully booked so I rang it up and guess what? It wasn't. Then Nick tried to complain about me to Martin and said that he was on a budget but Martin wasn't having any of it either. He told Nick that our hotel was beyond expensive and it was just that the other hotel was beyond expensive - plus.

What really annoyed me though was in the weeks running up to the holiday. It wasn't that Patrick had gone off on his own and booked the posh place, he just assumed from our conversations, as did I, that we were all going to be staying there. However, once he realised that the four of us would be slumming it all he could do was rub it in at every opportunity. It came to a head on the day of travel when we were on the flight together. We discovered that Patrick had a private transfer from Denver that had been arranged by his hotel while we had to go on a shuttle bus. Disgraceful! I was not happy.

I tried not to moan too much as I seemed to be alone in my annoyance; even Val didn't seem that bothered, but when Patrick 'phoned from his car to tell us that they were only an hour away from Aspen and he had just rung the hotel to book a spa package for them both for the moment they arrived, whilst we were at least two hours away with nothing booked I actually felt the tide was turning in my direction. Val said that Penny had asked her on the 'plane if money was an issue and she said that it wasn't and that there had been a bit of a mix up with bookings to which Penny had just said, "Oh," like she totally disbelieved her. "Let us ring the hotel for Patrick," Nick suddenly suggested, "and order a few extras."

Martin found the number online and when the minibus driver pulled over for a comfort break we all jumped out and Nick rang the hotel. When the 'phone was answered Nick put it on loudspeaker and said, "Oh hello, it's Mr Kee here. I rang a short while ago to book a spa and I wonder..." "Yes, Mr Kee," said the voice at the other end, "You spoke to me, David. What can I do for you now?" Nick looked a bit worried but he needn't have. English accents sound all the same to Americans and vice-versa. "The thing is David," said Nick. "We've just stopped for a quick break and my wife has gone off to the toilet. What I couldn't tell you before is that it's her birthday today and I wonder if you..." "Mr Kee," said David. "What you need is our birthday celebration package. Say no more. I will get onto housekeeping immediately and they can pop everything in your room. Would you like white or pink Champagne?" "Er, white please. Is it French?" "Of course sir. Leave it to us. Will there be anything else?" "Could I have some flowers?" "That's part of the package, you won't be disappointed." "Just one last thing," said Nick. "Please don't mention the birthday to my wife or leave any cards or tags with 'Happy

Birthday' on them. She's a bit sort of sensitive about this kind of thing now she's getting a bit, um, older." "Certainly sir, we can manage that for you."

How Nick managed to keep a straight face I've no idea but as soon as he rang off we fell about laughing. We were still giggling when the driver returned. He must have thought we were mad! We heard no more from Patrick and Penny as it was quite late when we arrived in the resort but we met up on the slopes the following day at the top of Summit Express. It was Martin who asked first, "How's the hotel Patrick?" It was Penny who replied first. "It's delightful. Even better than last time. You really should have made the effort you guys." "So what's improved?" asked Nick. "I'll tell you what's improved old chap," said Patrick unable to contain himself any longer, "it's the welcome. We've been greeted like old friends. They obviously remembered us although frankly that's the sort of thing that happens with top end hotels like ours. When we got to our room there was a bottle of chilled Champagne on ice with two flutes, a huge bouquet of flowers, an enormous box of chocolates and some Champagne truffles, rose petals sprinkled liberally all over the bed, and a Water Wood candle. It was totally unexpected but that's what you get when you stay at the best. We opened the Champagne and had a quick glass before we went for our spa that was also wonderful. And now we need to do some skiing to blast off the cobwebs. When we stop for elevenses the drinks are on us!" They certainly were and I made sure that I got a glass of Champagne as did Val. And a top up.

The skiing was superb with plenty of blues (which are European reds) and blacks; we had a great ten days. We even went to Patrick and Penny's hotel for a drink once or twice. We didn't see David but just to make sure that nobody recognised his accent Nick did plenty of nodding and not much talking when there were any staff around. It wasn't until we met Patrick and Penny back at the airport that we revisited the deception. "How was your minibar bill Patrick?" Martin innocently asked. "That was the least of my problems," he replied morosely. "When I went to settle up, the biggest individual expense on the bill was for a birthday celebration package. I had no idea what it was for and, in any case, it's certainly not mine or Penny's birthday, so I queried it. The receptionist said, 'Didn't you get Champagne, flowers and chocolates and maybe a few other bits in your room?' and I said that we had but we assumed it was because we were regulars and that the hotel was just making us feel welcome. Then she tapped a bit on her keyboard and then told us that according to her records we had only been to the hotel once before. I didn't disagree but said that how was I to know that the hotel staff didn't make friends quickly? Then she said that the birthday celebration package was never free and that someone called David had placed the order and she would need to speak to him and I said, 'Fine, sort it out while I wait.' Unfortunately she couldn't get hold of him as it was his day off. Then I started to get a bit annoyed because we needed to get to the airport but she said that she had to speak to a manager and told us to go and sit down. After about ten minutes she came over and said that we could go." "And what happened to the birthday celebration package cost?" I asked trying not to sound too interested. "They just scrubbed it off the bill," said Patrick, "and then we left."

We've never told Patrick and Penny what really happened but we will one day. However, I've got a feeling that they're now just about to find out.

Avoriaz

Red run bombing with a ski glove.

The first time I went here when I was thirteen I was very impressed by much of the futuristic architecture that is quite a talking point in ski circles. The resort is part of the vast Portes du Soleil area that takes in twelve villages. You can even go and ski in Switzerland!

I considered myself quite a good skier even then as did my friend, Ali, who came with my family on the holiday. I was mortified to discover that mum had put us both in one of the beginner but not absolute beginner classes. I was super unimpressed. There were eight of us in our group and a couple of them weren't very good but that was their problem. We went up this six-man chair lift called *Grandes Combes* and then we had to ski down this boring blue and then up again. The two of us were allowed to go up unaccompanied because we had skied before. Our ski instructor, Julian, was very nice so we asked him if we could do some reds but he said no as that was too advanced for the group we were in. It was time to hatch a plan.

One year my mum had dropped her glove off a chair lift by accident but unfortunately the place that she chose was manky off piste that wasn't suitable for skiing on. It was all hard windblown ridges but she had to go down it to retrieve her glove, much to the amusement of those in the chair lift above. Every few seconds she would look up above her and respond to shouted comments with, "I'M GETTING MY GLOVE!" The *Grandes Combes* went over the blue that we had skied down but it also crossed over a red. Ali took off a glove and, with precision targeted bombing, dropped it so that it fell at the side of the red piste on a steep section and behind a small mound of snow. She had decided that no one was likely to stop and pick it up and she was correct.

When we reached the top of the lift, just as Julian made to take us down the blue yet again, I said that Ali had dropped her glove and that it had landed on the red run. There was nothing for it but for all of us to ski down the red after Ali said that she had to get it or her mum would go mad. "I can always go on my own," she said, knowing full well what the answer would be. It was red from almost top to bottom and was exhilarating though some of the others struggled and Julian wasn't very happy but at least we were doing some proper runs. We were onto a good thing - what a team! We repeated the same trick only this time with my glove. However I think our mistake was to drop my glove in exactly the same place as Ali's before because when we told Julian at the top this time he didn't look very impressed. He didn't say anything though so when we got to the bottom of the red we decided that we were both going to drop our gloves onto the black that we crossed at the top. The only problem was that Julian by now had smelt a rat and rather than let us go up by ourselves again he got on the lift with us and between us. This was a real pain because it stopped any communication between the two of us. I did consider for a moment texting but that would have looked a bit suspicious apart from the fact that I may well have dropped my 'phone and not even on purpose so it could have ended up anywhere and, if on a piste, skied over. "Now then ladies," he said once we started to ascend, "I don't know how you managed to drop your gloves, one after the other, in exactly the same position so I feel that maybe there's more to it. I'm not accusing in the strictest sense; I'm just suggesting. So, as we need to do some more blues so that I can get some teaching in and do some exercises, I've come on your lift just to make sure that this time you keep your gloves on and don't, um, accidently or any other way drop one or maybe two of them or even three or all four of them."

I thought at this point that our luck had run out but I hadn't reckoned on clever, intelligent Ali. I underestimated how determined she was to get on the black. I couldn't work out what she was up to but as she was squirming about in her seat I thought that she maybe had piles. As we crossed over the black at the top of the lift and with Julian staring at us both in turn as he had earlier when we were going over the red Ali let out a little squeal. "What's the matter Ali?" Julian asked, slightly shocked. Ali dramatically peered over the side of the chair we were on. "Oh dear Julian, look! I seem to have dropped my skis!"

Five minutes later and I was on the black with Julian and a load of screaming kids. Ali hadn't thought it completely through though. She had to walk down - the blue. She even had to endure some guys going past shouting, "Get some lessons!" Still, it was worth it and the following day mum put us in a proper class.

Banff

A janitor in the john causes cringe worthy confusion.

A few years ago when ski brochures were printed by all the major tour operators, I picked up a Thomson Holidays' copy and turned to the first page. "NEW for..." whatever year it was. "CANADA!" "Why not?" I thought and turned to the prices. The pound was going through one of its regular downturns and holidays to Europe were looking quite expensive. Canada, by comparison, seemed good value especially as a trip would have been for ten days.

Thomson was offering Banff Springs Hotel, a huge seven hundred and fifty plus bedroom building that looked as though it had been modelled on a baronial castle. The only connection with Scotland is that the name was chosen for William Davidson, the first European settler to that part of Canada. Davidson had grown up near to Banff in Scotland as had another Scotsman after whom the town was named. I rang Thomson up and was surprised to find that the hotel was fully booked for the dates that I wanted. With over seven hundred and fifty beds I surmised that possibly what was meant, to be more accurate, was that the Thomson allocation was fully booked so I rang the hotel direct. They had plenty of availability. It was time for a spot of D I Y.

I booked a flight to Amsterdam then a jumbo to Calgary, hired a car and then reserved a room at the hotel for ten days, all for less than a package to France for a week. The hotel was magnificent, out of this world, certainly by Alpine standards. I went with my wife and she was equally impressed. There were several themed restaurants in the complex including Italian and Japanese and in the grounds you could have German-inspired mountain dishes in a

Bavarian-style cottage which we booked for our second evening. The lower ground floor of the hotel was almost completely taken over by shops.

On the first afternoon after skiing we met a load of sales reps, huge hunks of meat with necks as wide as their heads. Sometimes it was difficult to work out where their necks stopped and their heads started. They were everywhere! A group of them were in one of the large lounges necking beers and scoffing nachos. My wife and I squeezed in-between a couple of them on a sofa and started to chat. We discovered that they all worked for Compaq, at the time a huge, American computer company and our trip coincided with Compaq's North America sales division's annual convention in the hotel. There was much loud, testosterone-fuelled talk, back-slapping and high jinks in evidence, mostly exclusively male. My wife was terrified and so was I! Nevertheless, seated among the reps (we had no choice as they were sprawled around the large lounge) we soon became their greatest friends. "You're from Eeeenglaaaand?!" (There weren't many Englanders in the hotel apart from, presumably, a smattering of Thomson clients but we never met them.)

My wife lost no time in starting to work through the facilities and services that were on offer. That first afternoon whilst we were having a drink and wondering where the Compaq boys put all the nachos that they described as a light snack, she sneaked off for a few minutes and booked up a full-body massage for the following evening.

The skiing was great. Although the ski resorts are a drive away the nearest is only ten minutes in the car. There are three resorts, the nearest is Mount Norquay, then Sunshine

Village and then Lake Louise which is a forty-five minute drive. Mount Norquay is the smallest of the three but there's still plenty of skiing, Sunshine Village has some of the highest skiing in Canada and Lake Louise has one of the largest ski areas in North America so there's plenty of variety.

In the late afternoon the following day, once we had returned to our room (number 716 - it's ingrained on my memory), a room that had a similar floor space to that of the whole of some houses in the UK, my wife said that she had to go downstairs to make her spa appointment. She left me to sort out getting our toilet fixed as it wasn't flushing properly. I 'phoned reception and spoke to a very pleasant-sounding young lady who put me through to housekeeping whereupon I advised another helpful female of our small issue. She said that she would send someone up immediately, which she did. A smart uniformed man appeared. He gave the appearance of not having had to stick his head down too many lavatories that day and who, after I told him the problem, disappeared into our toilet with a large, very clean canvas holdall. I sat on the emperor-size bed and picked up a book in order to fill a few minutes. Suddenly the 'phone rang. Not my 'phone, the room 'phone. This was something of a novelty; I don't remember my hotel room 'phone ever having rung before. I picked it up. "Er, hallo." "Oh yeah, er, hi there." It didn't sound like a receptionist, it sounded like a Compaq North America sales division rep. But what did I know? "Can I help you?" I asked. "Er, yeah sure. I'm, er, wanting to speak with Greg. Is he there? You're English. You're not Greg are you?" "No I'm not. But just wait a moment and I'll get him." I put down the 'phone and route marched over to the bathroom. "Excuse, me," I said to the janitor who was wielding a very large spanner as I stuck my head around the door "but is your name Greg?" "No sir, it's not," came the reply. "My name is Jack." "Oh okay. Sorry. It's just that, um, there's someone on the 'phone asking for Greg." "Maybe a wrong number?" he suggested. "Maybe," I replied and left him to go back to his work. I went back to the 'phone. "I'm sorry to keep you waiting but it probably needs some explanation. You see, there's a man in my toilet but I didn't know his name. I hadn't got that far. But now that you're asking for a man I thought that he could be the only person, but it turns out that he's not Greg. His name is..." "Excuse me sir," Compaq interrupted. "If I'm understanding you properly, you have a guy in your john and you don't know his name?" "Correct." "May I ask as to how long's he been in there?" "Oh, only a few minutes but I wasn't going to bother with his name because he was only going to be with me for a few minutes at most unless things got a bit complicated and we needed to chat. Hallo? Hallo?" There was a long pause and then my interlocutor asked, "Is that room one seven six?" "Um, no, it's not. It's room seven one six." Another pause. "Okay. Sorry. Looks like I've got a wrong number. Anyway, have a good evening with the guy in your bathroom whose name you don't know but why should you if it's only a quickie." "No, wait," I replied but too late, Compaq had rung off.

"All sorted," said Jack as he emerged into the bedroom wing looking no different from ten minutes earlier. "Everything's fine now and you should be having no further problems. I just had to change a small pipe that was leaking." "I think, actually, my problems are just starting," I replied. He gave me an oblique glance as he reached for the door knob, pulled open the door rather too quickly for my liking and scuttled out.

When my wife returned she was bright red but not from heat but from embarrassment. "No one told me that my massage was going to be by a MAN!" she exclaimed. "He was huge, like one of those Compaq guys. He had great big fingers and his name was Sven and he was Swedish. 'So, we ef you down for a full body massage?' he asked but all I could squeal was, 'Just my back please Sven.' Honestly, I could have died! I was sooo embarrassed, but it was quite nice though. However I couldn't help lying there thinking of you up here having to do no more that deal with a dodgy loo. Is it fixed?" I nodded. "Still, I'm looking forward to trying the German restaurant tonight." "Darling," I replied, "I think we should go into town to eat tonight. The thing is there may be the slightest whiff of scandal drifting under the Compaq boys' noses this evening; I expect they're all aware of it by now already and we don't need to sniff as well." "Ooh," my wife replied. "Who does it involve?"

"Er, me," I replied.

Beaver Creek

Bargain basement skis turn out to be not quite what was expected.

I was very excited at the prospect of a trip to the States as I had never been there before, let alone skied. We were a large enough party of three families comprising different skiing abilities so had to get the resort selection just right as it needed to cater for everyone. We settled on Beaver Creek. It's only ten miles from its more famous neighbour, Vail, but no less luxurious with heated pavements, escalators up to the slopes instead of steps and people at the back entrance to the hotel we stayed in who will put your skis and boots away for you. Bonkers but fun.

One of my friends, Duncan, who was in our party is a mergers and acquisitions' accountant and is very, very rich. Naturally he's a Club World traveller and this is where the fun started. All twelve of us were in the single check-in queue at Heathrow, snaking left and right, when one of the BA staff spotted Duncan's Club World luggage label fob that was dangling from one of his suitcases. She tapped him on the shoulder as he negotiated one of the queue's hairpins. "Follow me, sir," she gently commanded as she unhooked one of the lengths of black tape that was keeping us all in line. He did as instructed and the eleven of us followed him. The BA woman ushered Duncan to a fast-track check-in desk that was tucked away in a corner. It had no queue. She asked the staff member to look after my friend and then turned round. Her face was a picture. "I'm sorry," she mumbled to her colleague. "I didn't realise that they were all with Mr Hobson." "That's fine," I said. "No need to apologise." Duly checked-in Duncan then attempted to get us all into the Club Lounge but we had ridden our luck and were unsuccessful.

For many years I had owned my own skis but the previous year they had been stolen overnight from a ski locker room in a European resort so I was on a mission to buy a new pair. Not to be beaten Duncan had decided that he and his wife should buy skis also as did the other couple. Duncan was beside himself with excitement at owning his own skis. He could talk of nothing else on the flight over. He was just as bad during the coach transfer. "The thing is Mike," he kept saying, "I've done my research. Down the road from the hotel there's a small town called Avon and they have a sports shop. A proper, big sports shop like a hypermarket but with no food. In there they do skis for twenty-five dollars. I saw an ad in one of the ski magazines." I raised an eyebrow in surprise. I knew everyone liked a bargain but I was a little concerned that the man who could probably buy the shop was so excited about spending so little on a pair of skis. It did sound a bargain though considering they cost several hundred Euros in Alpine resorts.

No sooner had we reached our hotel than Duncan was ordering a people carrier to take the six grown-ups back down to Avon that we had only just driven through on the way to Beaver Creek. We all piled in and in a few minutes found ourselves inside the most enormous sports shop. It looked similar to one of the warehouse-type stores back home apart from the huge collection of basketball apparatus, row upon row of semi-automatic rifles - and skis. It wasn't long before a sales assistant sidled over. "D'ya need some help?" the assistant drawled. "We're looking to buy some skis, six pairs," said Duncan authoritatively. The man's eyes lit up. He guided us over to mainly K2 and Völkl skis. He looked our wives up and down and selected three pairs. "How about these?" he asked. Then it was our turn. We examined lengths, discussed performance and suitability for our varying abilities but all Duncan was trying to do was look at the prices. They were on average around three hundred dollars. Finally Duncan could contain himself no longer. "Do you think we could have a look at the twenty-five dollar skis please?" "Twenny-five bucks?" I thought the guy was going to explode. "You wanna buy kids' ex-rennal?" I butted in and assured him that we didn't and in due course we left the building with six pairs of new ex-nothing skis. I also spent a hundred dollars on a pair of Völkl carbon fibre ski poles. They were excellent. They had a bit of give in them so when I pushed on compacted snow they would spring back a bit and give you a little extra acceleration; only a touch but they looked and felt very cool. They didn't last long though. The following year I took them down the unpisted black Forêt run in Val d'Isère. I never wrap the pole straps round my hands so when I hit a bit of powder and took a tumble I let go of a pole. It was as if the snow had opened up just to swallow it. The surface was as smooth as silk. I couldn't find it anywhere. What a waste of one hundred dollars and twenty minutes of my life! I should have bought a pair of kids' ex-rennal poles maybe. Or a rifle.

Peppermint liqueur with a dash of hot chocolate.

One morning out on the piste we skied down a long blue that came to an abrupt halt outside The Ritz-Carlton, a huge and imposing hotel that looked like the one in *The Shining* apart from its being brown not white in colour. It describes itself as being inspired by a traditional mountain lodge but with one hundred and eighty bedrooms I reckon someone's been having a funny dream. We decided to take a look inside; coffee would be the excuse.

Once we were settled down in some easy chairs in the lounge a waiter came over. My wife said that she fancied a hot chocolate but thought it was too late for elevenses and too early for lunch. "How about a hot chocolate with a shot of peppermint Bols in it?" he suggested. His proposal went down well, too well in fact. The following day Duncan and I were stuck in a snow bowl. There was no way out other than by lift but both were closed due to a storm that was passing overhead. All that was in the bowl, apart from a few other skiers, was a small café. We went inside for a drink until the storm blew over. Duncan decided to have what my wife had had the day before. Unfortunately the woman at the counter hadn't heard of peppermint Bols. "That'll do," said Duncan pointing at a bottle on a shelf behind her. She unscrewed the cap but instead of measuring out a shot she just poured it into the hot chocolate, glug, glug, glug, enough liqueur to keep several alcoholics content for a month. "I'd better not stir," Duncan thought aloud. He drank it all though. However, when the lift reopened and we escaped back up to the top Duncan said that he had temporarily forgotten how to ski and so had to get the lift back into town whereupon he returned to the hotel and slept through both lunch and dinner. And he lost both his poles. I shouldn't have smiled; mine weren't going to last much longer.

Bourg-en-Bresse

The children are sent out to fend for themselves with their mother's debit card in a pizzeria.

This was my family's (mum, dad, brother, sister, me) stop for the night on the way back from skiing a few years ago when I was about twelve years old. My brother is two years older, my sister two years younger. We stayed in a hotel that had just been completely refurbished. Everything was bright colours - reds, yellows and greens - the walls, the furniture, the reception area. It was everywhere. Dad said that it felt like he was in a pre-school nursery. Apart from that mum said that she loved the town and we should make it our new stop back from skiing instead of Dijon. Soon after we arrived mum said that she needed to go for a walk. She disappeared off and whilst out tried to book a table for all of us for the evening. (The hotel didn't do food, just breakfast.) Eventually mum returned back to the hotel. Apparently she couldn't find anywhere that was reasonably priced but not fully booked so on the way back she went into the restaurant on the corner which was part of the theatre and which was called Brasserie de la Théâtre and very expensive she told us. She said that they only had one table for two available and so she booked that for her and dad and us children were to go to a pizzeria next door to the hotel. It wasn't particularly cheap but had space she said. Mum gave Sam, my older brother, her debit card to pay for the meal. To this day I don't know why my parents couldn't have had a pizza with us. There's never been a satisfactory explanation. Mum once said that it was because she had already booked the posh place but given what happened she probably wished that she had come with us.

Mum and dad got changed and went out looking quite smart and the three of us children went next door wearing the same clothes that we had been in for the car journey.

We all left at seven o'clock as mum didn't want us out late, or so she said. When we arrived there was no one else in the pizzeria so we were allowed to choose which table we wanted. We chose the biggest one which was just as well. The waitress who served us was Italian but she didn't speak any English and the menu was all in French and Italian so we decided just to have a bit from each section. As you do. She wasn't your average student type doing a stint of waitressing on the side; she was a bit older and we thought that she was possibly the owner. The first dish was from "Primo" and it was mostly salads so we ordered one each. The waitress kept putting one finger up as if she wanted us to have one between three but we were hungry so we had a salad each. Then the next section was "Bruschetta" and Sam knew what that was. He told us it was like pizza toppings but on bread so we ordered one of those each as well. The waitress kept smiling at us still waving her one finger in the air. We felt very sorry for her because there was no one else in the restaurant and so she wasn't going to make much money. We thought it best if we helped her out. We then looked at the menus some more and found pizzas. We ordered one of those each. Then she made a drinking sign so we ordered some lemonade by making fizzy noises but something went wrong and Sam got a bottle of grand Prosecco! He didn't look eighteen and wasn't but that wasn't our problem. We ate the salads okay but they were quite big and when the bruschettas came Sam was right, they were like pizzas only bread instead of pizza base (which is like bread anyway). We managed to eat them and then the pizzas turned up. They were enormous, however we ate them but very slowly. We were really stuffed and

Sam had to help my sister Olivia out but we managed them all apart from the crusts which we hid under the tablecloth. By the time that we had finished Sam had drunk all the Prosecco. Then he complained that the room was moving but it wasn't. I tried to explain to the waitress but she had no idea what I was going on about. There still weren't any other people at the other tables so we thought we should ask for pudding. Then the waitress took the tablecloth off and found our crusts. We shook our heads at her and said that they weren't ours but unfortunately they were still warm.

She said that pudding was "glace". We knew what that was and she said it was "homemade". She managed that word in English. Sam had lemon sorbet and I had a berry one and so did Olivia. Then she held up one finger but Sam held up three on each hand but he had no idea what she was on about because we weren't going to share an ice cream. We found out soon enough when they turned up and we had six scoops each. Then an old boy tottered over with a bottle of vodka and poured loads of it over Sam's sorbet. We didn't really need a drink after that but we felt sorry for the waitress and the man who we guessed was her husband and their empty restaurant so we ordered a hot chocolate each. We can manage those in French. Just as they turned up Sam said he needed to go to the toilet. He didn't know how to ask for the toilet in French or Italian so he just stood up and pointed at the relevant mechanism in his trousers and the woman smiled and showed him a door down some steps.

When he returned a few minutes later he was giggling like a juvenile hyena. He told us that downstairs there was another part of the restaurant that opened onto another street. We were on a bit of a hill and we must have come in the back way as there were loads of people downstairs. Of course then Olivia and I both had to go to the toilet so we could have a look and it was true - downstairs was full up and very, very busy. We felt a bit happier then and decided that we didn't need to order anything else apart from the bill. The waitress understood "bill" alright though. When it arrived Sam looked at it then went a bit pale. We had managed to spend about four times what mum had suggested to him but we had to pay it. It didn't end there even though we were ready to leave. The waitress brought us another drink each. I've no idea what it was but we drank it. Anyway once we were all properly finished and just about to leave again we got a bit of a shock - mum and dad came in. Sam gave the receipt to mum and told her, "I've been on a bit of a bender." Then mum gave the bill to dad who asked Sam if the total was in Euros and was the dot in the wrong place? Sam said that he had no idea and he was just helping the poor waitress out. When dad felt it necessary to inform us that his abandoned children's meals were more than double per head what he had just paid in one of the most expensive restaurants in Bourg-en-Bresse Sam went even whiter then said, "In that case I'll put some of it back," and promptly threw up.

The following year we returned to Dijon.

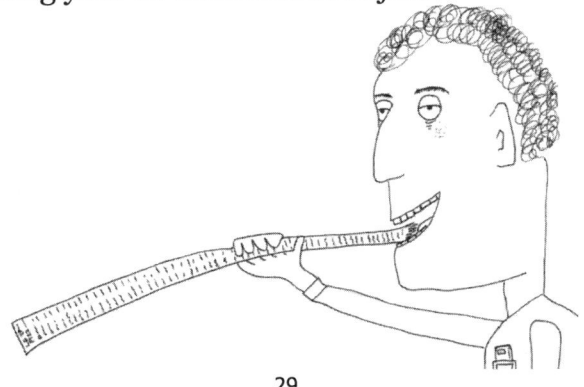

Bourg-Saint-Maurice

Never order anything from a menu in France without knowing exactly what it is.

Not a ski area in its own right but a gateway to several resorts as it's where the snow train from London terminates.

Three friends and I were on our way to La Plagne and had just stepped off the train when we decided that as the evening was getting on, to be sure of getting a drink we should have one sooner rather than later. We found a very small local bar and elected to embrace the full French experience by ordering a pastis each, it being an aniseedy liqueur. We weren't going to eat as we had had breakfast and lunch on the train (and plenty of drinks) but the food had been a bit crap so when monsieur le patron came over with the drinks and asked simply, "Manger?" who were we to say no? There were no menus, just a rundown of various items. We caught "croque monsieur" so my three friends had that. However, I had heard the words "salade" and "gourmande" so I ordered it knowing that I would be in for a treat; I didn't know what the rest was. It sounded like "gesiers".

The croques were fine but when my salad turned up it wasn't. It comprised a mixed green salad that was okay, then mushrooms, potatoes and figs that looked great but it was topped with dark, diced squares of meat that absolutely stank! I chewed on one solitary piece and swallowed. Almost immediately I retched and back up it came followed by lunch and then breakfast, all enveloped in an alcoholic liquid sauce. How did my body know?

I asked around whilst on holiday but no one seemed to have heard of the word gesiers, jesiers, gesieurs, gesiay etc. The first thing I did when I returned home was look it up in my French dictionary. Nothing. These were pre-internet days. I asked some friends who had studied French, who had lived in France. Still I drew a blank. It was only when I was wandering round London the following summer that I walked past a French restaurant. "I wonder?" I thought and stopped to look at the menu. And there it was - gesiers. Salade aux gésiers de poulet. *Chicken gizzard salad.* Back at home I consulted another dictionary. Horrors! The gizzard is the lining of birds' secondary stomach where food is ground up. No wonder I was sick.

The following year the four of us returned to La Plagne. I insisted that we pop into the bistro and apologise as we had left in something of a hurry after I had deposited the contents of my stomach over the table and floor of the establishment rather than down myself that would have been preferable for the bistro as I could have just taken my stinky self outside. No sooner had we sat down than monsieur le patron ambled over and asked in almost perfect English, "Four croques?"

Brides-les-Bains

Insightful interlocution on the chair lift.

I always wanted to ski the Three Valleys but couldn't justify the cost of staying in Courchevel. This was despite knowing that everywhere would be a load of money. (My wife says that it's the only sport that costs an arm and a leg to break and arm and a leg.) Then a friend of my wife suggested basing my family in Brides-les-Bains which is the lowest place of all this particular ski area at only six hundred metres. She told me that it was where all the ski instructors live and, "...it's just a gondola ride up the valley each morning." My wife said that it sounded like just what we needed. What is it with women and ski instructors?

The holiday itself was fine but the gondola lift was a bit of a pain as it used to take about half an hour to reach Méribel at which point more lifts were needed just to start skiing. There were advantages though. Méribel is the middle valley so we could then go straight up or left to Courchevel or right to Les Menuires; everywhere was very accessible.

One morning, after our usual poodle up to Méribel via Les Allues which is the halfway stage for the gondola, we skied down to a chair lift that had a very small queue, probably because it comprised a load of ski school kids who, when they get going, can cause all sorts of grief. I skied up to the gate and an instructor indicated that I was to accompany a ski school child. This was always a very sensible precaution for the kids because, until very recently, chair lifts had no restraint other than a horizontal bar to prevent smaller skiers from slipping out from underneath which tragically has happened in the past. Now there's a long, thickish bit of plastic that resembles a, um, banana that is bolted to the underside of the restraining bar for each skier. Once the bar comes down there is no escape. It also doubles as a cheap thrill giver or a member molester, depending on whether you're female or male. I've seen some skiers trying to remain on with the restraining bar still in place once they've reached the top but that's for another book.

I didn't want the poor child to sit on the edge of the chair saying nothing so I thought I would speak to him. He could always refuse to say anything which would have been fine but I wanted to make sure that he was okay. First I had to find out whether he would be able to understand me.

"Are you English or tu es Français?" I asked. The young boy sounded, and was, very polite and he said, "I am English." Then he added, presumably just in case he thought I wanted to speak in French (which I didn't), "I do speak a few French words also." I didn't ask him which words they were though as, from my own French lessons with a group of French girls that I once met in a record shop in Rochester when I was supposed to be in class, they were probably the wrong ones. "And how old are you?" I asked.
"I'm eight."
"And are you staying in Méribel?"
"I'm not sure. Somewhere near here but I'm not exactly sure."
"That's understandable but not very useful. Don't get lost. Have you skied before?"
"No, this is my first time."
"Put your feet on the bar. That's for your skis. And sit up straight. Are you enjoying it?"
"Yes. It's good fun."
"And you're having lessons?"
"Yes."
"Are you with your friends?"

"Yes. I have my sister Harriet and our friend Noah. All the other children are French."
"It looks like you have a French instructor?"
"Yes. His name is Christophe."
"Do you understand him?"
"No. He speaks English but it's not the sort of English that the three of us understand so we just follow the French children."
"That's a good idea."
"Not always. Because sometimes we follow them when they do the wrong things."
"That's not so good. Are you staying in a hotel or a chalet?"
"We're in a chalet. There's me and my mummy and daddy and me and Harriet. Then we have the Billinghursts. They have a mummy and a daddy and there's Daniel and Jack and Katie. We also have the Eyres family and their children. We did have Jamie as well but he's been sent home and he's staying with his auntie."
"Oh dear, poor Jamie. Has he been a naughty boy?"
"No, not really. Someone skied into him on the first day whilst he was at ski school and broke his leg." That floored me for a moment but I soon regained my composure.
"Oh dear, that's terrible," I said. I was genuinely shocked. "And is he eight also?"
The little boy thought for a second then he said, "No he's not. I think he's about forty-seven." I'm glad I had a snood over my mouth. Deep breaths, regain composure again.
"Oh, I see. That's still pretty dreadful."
"Mummy says that the only dreadful thing is that when it's time to go home his wife will have to drive their family which is a bit of a concern to mummy because mummy say's that Jamie's wife is normally plastered."
"It sounds as though they're both plastered," I heard my mouth saying without being able to stop it; it just came out. The boy remained silent.

By this time we were at the top of the lift so I raised the bar and the young lad skied off to find his friends. I have to say I spent the whole day keeping an eye out for a group of children with a woman who was ever so slightly wobbly on her skis and looking more than a little out of control. The trouble is I saw loads of contenders. That's Méribel for you.

I often wonder if Jamie's family managed to get home okay.

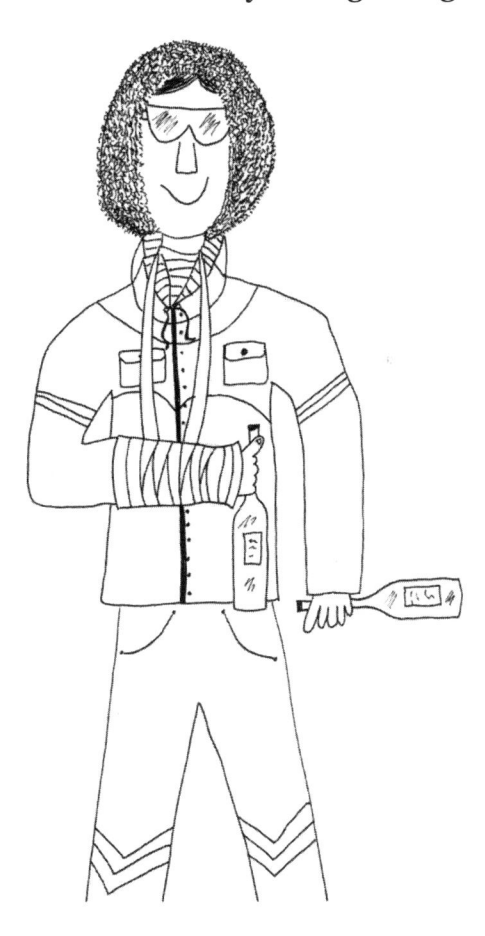

Calais

A playground for the British and an amusement park for the French.

After a long drive back from the Alps via a night in Troyes we arrived at Calais and went to Eastenders.

There were four of us in the car, two couples, and at the time a trip to France wasn't complete without stopping off at this huge warehouse on the outskirts of Calais. It was a pile 'em high, sell 'em cheap operation that was run by the irrepressible Dave West, a multi-millionaire who took full advantage of France's much lower duty rates to sell shed loads of booze and fags to the ferry customers. He was later to be killed by his son who was subsequently jailed having been found guilty of manslaughter.

On this particular occasion we happened to meet Dave in his warehouse and he plied us with free "samples." My friend Mike's wife, Carol, bought enough wine to keep her going up to the following Christmas and beyond. When we were leaving Carol suggested that Mike ought to see whether he was over the drink / drive limit. He had a breathalyser kit in the car that I think we were supposed to carry. Unsurprisingly the reading was positive and so Carol had to drive at least to the ferry terminal; she was the only other one who was insured. The first thing that she said when we were all back in the car was, "I've never driven on the wrong side of the road before." I should have made the decision at that point to walk - it wasn't far.

It was a short but hair-raising journey. I was convinced we were going to end up in the marina. When we got to the roundabout by La Quai de la Loire Carol had a bit of a meltdown. She was trying to go round clockwise but the arrow in the road was pointing her anticlockwise. So what did she do? She didn't go round it, not even the wrong way. She just drove over the middle of it. She left two rather obvious tyre tracks in the flower bed and then got tooted at by another English car as she bumped down off the roundabout on the other side. "I thought we were friends!" she shouted at the woman in the Volvo who was driving but the woman just tooted again and drove off.

"Follow her!" commanded Mike. At least it meant that Carol was able to stay on the right side of the road, so that she could "regain her bearings." She managed to get into the port okay whereupon my friend took the driving back over. He said that there are no driving laws inside the port which is cobblers. What wasn't okay was that we had missed our ferry and because Mike didn't have a flexi-ticket he had to pay rather a lot to get on the next sailing. What's more we weren't allowed in the club lounge so had to "sit with the chavs" which is how Carol described it. Mike didn't sit with the three of us though because he wasn't very happy that all the money that Carol had saved by buying her wine in Calais he had spent on the excess ticket.

When he finally returned to his seat with us Carol stomped off. When she returned Mike stormed off again. Carol said that she had had to bite her lip in the toilet when a woman came up to her and said, "It's called a 'roundabout' not an 'overabout,'" and then left. When Mike reappeared for the second time he said that he had met a man who had been in a bar in Calais and he had missed his ferry also. He was held up because he had wanted four straws for his family's drinks and asked for them in French which apparently is, "Je voudrais quatre pailles." The waiter disappeared and didn't come back with the straws. Then the English family decided to swig their drinks out of the bottles and told the waiter not to bother with the pailles but he wouldn't let them go. Then the English family stood up and so the waiter locked the front door and looked angry! Eventually, just as the Englishman pulled out his 'phone, pointed at it and said, "Police!" another waiter appeared with four huge plates of meat pie, chips and vegetables. "SIT," he commanded and they did. And they ate the pies even though they had just had lunch. He wasn't talking to his wife on the ferry either.

The Channel ferries are funny places really. Dover-Calais ferries are usually full of noisy Englishmen getting drunk at breakfast time whilst on the Calais-Dover ferries in the evening everyone's asleep apart from the French children all going to England for a holiday. Their first impression of the English must be that everyone snores.

Calais

The Burghers of Calais weren't what was expected.

One year when we were driving back as a family from the Alps we reached Calais with far too much time to spare. My dad was so mean that he had bought the cheapest ferry ticket available. This was one that meant that you had to sail on a specific boat or pay a huge sum to change. He was also so mean that he wasn't going to pay the fee to change sailings so we ended up in Calais town for three hours. Dad told us that we could go to the "Six Burgers of Calais" so my sister and I stopped making a fuss because it was lunchtime and we fancied something to eat and we love stringy French chips. Unfortunately, when we found the burgers they weren't in the posh hotel that looks a bit like Big Ben and the Houses of Parliament but outside in front of the town hall in a park. We didn't get grilled minced beef patties in buns with chips but a few minutes to gaze at a statue of six bronze (as opposed to bronzed) men dressed in bed sheets.

We eventually got a bit of lunch in Au Café de Paris down by a large square called Place d'Armes. The name of the restaurant is a bit odd for Calais but we weren't complaining because this time the burger was something we could eat. The best bit was we were held up going through passports and so we missed our crossing and dad had to pay a huge supplement. To rub salt in his wounds the girl at check-in said that had dad arrived in time for the earlier crossing to the one we were booked on she could have put us on that for free because it was fairly quiet.

Hopefully he's learnt his lesson and we won't have to have some weird French culture thrown in next time.

Calais

Mother has a meltdown in the hypermarket.

We had a bit of time to kill in Calais on the way back from skiing a couple of years ago, before getting our ferry.

We went to the huge hypermarket and mum stocked up on wine as usual. And cheese. Then she said that she was going to buy loads of fruit and veg. Her reasoning was that they sold nicer stuff in France than back at home. I don't understand myself because to me a tomato is a tomato but mum said that it didn't have to travel so far in France so the flavour is better. I don't know what she was talking about because we still had to take it home so it will have travelled just as far eventually only in our car and not a lorry.

When we finally got to the till - it was quite busy and mum was tut-tutting all the time because she was now in a hurry and didn't want to miss the ferry - the wine and cheese went through fine but when it came to all the apples and oranges and courgettes and peppers and things the woman looked at mum and shrugged her shoulders and said "posy" in French. Mum shrugged her shoulders too. Fortunately there was a little French girl with her mum behind us. The little girl spoke English and she asked us if we needed any help. Mum asked her what "posy" meant. The girl said that mummy had to go and weigh the fruit and veg. and salad bits over by where she got it all from and put it in plastic bags and then tie them up and put a sticker on each of them. What a performance! Mum wasn't very happy. She said that she was trying to stop using plastic bags (that are now banned in France for fruit and veg.) and in Reading where we live you can simply dump your stuff at the till and the sales assistant weighs it all loose and what's the point of having to do it all yourself and whatever happened to service? The lady on the till didn't understand but the girl did! She said that it was to save time at the checkout and to stop English people moaning. This girl was only about twelve! We all laughed except mum. We had to put everything back in the trolley and go and find the scales. Once mum had found them and put on the tomatoes in a plastic bag she then had to press in a code next to "Tomates." Oranges were next and that was easy enough as was "Courgettes" because they're English words or foreign words that we use, but then we had a problem with "Apples" so then mum tried "Peppers" and they weren't listed either because it was all in French and mum was getting very agitated. "You would have thought that in Calais they would have put everything in English, wouldn't you Toby?" she said to dad. She sounded very exasperated. "After all, everyone here speaks English, even the kids, apart from the checkout people, so why don't they make it easier for us?" Mum got no reply because dad had wandered off so mum told my brother to go and find out what "potatoes" were in French. He wandered off as well. By the time that he came back mum had stuck all the other fruit and veg. and salad bits - all the stuff with foreign names that we didn't know - into the largest plastic bag that she could find and pressed "Pommes de terres." That made everything a lot cheaper as well, especially all the posh stuff. Mum then tried to go through the self-service but was told by a man, "Non." He pointed at all the shoppers with hand-baskets. Mum asked, "What sort of idiot goes shopping in a hypermarket with a hand-basket?" She didn't get a reply obviously and we went back to our cashier lady and had to queue again.

When it came to the large plastic bag with all the food with weird French names in it the woman took one look at it and said, "Non." She waved mum away having given her a handful of plastic bags. "I have an idea," mum said to us. "I'll pay for everything except the big bag and you wait over by the window whilst I sort the extra fruit and vegetables out." Which is what she did. We wheeled the trolley through and sat by the window and waited as mum didn't go and rebag everything separately but went and got a handbasket, put her plastic bag in it and marched over to the self-service, swinging it in front of the man. Mum scanned the bag label and was just about to pay when her till started to make a very loud peeping noise. Everyone turned round. The man went over to mum and beckoned for her to follow him. By the time that dad had reappeared, having spent the last twenty minutes tasting Beaujolais, we had to explain that mum had gone off somewhere with a man which wasn't the best explanation but it was all we knew at the time. Anyway, she reappeared after another ten minutes and she was still with the man. As she walked over to us with a very red face she turned round and said that she didn't want his (very rude word) vegetables anyway and then said, "Come on you lot," to us and marched out of the store.

I often wonder who upsets the Calais people more: refugees and asylum seekers passing through or the English. I have a good idea what the answer is though.

Cervinia

Safeguarding shocker with the ski instructor.

I learnt to ski in Cervinia whilst I was at school and so it will always have a special place in my heart. There's plenty of skiing there because it's linked to Zermatt in Switzerland. It's also great for beginners because the nursery slopes are at the top of a gondola so you feel you're in amongst it even as a complete novice.

I did okay on the first day but I don't think that our instructor, Diego, was too impressed as I couldn't stop without falling over. I was trying to ski parallel because that's what all the other skiers were doing outside of my class. He kept on and on about transferring my weight and bending "zee" knees to no avail. After day two he suggested to my teachers that he should take me for a private lesson on Wednesday afternoon and they readily agreed. They had parents to please after all, especially my mother.

I did okay and didn't fall over much. He had me holding his poles that he was putting out behind him and then moving them away from each other to get me more in the snow plough position. "Zis way you can at least stop and zen we move to parallel maybe tomorrow. Practiz, practiz, practiz." He looked at his watch. "Okay, vee need a break. Do you drink coffee?" "Yes," I lied. "Espresso?" "Cool," I said. "Double?" "Why not?"

There was no tomorrow for us and Diego.

As we sat in the glorious sun's rays on the terrace of a restaurant next to the gondola station that was by that time mostly empty, Diego's main advice was, "I vant you to open your legs more. It is zo much easier zat way." I nodded but I was more interested in getting through my disgusting drink. It was only about four sips' worth and he spent an age drinking his. "Finish," he said suddenly and stood up. "I'm just going for a, um..." "I know," I said, seizing my chance. No sooner had he disappeared inside than I took my cup that I had hardly touched and carefully poured the contents between a couple of the slats of the wooden floor. It took too much time and was much slower than simply chucking it over my shoulder but the drink was so black that anyone passing and looking at the unusually coloured resultant snow (that, in my experience, if not mud - because it is mud - is red (splatters) or yellow (stream)) would think that a fully laden squid had been murdered.

In the evening our Head of Sport, Mr Berrow, asked me how my one-on-one lesson had gone. "It was great," I said with a smile. I really felt as if I had learnt something and told Mr Berrow so. "Tell me what you got up to," he commanded and so I told him, most of it.

"We went up the gondola and tried the runs up there and then Diego showed me a few things that are a bit difficult to explain but I soon go the hang of it and then he took me for a quiet coffee which I didn't like and told me that he wanted me to open my legs..."

The following day we had a new instructor. Her name was Giana. She didn't seem to know a Diego. I hope he was okay. Looking back I reckon I should have just kept my mouth shut.

I've never sipped on an espresso since without remembering Diego.

Chalet Girl Shorts

A few shorter stories in no particular order from chalet girls past and present...

Burnt croissants.

I was mostly waitressing in a large chalet-hotel in Alpe d'Huez. To encourage us not to over order from the central store or waste food we had a maximum allowance placed on us - the total depended on how many guests we had. If we went over the allowance something was wrong. My boss would investigate if there was a complaint such as not enough food and we would end up paying, so had to find other ways round any problem. Breakfast was actually the worst meal to deal with because we had to be up and dressed by 6.45am, having sometimes only gone to bed about an hour and a half earlier. Croissants were my bête noire. They would arrive in the kitchen from the bakers basically in the middle of the night and all we had to do was heat them gently under the grill for just fifteen seconds. One morning I put them under the grill, and we're talking all of the croissants, fifty or so, with a huge oven - they could all be done at once - when I needed to go for a pee. I thought I had time but then I got chatting and although I had been less than a minute all the tops of the croissants had burnt black and were ruined. I couldn't afford to have to get another fifty and I could hardly serve them to the guests in that condition so I carefully cut all the burnt top bits off with a bread knife then squirted Chantilly cream on top of them all and served them. I told the guests that it was a tradition in Alpe d'Huez on saints' days to serve them like that although I didn't know which saint it could be, Saint Huez, I suggested. One pretentious idiot git of a guest said,

"Oh yes, I've heard of that tradition. Full marks for keeping to it"!

***

Stale croissants.

One of my jobs when I was working in a chalet in Obergurgl was to heat up the croissants in the morning. The resort manager was so tight that he bought the croissants from the bakery at the end of the day when they were selling them off at a quarter of the usual price. They would sit all evening and overnight in the kitchen. Then, in the morning, I used to turn the oven on, put the stale croissants on a baking tray, sprinkle water lightly over them and bake for about five minutes. I would then tell the guests that they were freshly baked which they were sort of. I didn't tell them they were freshly baked then stale then baked again. No one ever said anything other than how good they tasted!

***

Double trouble.

I worked one season in a top end hotel in St Moritz. I used to clean, tidy up and generally sort out all the bedrooms every morning with another girl, Jackie. You wouldn't believe how messy and dirty some people can be! We used to go down each corridor and do alternate rooms. If it was a really messy room we would always groan, "Oh my God!" out loud and shut the door before reopening it and going in.

One day I opened the first door, which was room 101, to be confronted not by mess but by a man standing in the middle of the room, completely stark naked apart from a pair of socks on his feet. I didn't know where to look! He didn't seem at all embarrassed and he didn't say anything. "Oh my God!" I shrieked and put my hand to my mouth. Then I shut the door. Jackie was obviously feeling magnanimous for she grabbed to door knob and before I could say anything she had flung the door open saying, "Don't worry Mel, I'll do the first one." Then she looked up and saw exactly what I had seen a few seconds earlier. He was still standing there. Poor man. "Oh my God!" she shrieked but instead of shutting the door she just froze. I had to pull her out of the room whilst muttering something like, "We'll be back later," but we weren't, not until the following day. After that, for the rest of the week, instead of starting at room 101 we finished at room 101. This gave our *déshabillé* friend time to get up, dress, breakfast and leave for a day's skiing, thank goodness.

***

Massive injury on the slopes.

I was working as a chalet girl in Grindelwald last year. I had a couple of hours off every afternoon and then evenings once dinner was cleared away, usually by half past nine. One day the guests were very slow with their meal and I couldn't get them to budge. Once they had left the dining table we were allowed to clear up but not before. A couple of tricks that usually worked were to tell them they could have their puddings sitting on the sofas if they wanted a break between courses or tell them that I would pour their coffees and put them on the coffee table. However, neither of these suggestions worked and they were lingering far too long with their glasses of wine, just chatting. I didn't blame them but I needed to get out for a few drinks. I finally escaped at gone ten thirty so was not too impressed at having to drink more quickly than I usually did in order to catch up with my friends. When it was time for me to get up to prepare breakfast I felt very tired and so it remained all morning. After I had done all the chalet chores I headed up the Wengernalpbahn train to the top for a long red all the way back down. I was feeling so tired still that I bought a couple of cans of Red Bull and drank them both on the way up the mountain.

I had had no lunch - no time for lunch - and was feeling a little bit woozy as I started down the slope. I knew I was going to be sick but there wasn't time to ski to the side and make a small hole in the snow which is what my manager said was the best thing to do. "Just cover it up, like a cat," was his suggestion at our training meeting. He was talking about peeing in the main but then added, "...or any other unwanted bodily excretion." We all let out a groan of disgust, "Not us!" we girls more or less all said in unison but over the following weeks everyone had occasion to put this suggestion into practice - except me. (As an aside, never let your children have snowball fights on the piste. There's a fairly high probability that they will scoop up more than white solid precipitation.) It came out so suddenly and I couldn't stop. As I went into a schuss, going far too fast and probably out of control, I turned my head. The dark red mixture of Red Bull and everything else in my stomach came out without much retching like a Red Arrows' vapour trail. Fortunately there weren't too many people around. I coughed and spluttered and let out a few squeals but I kept going with only a couple of quick get-your-breath-back stops until I reached the bottom where I soon discovered I had a welcoming party.

I was going to ski straight past them but one of the police officers held out his hand and so I felt obliged to stop.

Another of them was armed. Another then explained that they had received reports from an anonymous source on the mountain that a young lady wearing a ski suit matching mine had apparently been shot and probably needed medical attention. Instinctively I gasped but then, showing remarkable composure and a worryingly good ability to lie under pressure whilst also not wanting the police to waste their time, I said, "Oh, it's okay. I saw her. She hadn't been shot, she's just been very sick. Red sick. Silly girl. She's having a rest and some water about halfway down." "Thank you," said the officer. "That has been very helpful." Just at that moment one of my friends came over to me. "My goodness!" she exclaimed. "You were going fast! That was some trail of red sick you left! There was never going to be a hole big enough to accommodate that lot!" My cheeks exploded with embarrassment as the officers shrugged their shoulders and fortunately left without saying a further word. I went back to bed.

***

The mystery of the severe allergic reaction.

After uni. I worked one season at a very exclusive ski chalet in Davos that cost over ten thousand pounds to rent for a week. The owners lived nearby and were a bit obsessive about cleanliness during the pandemic. There were sprays and wipes everywhere. I had read chemistry so approved.

One evening I was asked by one of my guests how he could get hold of a doctor. We had well-worn routines for both emergencies and matters that weren't. I have been trained in first aid and I was allowed to ask the nature of the illness. "It's a bit embarrassing but I have come up with a rather nasty rash." "Where?" I asked. "I would rather not say," said the man. I said that there was no need to be embarrassed as I had had some first aid training and there was nothing that he could show me that I hadn't seen a thousand times before (not true) but I didn't pursue the matter. Instead I rang the 24-hour emergency number and arranged for a medic to call round. Then I went out for the evening and told the guests that they could 'phone me at any time if they needed more help and I would assist further. No call came.

In the morning the guest that had needed a doctor said that one had come round soon after I had gone out. He had said that he had had a severe allergic reaction to something unknown and that he had been prescribed beclometasone skin cream. I just nodded wisely. "Must be quite serious then," I suggested. "It is!" said one of the other men. "It's all over his anus! We've had a look! See for yourself!" I declined the invitation, despite my previous assertion that I had seen everything a thousand times before, telling the patient that if he was under the doctor then that was good enough for me. Then he said. "If the truth be told, it is a bit of an embarrassment." "And why would that be?" I asked. "I've been told to stop using the wet wipes and go back to toilet paper," he replied. "What wet wipes?" I queried with a slight frown. "There are no babies here this week." "Dur, the ones in the cupboard in the toilet," he replied, sounding like he thought / knew I was stupid. "There are no wet wipes in the cupboard in the toilet," I said sounding calmer than I should have done, "unless someone from your party has put them there." They all shook their heads. At that Mr sore arse got up and marched off in the direction of the bathroom. He soon returned waving a plastic pouch in the air. "I present the evidence! And that concludes the case from the counsel for the prosecution," he announced with a flourish. (He was a lawyer after all). He then slapped the packet down on the coffee table. "See for yourself!" he all but shouted triumphantly. However, even calmer than I had sounded when I last spoke I said, "They're not wet wipes, they're toilet wipes." "And the difference?" he asked, expecting a full analytical presentation from a chemist. "Wet wipes are for babies and those with sensitive skin," I replied. "They're PH balanced and comprise mostly water and plant derivative. Toilet wipes on the other hand contain loads of chlorides and kill 99.9 percent of toilet germs - so at least you're properly disinfected - but their main purpose is to wipe toilet seats, not bottoms." There was silence for a few seconds and then all the other guests burst out laughing. The patient remained silent.

"Shall I inform the doctor or will you tell him?" I asked as I headed for the toilet myself. I had a feeling I was just about to wet myself.

***

How the French pistes are graded.

One thing guests always seemed to ask me was how are the pistes graded? I was working in France where the blues can be quite steep. I used to explain it like this. "It's all to do with what happens when you fall over and it will happen within a few seconds. On a green nothing. On a blue you will soon come to a gentle stop but may be moderately injured. On a red you may come to a violent stop and be severely injured. On a black you may take off and be maximally injured." "And what does 'maximally injured' mean?" they would then ask. "Untreatable." "Like, er, dead?" "Yes."

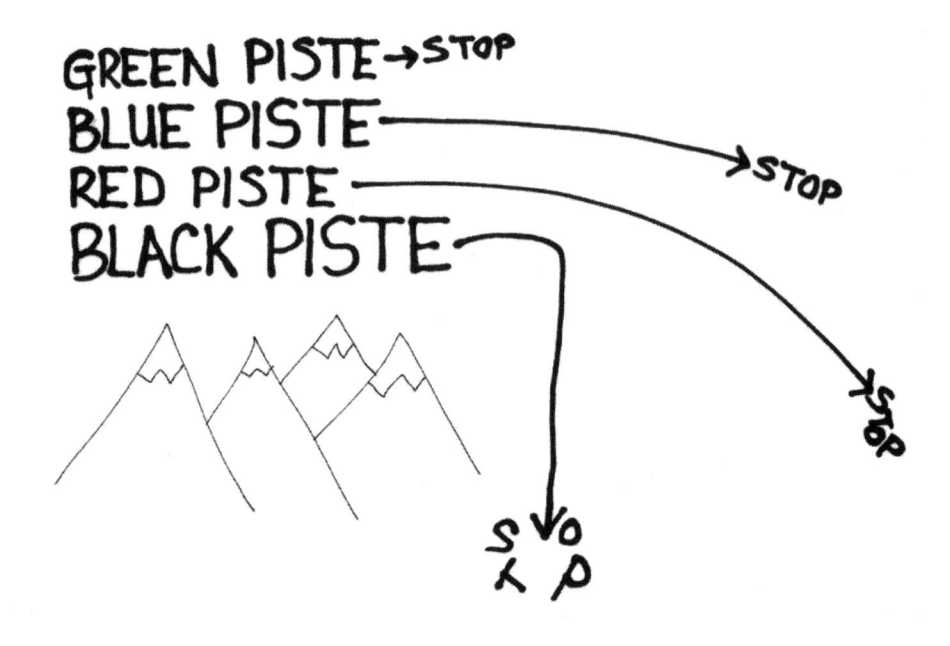

Chamonix

A not-very-friendly Café de l'Amitié.

Chamonix is one of the oldest ski resorts in France. It is also a town in its own right, not a concrete jungle thrown up merely to satisfy a short ski season. It can be visited at any time of year and there will still be "things to do." I shouldn't have been surprised at the reaction I received from my elderly neighbour, a very graceful lady from another age, who usually looked at me blankly when I told her where I was to be skiing that year. However when I told her "Chamonix," her eyes lit up. "You know it?" I asked. "Oh yes, I used to go as a child for the summer. By train. The Gustavia hotel. It's older than I am don't you know? Chamonix was discovered by two Englishmen don't you know?" I didn't know. "It's fondly held in the hearts of the English." "Of course," I replied, not knowing anyone who held it fondly but it's indeed a great place.

The first time I went to Chamonix I was on half board but I didn't make that mistake a second time. There are so many fantastic places to eat, including the Gustavia with its legendary Chambre Neuf après ski bar, and I wanted to try some of them. I went with my wife and another two couples. Another couple, who couldn't get into our hotel, was staying nearby on half board.

On the first evening four of us were strolling down Rue des Moulins when we came across Le Chaudron, a restaurant that looked warm and welcoming. Outside there was a large pot, a cauldron obviously, the sort that you see in cartoons of cannibals cooking up a feast. "Stick together," my wife suggested with a wide grin as we went inside.

The middle-aged waitress and probably owner was charming; she spoke not one word of English to us. My French is good enough though and we succeeded in ordering four entrées and mains - steak and chicken dishes. Then the wine. I chose one bottle of white and one of red. That is when the trouble started. I'll translate the conversation into English.

"Oh, no, no, no. You can't have either of those with the chicken," said the waitress. "If you want chicken you need this one or this one. The red that you have chosen is good for the liver, the white for the veal. You must have this and this."

"Er, okay."

"What a great place!" I told my small party once she had gathered up the menus and wandered off. "Basically, you choose the food and drinks and then she'll change the wine order."

"We need to bring Steve here," my friend, Mark suggested. "He knows his wines."

The meal was a great success and we decided to finish with coffee. On the menu was an intriguing item: "Café de l'amitié." Next to it was the slightly corrupted English translation, "Friendly coffee." We decided that that sounded sufficiently wacky so ordered it. "Pour quatre?" "Oui s'il vous plaît." What turned up was beyond our wildest dreams. It looked like an outsized ashtray with four spouts that resembled cigarette rests. It was a wooden bowl, ornately carved, about the size of one of those Japanese, trendy, round cast iron tea pots but with no handle. We had many questions. Madame explained that the "ashtray" was called a "grole" and that it contained hot black coffee with various liqueurs including Marc de Savoie. "Marc" is a disgusting local spirit that is described as brandy but with none of Cognac's qualities apart from the alcohol content. Some sugar is mixed with the Marc, added to the concoction and then lit to add a caramel flavour. The lid is replaced to extinguish the flames and to encourage the alcohol fumes through the spouts for the participants to inhale as they imbibe. We were told that we had a spout each. Once someone picks the grole up they have to take a mouthful of the potent mix and pass it round. Everyone takes a sip from their spout and the grole, once up, is not allowed to be put down until all the drink has been consumed. We staggered out and home having booked to come the following evening with the other couple.

(The joys of the English language! There is a world of difference between the more correct translation of "Coffee of friendship" that describes the ritual perfectly and "Friendly coffee" that still makes me think of a frothy cappuccino that someone has made a smiley face on top of with the cocoa shaker.)

Forewarned, on the second evening, having ordered our food, madame enquired of us what wine we would like to drink. The diplomatic Will asked, "What would you suggest?" I translated but she seemed to understand the English. She recommended some wines and we nodded cautiously in agreement. We hadn't been given the most expensive wines the night before and so we decided that we were safe - and we were.

Once again we ordered the friendly coffee. This time we had a bigger ashtray. It had six spouts. We explained the procedure to the other couple and then we tucked in. It didn't taste any better but sharing is caring. We booked for the following night and this time we added Steve, our wine connoisseur, and Annie who were happy to miss one evening's hotel meal in order to meet our exacting waitress. "She'll have you on the wine," I warned but Steve was unfazed and having none of it. "I know what I'm doing," he replied.

Once seated madame brought over the menus. Steve picked up the wine list and opened it. Our waitress hovered behind him. "I would like a bottle of that and a bottle of that," he asked pointing. I didn't need to translate. "Now, what do you suggest I have to eat with those wines? Can you help?" "Nice move Steve!" I thought. "Mais oui," madame replied. If she now understood English she wasn't about to speak it. She told Steve what he should have for his first two courses and of course, to avoid any dissent, the rest of us had the same. We had a friendly coffee for eight (eight spouts) and then decided that with three nights at the same restaurant we should try somewhere else or we might as well have had half board again. We spent the rest of the week going to different places but nowhere lived up to Le Chaudron for food, drink, atmosphere and - of course - our wonderful waitress.

The following year I was back, this time with a group of my male friends. There were eleven of us in total. On the evening we had booked a table in Le Chaudron we had started in a bar in the same street that was offering half-price "happy hour" drinks. We thought that we would only have a quick pint each so someone suggested that we order five and a half pints and get eleven. But with the variety of beers requested and the fact that we sort of learnt that it was more of a BOGOF (Buy One, Get One Free) deal we somehow managed to end up with four pints each and charged for two.

After a quick four pints, forget staggering out of Le Chaudron, this time we staggered *into* Le Chaudron. We were greeted like old friends and were shown to a long table with five places either side and one at one end. Phillip needed space and so plopped himself down at the end. Billy likes to be in the middle so that he always has plenty of people to speak to and positioned himself likewise. As an aside, it is fairly amusing to see Billy at work. Normally diners sit down from one end of a table as they enter a restaurant; Billy starts in the middle on either side. My wife, on the other hand, sits in the middle on the side that backs onto the wall as she likes to see what's going on. Everyone had been forewarned about the wine débâcle and there were now present those who thought they could get even. Billy gently held madame's wrist. He speaks not a sentence of French: he wasn't deterred. "Now then, please help me with what I should be having with my meal and what is your name?" She replied in almost perfect English, telling Billy that her name was Chloé, guiding him through several options. "I am most obliged Chloé," said Billy at one point. "You really do know your wines." Then he stopped, only for a moment. "My goodness Chloé, I do believe you're blushing!" he remarked softly. Indeed she was! "Oh là là monsieur!"

One of our party ordered a lager and was then mostly ignored whilst Phillip had gone a little off-piste with his entrée and ordered Parma ham and figs. Once the mains' wine merry-go-round had finally been completed Phillip was then targeted. "Of course, you won't be drinking what they're having. May I suggest a large glass of chilled Sauternes?" Phillip was more than happy to accept.

Once again the meal went well and eventually it was time for the friendly coffee. This is where it all went terribly wrong. The grole came up and we began by counting the spouts. There were twelve. Ordinarily this should not have posed too much of a problem as all we had to do is miss out one spout but the problems started even before that. The bowl had only been sitting on the table for a minute when Billy picked it up! He took a gulp, swallowed, screamed and passed it on. By the time that the first circuit had been completed we were all suffering from scalded roofs of mouths. Then Billy decided that he wanted a clean spout so used the one that hadn't been touched. Soon no one could work out which was their spout. This shouldn't have been an issue given the amount of germ-killing alcohol we were drinking but somehow it was. Then another member felt that they had had enough but instead of simply bypassing them it was determined that the grole should go round anti-clockwise. Now some were getting more and so those that were getting less ordered another alcoholic ashtray even though the first one hadn't been finished. There was only one twelve-spout grole bowl in the restaurant so we were now given two six-spouts. Naturally it was suggested that we pass the two around together with one for six of us and the other for five of us, alternating and so continually leapfrogging each other "just for fun." Now we had three going round with the original one still going anti-clockwise. Soon one of my friends had two bowls, one in each hand, so said that he would execute a double-sip. It didn't work. Then someone else said that we should combine all three into the largest one. He took the lid off the twelve spout and began to pour. When there's only one person sipping the drink only comes out from one spout but if the bowl is tipped too high then three spouts come into service. The middle one hit the target but the other two poured the precious liquid all over the tablecloth. I complained that they were doing it all wrong. Billy was cross because of the waste of alcohol. Steven was only concerned about his trousers that had been soiled by flying coffee that he said would make a stain that would never come out. Phillip blamed me for ordering them in the first place although I pointed out that I had only ordered one and the ritual was being played out perfectly well until Gary wanted to reverse the direction and then ordered a couple more. In the midst of this Gary "froze" and so we all had to follow suit. Lager man said he had put a spout to his mouth but not sipped so he wasn't going to pay then someone pointed out that the top of his spout was wet so some must have gone into his mouth. Lager man replied that he hadn't swallowed so was challenged as to what he had done with the liquid. As with all booze-fuelled male-only events a punch-up seemed inevitable saved only by Chloé bringing over the bill. The fight was taken to the streets (although we were mates again by the morning).

"Not that friendly a coffee then," Phillip remarked as we left the restaurant.

The following year we returned and we all had cappuccinos.

Courchevel

L'andouillette AAAAA. Possibly the worst thing you can ever put in your mouth.

Said a pig to its colon, "With no warning,
For you I will be in deep mourning.
The French are in town
With scalpel and frown.
An andouillette dish soon adorning."

When you think high-end ski resorts first you have most of Switzerland followed by Courchevel in France. It has loads of greens and blues so great for beginners. Then there's the chic boutiques and high-end dining, especially at 1850. I haven't stayed there though. I've spent a week slumming it (it's all relative) at 1550 Courchevel-Village. We stayed, basically, in a pub with rooms and there I learnt a drinking game with a kids' toy - Pop Up Pirate.

My wife and I had met a couple on a summer holiday. They came from Portsmouth and had a huge group going skiing and we were invited. Several of our number were British Airways' pilots and there was a fair smattering of BA air hostesses for good measure. They knew how to party and they also loved good food.

One lunchtime one of the BA air hostesses, Genevieve, who was something of a gastronome, had booked us in to a bistro behind the *rond point* at 1850. Small, intimate and with just enough seats to accommodate us all outside we plonked ourselves down and picked up the menu. As usual I thought I would try something regional. "That looks good," I said to Genevieve who was seated next to me. "L'andouillette AAAAA." "Vraiment?" (Really?) she asked.

"Do you know what it is?" "It says underneath, 'Spicy sausage.' That sounds good." Genevieve gave me a funny look. "But it's not like sausage as in England. It's a speciality of Lyon. It's a very French thing." "So what are you having?" "I'm having a mushroom omelette." "That doesn't sound very French," I told her. "'Omelette'? It is French!" she complained.

When the waiter came over to take our order I said that I was going to have l'andouillette AAAAA. "Vraiment?" he said. "Oh, my goodness," I replied. "What's wrong with it?" I looked at Genevieve. "Tell me one thing, is it dick?" Genevieve laughed. "No, it's not dick." Then she laughed again.

When l'andouillette (the AAAAA is a mark of its top quality) arrived my first impression was that it looked like an outsized spring roll that you get in Chinese restaurants, the only difference was, apart from it appearing to be furry, that it stank! Long, big, fat, furry, stinky: I was beginning to wonder. Genevieve took a bite of her beautifully fluffy mushroom omelette and watched me cut into my dick, so to speak. I cut straight across the middle and opened it up. There it was - a large tube running through the centre. It was dick, donkey's dick! "Spicy sausage" my backside! I did try a bit though and it was fine. Smelly, chewy, garlicky - but fine. Genevieve had other ideas. She had been eying it suspiciously for several moments. "You don't like it?" "It's okay," I said, "okay" meaning good. "I knew you wouldn't like it, here, have my omelette," and before I could grab hold of my plate it had gone and in its place an omelette with a tiny bit missing from one end. Genevieve cut a large slice of the dick and stuck it in her mouth. She shut her eyes, chewed then smiled. She looked as though she was in heaven. I had a funny moment but then I came quickly back to earth. She had garlicky juices pouring from her mouth. "Mmmmm, délicieux!" she purred. Another slice went into her mouth, then another. Soon she was halfway through it. Then she looked at me. "'ow is your omelette?" I pushed it away. "I don't know," I said, "I can't eat eggs."

I was only joking of course; the omelette was lovely. But whenever I go skiing and I see l'andouillette on the menu I remember garlic Genevieve and have a little smile to myself. Then I order something else; pig colon is not for me.

Davos

You never quite know who you might meet on a chair lift.

Way, way back, when I was in my twenties, I was very fortunate to be invited to stay at a wonderful Swiss chalet belonging to a close friend of my father's for ten days' skiing. He had a son of a similar age to me and he was keen for him to be in the company of someone with whom he would be able to ski and socialise. It was something of a risk though as we had never met.

The first impressions were positive; we soon became firm friends and remain so to this day. Although neither of us ski any more we often get together and reminisce with a plethora of anecdotes. However, that first trip to Davos remains the location of my favourite.

Back in those far-off days skiing was even more the preserve of the wealthy and in Switzerland many had their own chalet in the mountains, something that remains to this day in some respects. My parents sent me off on the train with plenty of Swiss Francs in my pocket and a book of travellers' cheques. I was young and desirable though I say so myself, with an aura of the rakish about me according to my friend. I walked in fairly high society in London and shouldn't have been surprised to see more than one familiar face in the village.

One morning I jumped on a two-man chair lift ahead of my friend and found myself in the company of a young lady, around thirty years of age. She bade me a, "Good morning, good to see you," and smiled; I returned the compliment. As we started up the mountain I noticed that she was wearing no skis but otherwise could have been a skier as she was wearing a jacket, ski pants and sporting a pair of goggles. I was convinced that I knew her, had met her or seen her somewhere. I decided to break the silence that ensued and set myself the challenge of getting an answer before the top of the lift. In those days it wouldn't have done for the lady to initiate any questions so I asked simply, "How are you?"

"Very well, thank you," she replied. On the other hand too invasive a line of questioning from the man would have been considered not proper also. I had to tread cautiously.

"Not skiing today?"

"No, I've just slipped out for a quick trip to the top to take in the view. It's a favourite of mine. Skiing's a bit out of the question at present." Silence. I had no idea why and to ask would have been considered prying.

"Um, how are the children?"

"Child. Still a baby really, but he's fine." Oh dear.

"And, er, your mother?" I asked racking my brains. Where had I heard this voice before?

"Very well."

"Your father?"

"He's still dead." Now I was beginning to become just a little troubled in both my heart and soul. How deep could I dig my hole but I felt compelled to continue. She was giving nothing away. I wished I could just have asked, "How do I know you?" or "Have we met before?" but asking such questions would lay me open to charges of not being very attentive to any meeting we had previously had and we must have met before because she was just a tiny bit more familiar with me than had I been a complete stranger.

"Your brother but I can't remember if you have more than one. How is he?"

"I have none."

"It must have been your sister then," I flustered in abject desperation. "How's your sister?"

"Very well also, thank you." Finally I decided that I needed to caste all social conventions aside and probe. By this stage I was actually physically shaking but not from the cold.

"And what's she doing now?"

"She's still Queen."

Fortunately we had reached the top of the lift and it slowed to let my companion for the ride walk off. No further words were exchanged. As for me I immediately skied off down the nearest piste with my friend chasing me from a short way behind. I didn't stop until I reached the bottom whereupon I immediately went back to the chalet to change my jacket lest I be recognised. The shame! The embarrassment! That said, since that holiday I have, over the years, eaten out many a time recounting the story of that second meeting with Princess Margaret and I don't doubt she did too.

We never met again.

Les Deux Alpes

CLOSE / rhymes with dose / adjective 1. only a short distance away, or
CLOSE / rhymes with nose / verb 1. bring two parts of something together.

A great resort for beginners who want to feel part of the holiday as there are some easy slopes at the top of the mountain rather than down in the village which is often more usual.

When I went there with my wife and two children she was still very much a beginner, in fact more of a beginner than our children, but she wasn't going to let anyone realise it when off the slopes. Not quite, "all dressed up and nowhere to go," but not far from it. Unfortunately she had yet to fully master the chair lift and so her cover was blown on the first day before she had even started down a piste. To be fair, even seasoned skiers can have the occasional issue with chair lifts but most of it comes down to concentration which my wife did not have in abundance.

We had had a small argument over breakfast about when she could progress to red runs. I had said, "Wait until next year," but she wasn't having any of it. She then decided she needed a bit of time to herself on the chair lift without telling us. She managed to get on in front of us and was then all by herself. We were following her on the chair behind, having pushed to the front. I was watching her and it looked as though she was fiddling with her helmet then her gloves then her poles. Basically she was doing everything except keeping an eye out for the top of the lift. I've always said, "Lift up the security bar when you're at the last pylon" is a good rule of thumb so when my wife's chair went past the last pylon and she didn't do anything I waited for the crunch as her foot rest piled into the alighting platform but it didn't happen.

I wasn't going to shout at her but the lift attendant did. In fact he blew a whistle and gesticulated at my wife to lift the bar but by then she was panicking. She was trying to lift it up but she still had her feet on the foot rest but in her confusion she hadn't realised. The attendant had no alternative but to press the emergency stop. The lift quickly ground to a halt whereupon my wife calmly removed her feet, lifted up the bar and slid from her seat a couple of feet onto the snow at which point she crumpled into a heap. Cue more whistle blowing from the attendant.

I wasn't going to say anything after she had been rescued and dumped at the top of the piste to one side of the lift and we had caught up with her but she looked at me and said, far too aggressively for my liking, especially as I was going to say nothing much, "Well if you're going to say something, spit it out."

"I was just wondering why you didn't lift up the bar," was all I said. She glared at me and replied, "I was only following instructions on the pylon. It said 'CLOSE' so I kept the bar closed.

I said to her, "'C-L-O-S-E' doesn't mean put the bar down it means that you are nearly at the top you idiot." There was nothing that she could say to that and she knew it. I suppose she could have hit me but it doesn't really have much effect in ski gear. She took off her skis and stomped across the piste to the restaurant then disappeared inside. That was the last time that I skied with her on that holiday, in fact any holiday since because she's now my ex.

England

Drama on the dry slope with break-a-neck bindings.

I have lived in north-west Kent all of my life and have skied regularly since I was in my teens. I've become quite good! When I began skiing my friends and I used to have a few warm-up sessions at a dry slope down in Chatham before one opened up much nearer to home. It was in St Paul's Cray, Orpington and called "Bromley Ski & Snowboard Centre." It had a decent enough length of nylon tufted matting complete with "moguls" and to one side there was a smaller nursery slope. There was a drag lift on either side. It had a reception where you could hire kit and book lessons. There was also an alpine lodge that was home to a ski shop and a bar. It was a great venue for a social ski gathering and when it snowed, with a mulled wine in your hand, sitting on the terrace under the twinkly lights, you could almost be in the mountains apart from the view, from the top of the slope, of the A20 and the traffic going into and out from London.

It was still there in the early 2010s when my children were old enough to ski. They had been on a few holidays already but one year I decided to take them to the centre for a warm up and a bit of a practice. It wasn't strictly necessary for my children because young people are very good at picking up where they left off the previous year in respect of skiing lessons. Nevertheless I thought it would be a bit of fun. When I arrived with my wife I noticed how run down the facility had become compared to its glory days a few years previously. The bar had very few customers, there was a café area with gaudy florescent star-shaped price cards with FREE DRINK WITH EVERY SAUSAGE ROLL, that sort of thing. The ski shop had gone.

I had booked my children in for a lesson each so I went to reception and handed them over. I thought that whilst I was there I would have a little go myself as did my wife. I booked us both a half hour session. I collected my boots and went over to the ski section. This was still at a time when it was all about length and I was skiing in skis every bit as long as I am tall (over six feet) if not longer. The ski attendant grabbed a pair of carvers, not the best type for nylon matting, and took a boot. "Height? Weight? Ability?" he barked. "Fourteen stone, six foot one, advanced," I replied. "Do you think I could have some longer skis please?" He looked at me with a raised eyebrow. "Everyone's normally intermediate here," he said, ignoring my question. "That's because beginners normally say they're intermediates as do intermediates. But you won't get many who are advanced because they will be on snow," I advised. "My children are here for a lesson so I just thought the two of us would put a few turns in. Could I have longer skis please?" He looked at my wife. "Are you advanced too?" "Expert actually." "How expert?" "I'm a professional if you need to know. Won cups and medals, proper ones - real gold-plated, that sort of thing." "So why aren't you teaching your kids?" he asked. "Because I'm their mother," my wife replied shortly. She doesn't suffer fools gladly.

The attendant took my skis off the adjusting clamp. "Could I have longer skis please? About one nineties please." "No one has one nineties any more unless you're an expert." He looked at me in an attempt to stare me out, then leered at my wife. "And you're only advanced." He took one ski in each hand, put them upright with their ends on the floor and slammed them together so hard I thought they would break. "Off you go whilst I deal with the expert," he said. "Actually," said my wife, "I've changed my mind. I think I'll go and watch the children." "See ya!" said the attendant with a wink. "Only on the TV," said my wife and ambled off.

I went outside and put my skis on. They were definitely past their best. I grabbed hold of a button and up I went. At the top I looked down the slope and decided to tackle the bumps as there was no one on them. There had been a bit of rain so the surface should be fast enough I thought. I took off and went straight in order get sufficient speed to keep me going over the moguls. Before the first one I put in the slightest of turns to regulate my speed when something happened that had never happened to me before without first falling over or hitting something - one of my skis came off! Clean off, no warning. It carried on all the way down the slope to the bottom. (This is something that should never happen as when the boot heel comes off the brake pad then the brakes should engage.) I was left on one ski trying to put another proper turn in with a split-second's notice. I managed it but then I had the choice of going straight down or turning again. I took the latter course but soon decided it wasn't working. I was too near the edge of the matting and I was heading for the drag lift. If you push forward hard enough in your boots the back binding will release and that's what I did with the other ski. I then executed a controlled landing, bum first, on the matting. It's only when you're in this position you realise how forgiving snow can be but ice isn't and neither is nylon. I went over and then bumped down the surface for some considerable distance, taking the full impact of each tufted square hole, bumpity, bumpity, bump! It was agony!

Once at the bottom I picked myself up. Nothing broken. I retrieved my skis and headed straight for the reception area. I stormed in. I was fuming! If chummy hadn't seen me coming he would have heard me. He was out in the open boot-fitting area but when he saw me he quickly retreated back behind his counter. Before I had reached him he was shouting, "All right, all right! Keep yer hair on! You can have a pair of longer skis. I've got everything. Just take what you want!" I banged my carvers on the counter top. "It's not the length, it's the quality! Look!" I showed him the bracket that was supposed to hold the back binding in place. It had come unclipped and the rear binding was sliding up and down on its guide. "I didn't do that! It's not my fault!" "Yes you did and yes it is," I said, far too calmly. "I expect when you crashed the skis together the bracket came undone." "I don't think so," he said as he inspected the binding. He clipped the bracket back into place and unclipped it again. It came up far too easily. "I need to get these checked," he said a little quieter. "Who by? An expert?" I asked. "Yes," he replied. "I know just the person," I scowled. "She's not far away. I'll go and get her."

I went outside to my wife who had been so wrapped up watching our children on the nursery slope that she had missed the drama on the main slope. I told her what had happened then sat down. I had had my say and I vowed never to go back into the building again. And I didn't. The children finished their lesson and we left. The following day I had a bruise that would have won first prize in the right competition. The whole of the buttock that I landed on and halfway down the leg was black with bruising.

I suppose I could have sued but I couldn't be bothered. In fact none of my family ever returned to that dry slope and a few years later in 2016 it closed. The owner was reported as saying, "It's just not economically viable to run any more. There's been a decrease in volume over the years."

I wonder why.

Flaine

A very snowy lunch.

My friends and I were staying in a small chalet that was run by an old French lady and her daughter who was called Coraline. She was beautiful and had never married. She had lived in the Alps all her life and said that she was never going to leave. I was in love despite the fact that she was probably at least ten years older than me. I was twenty at the time. I didn't speak French but Coraline's English was fairly good although it was slow, thoughtful - as if she were translating every word in her head as she went along - and it came with a heavy French accent. This, however, just added to the appeal. I listened intently to her every word and always had a banal response along the lines of, "That is so interesting!" or "I feel so much better informed now that you have told me that!" I hung so much on everything that she said that my friends, rather unkindly, started calling me "lapdog". How rude. I figured that if I was responsive to everything Coraline said that she would reciprocate when I had anything to say and so the seed of mutual admiration would start to grow. I decided that I would have to become a little bit more French in order to close the gap between the two of us. I was trying to play it cool but whenever she was around I would get very hot under the collar, in fact a stuttering ball of sweat. I started drinking bowls of coffee and warm milk at breakfast because she said that that was what she had even though I hated coffee. I told her that tea was for wimps even though a cup of tea first thing in the morning is the best drink of the day. I started to eat croissants despite their being fifty percent butter which I also detest. When she said something to her mother (in French) I would nod gravely despite having no idea what she was saying.

In four short days I had matured considerably; I was cool, calm and eager for acceptance.

On the Wednesday of our week's holiday Coraline suddenly announced that she would come skiing with us for the day and take us all to an alpine restaurant for something to eat after a few hours' skiing. I was beside myself with excitement. I told my friends that I was reserving any two-man chair lift that we had to go on for Coraline and me. She would be a captive audience and I could continue to try to impress her with the few French words that I had learnt although I hadn't progressed much further than "Bonjour" and "Comment vas-tu?"

We had a few runs under our belt as well as several lifts, but so far they had been gondolas and drags. We then approached a chair lift. "Up 'ere," said Coraline waving her ski pole in the direct of a, sadly for me, six-man lift. We skied down to the gates and lined up ready to advance. Coraline was at one end and I was next to her with four of my friends on the other side. We plopped ourselves down without a hitch and I could soon feel her warm body next to mine as we started up the mountain. At least I imagined I could but it was a very cold, overcast day; visibility was poor.

We were high up over a piste with a huge valley wall on one side at the bottom of which I could just make out a few buildings. As we went higher and higher Coraline waved a pole in the direction of the buildings and announced, far too calmly for the subject matter of the statement, "That is where we 'ave, um, avalanche." My friends didn't say a thing but I did; I needed to respond and, for once, not with, "That is so interesting!" It was interesting but it was also shocking. I wondered how Coraline could be so complacent, unconcerned even. Maybe the emotion gets lost in translation. I turned in my small seat and looked over Coraline's shoulder down the valley. The buildings looked as though they had a fair bit of snow on their roofs but were certainly not buried: unless there were others of course. "That's dreadful!" I exclaimed. Coraline gave me a quizzical look. "Really?" She asked. "Yes!" I replied with a sense of urgency. "When?" "Today," she replied calmly. Maybe alpine people were used to death. Perhaps they just accepted that it was one of the hazards of living in the snowy mountains. I was still shocked though. I tried not to show it any more. "Where did all the snow come from?" "I'm sorry Paul?" "The snow; did it come off the top of the cliff?" Coraline sighed as if I had asked the stupidest question known to man. I didn't know why. I tried to stifle my shock and instead attempted a bit of empathy, not that Coraline needed it. "I 'ave no idea what you are talking about," she replied. "The avalanche," I repeated. "Where did the snow come from for the avalanche?" "No avalanche," she replied with a smile, looking straight ahead. "Oh dear." She shook her head slowly from side to side. "I said, 'Zat is where we are going to 'ave our lunch.'"

We 'ad a very good lunch but I had lost any smidgen of credibility big time with Coraline and almost as much with my friends on the lift with us.

The following morning as she started to prepare my goldfish bowl of coffee and warm milk I bit my lip and said, "I think I'll have tea today."

My ski friends, whom I love dearly, to this day never miss an opportunity to ask me, when we're going out somewhere to eat, where we are going to 'ave our lunch.

Le Fornet

Don't touch that!

I was recently skiing with a small group of girls on the Pisaillas glacier above le Fornet. We had a beginner with us, Chris, who was snowboarding but she had been on a dry slope with a couple of days' skiing under her belt. Also she was keen to progress so was happy doing the blues. At the bottom of the glacier there's a tiny run called Pays Desert. On the other side of the button draglift that you have to take back out of the "desert" there's a banked-up course for snowboarders that, naturally, us skiers had to go down also. At the bottom we all jumped, so to speak, on the draglift back up; our snowboarder was at the rear. Chris made it up to almost the top but let go just a second or two early and lost all momentum. As she shuffled forward she took my proffered pole then hooked it round a length of red rope that was strung up a couple of inches off the snow in front of her and pulled. She told me afterwards that she thought that the rope was merely marking where not to ski and that one had to turn, but no, it was an emergency trip wire. A claxon sounded, a red light started to flash and the draglift quickly ground to a halt. Now that's fun if you're actually on the lift, especially on the final approach when you're invariably going up a slope at a forty-five degree angle. The person on the lift behind our snowboarder was exactly in this position. He wasn't very patient at all having witnessed the drama unfold. We couldn't see much lower than his head with its stupid black woolly hat and John Lennon sunglasses but that was all that was needed for us to quite clearly hear, word for word, the torrent of invective that was pouring forth from his lips. I thought of going over to one of the posts and pressing on the large orange button but for all I knew that may have put the lift into reverse so we all just stood there wondering what was going to happen. We moved a few feet away so that we were physically as well as mentally detached from what had just occurred. With no lift attendant at the top and where we were not being visible from the bottom we watched and waited. Eventually a pisteur skied down from somewhere, looked around at no one in particular as we gazed at our ski boots, said something into his walkie talkie, examined the trip wire then, you've guessed it, pressed the orange button. An alarm sounded and the lift started up again. The first person over the top was the man spouting words that my teenage daughter had never heard before. "Watch out, here comes the manther," she warned as Mr Blobby emerged over the top, also let go too early, far too early, and very nearly gave us a quick demonstration of how not to ski backwards downhill. He waved a pole in the air at Chris. "You [bleep, bleep, bleep] pillock!" he shouted. "I nearly had to let go the strain on my [bleep] arms was so great." Chris wasn't at all put out. She was made of sterner stuff and could certainly look after herself. She said afterwards that she knew that she wasn't going to get thumped as it's almost impossible with skis on. "You should lose some weight then you miserable git, or do some arm muscle-building exercises. Skiing's a sport, not a recreation!" I thought for a moment that Mr Blobby was going to take some retaliatory action but with four of us stroppy females and only two of them (by now he had been joined by a friend who had been coming up behind on the drag), after another torrent of abuse from both they took to their heels, so to speak, and skied back down the blue.

It took us some time to get moving again. Chris was a little bit shaken by the experience and so we just stood and chatted for a few minutes whilst she calmed down after her adrenaline rush. We decided that we wouldn't do the same blue again in case we bumped into our new friend and that instead we would take the other short lift back to the main ski area. Suddenly our snowboarder was running. "What's going on...? Oh no!" Chris was standing by the red rope and just as Mr Blobby's head re-emerged at the top of the lift she shouted, "Loser!" stuck her fingers up at him then kicked the red rope. Claxon! Light! Halt! This time words poured forth from the manther's mouth that even I had never heard before. Then something unexpected happened - Mr Blobby's head disappeared. So taken was he with waving both arms in the air, one with ski poles in his hand, that he had lost his balance on the lift and had slipped off. Chris rushed over to the top of the lift just in time to see Mr Blobby cascading back down the ski tracks of the slope that the lift was on and then take out his friend who had tried to master the impossible feat of jumping up out of the way. The two of them tumbled over each other down the slope, finally coming to a halt on a flat bit about halfway down. Chris watched them slowly pick themselves up and then, happy in the knowledge that they weren't seriously injured, strolled back over to us and clipped herself back into her board. We skied over to the chair lift and jumped on as the same pisteur skied past in the other direction. Nothing needed to be said, we just smiled to each other. The moral of the story? Don't mess with the girls, not now, especially near a draglift - we have a secret weapon!

Geneva

The four-year-old bobsleigh smuggler.

The first time that my husband and I took our son, Rodney, skiing in Switzerland he was four years old. We put him in ski school in a resort that shall have to remain anonymous. He wasn't very interested in putting on a pair of skis, he was perfectly content just playing in the snow. A few days in we took him shopping in one of the lovely gift shops stuffed full of fun things to take home, not least of all the cuckoo clocks. However his eyes, wide open in amazement, landed on a toy bobsleigh, red and white plastic, about eight inches long. It was very heavy. The saleswoman explained that it was designed to go down the gentlest of slopes; we soon discovered that indeed it did! The following afternoon we took Rodney and his real sledge and his toy bobsleigh on the shortest chair lift in the resort. From the top we aimed the bobsleigh down the piste and when there was no one in the vicinity we let go. It went off like a rocket! It was going faster than I could ski. I left my husband in charge of Rodney and set off after it. At the bottom of the piste there was, to one side, a narrow road about ten feet below the slope and on the other side of the road a row of six old houses. As I chased the bobsleigh down the slope I was horrified to see it go straight under the orange netting that stopped people, but not toys, from sliding into the road. It took off and with so much momentum flew across the little road and straight through the large glass front window of one of the houses. I stopped and stood by the netting trying not to stare at the shattered glass but it was obvious that the bobsleigh had caused quite a bit of damage. And it had disappeared, presumably inside the house. Then I did something that to this day I am ashamed of - I skied away. No one was paying any attention, no one had seen what had happened so I skied off to the far end of the piste where the road comes round the corner and there I waited. Eventually my husband and Rodney found me and I pointed to where we had been. I indicated an imaginary line from the top of the chair lift to where we were now standing. "I just can't understand how it can just have disappeared," I said to my husband, sounding far too convincing, but then I am an actress. This was not quite a lie because it had disappeared, the only thing was I knew where it had disappeared to. Then Rodney began to cry. "It could be anywhere, round here," my husband said. It was getting very busy where we were standing with all the skiers gathering after their last run of the day so I suggested that we go and buy another one which is what we did. The following afternoon and for the rest of the week we took the replacement to one side of the nursery slope and were very, very careful. I made sure that we didn't go anywhere near the piste on the other side again.

We flew back to Gatwick from Geneva. We had minimal hand luggage but Rodney had his rucksack into which he kept his most precious possessions including his favourite monkey and a colouring book. All was going along quite happily with check in and passport control and so on but in between we had an incident. Rodney put his rucksack through the x-ray machine but once we had been through the scanner we were surprised to find that his rucksack had been taken off the conveyer belt by a member of staff. We were called over to one side and told by one of the security team that there was a suspicious item in the rucksack. "It's my son's rucksack," I wailed, "and he's only four!" There was no response, only a request for me to take everything out. I took out the colouring book and pens, the monkey, the bobsleigh... Then one of the security team pounced. He picked up the bobsleigh and examined it very carefully as if looking for the slightest scratch. I was asked where I bought it and when, and how much I had paid for it. I began to sweat. I suddenly worked out what I presumed had happened. The person with the broken window had reported the matter to the police, suggesting a non-Swiss national as being responsible, and the airport authorities had been alerted to look out for a bobsleigh matching the description of the one that had caused the damage. They had rightly surmised that a replacement would be bought and that it may well go in a young person's hand luggage. I suddenly began to feel quite light-headed and I started to sweat even more. "Are you okay madam?" a lady asked who had just joined her colleague. "It's my menopause," I blurted out. The lady grabbed my passport from my hand and opened it. "You're only thirty-nine," she said as she took the bobsleigh from her colleague. I started to whimper then it all came out. I couldn't stand the tension, the lies and the deceit any longer.

"Look, I'm so sorry about the window in [the ski resort]. We didn't know that it was going to go so quickly and it took off and I was just in shock and I then had to buy Rodney a new one and I'll pay for the window that I broke..." "What window?" asked the lady and my husband in unison. I immediately tried to think how I was going to get out of the hole I had just dug for myself but despite the adrenaline rush I was experiencing, or because of it, I was very confused and nothing coherent was forming in my brain so instead I simply stood there sobbing, as well as Rodney crying, telling them exactly what had happened whilst all the passengers going past stared at me. Finally the lady spoke as she handed the bobsleigh and passport back to me. She said gently, "I know nothing about what you are talking about and especially not about a broken window madam. We're mostly only interested in the safety and security of your flight. The only reason we pulled your son's rucksack to one side was because of this item that has a large block of lead in it and the x-ray machine can't see through it so we needed to see what it was. That's all."

You can imagine what my husband said to me on the 'plane.

The following year we returned to the same resort. I had some unfinished business. On the second day I went to the house that had had the broken window. It had obviously been replaced. I took a deep breath and knocked on the door. After a minute or two I thought that I should just leave but Rodney who was with me, my husband had refused to come, said that he could hear someone. The door opened and an elderly lady was standing there. The room she was in was large and modern. Then my heart froze. On the coffee table in the middle of the room - was the bobsleigh. I was ready to blurt out my, "You're not going to believe this but...I am so sorry...I know I did wrong...Please let me pay..." speech but Rodney got in first having also seen his bobsleigh. "Please lady. Please can I have my bobsleigh back?"

We were ushered into the room and asked to sit down. Then a man appeared, probably not much older than me. I thought we were then in big trouble but it turned out that he was acting as interpreter. "I thought you would come back eventually," said the old lady, "but I didn't think that it would take you a year." She offered us some tea and produced a large bowl of almonds. I thought I should eat a few just to be polite. I don't really like them but my husband does and I told her so, the latter bit. She was very forgiving and insisted that she didn't need reimbursing as the insurance paid for the replacement window. Then she said, "A small toy coming through my window is nothing.

One of the reasons the authorities put up the netting a few years ago was because one day a snowboarder came through my window." I gasped. "A toy one?" "No, a real one. A full size one. Have some more almonds." I didn't feel so bad after that. I was concerned that the old lady wasn't having any almonds so I suggested that she join me. Then her son said, "She doesn't like them." "Then why does she buy them?" I asked. "To give to people who have crashed through her window?" The man laughed. "Oh no," he said. "She buys them as sugar almonds because she likes the taste of the sugar coating. So she licks all the sugar off but doesn't like to waste the nuts so she puts them in a bowl for her guests." "As punishment," I thought to myself feeling suddenly as if I was going to throw up.

As we stood up to leave the old lady pressed the bobsleigh into Rodney's hand. "Next time, tie a long length of string round it, like a dog," she suggested. Then she asked me where Rodney's father was. "Back at the hotel," I replied. "He was such a coward. He was not prepared to come and hold my hand whilst I came to apologise. I was so upset." Then I'm sure I saw the trace of a twinkle in her eye.

"Would you like to take the almonds back for him?" she suggested. "All of them perhaps?"

How could I say no!

Les Gets

Live no Lies.

Last summer I graduated from Cambridge University with a first class degree in Theology, Religion, and Philosophy of Religion. Though I say so myself, I had worked very hard for three years and was now well-versed in asking and answering fundamental questions from theological and philosophical standpoints. I think! What I didn't realise was that my knowledge was going to be put to use sooner than I had expected. After my A-levels I didn't take a gap year as I went straight into my degree course. Now I needed some fun!

Many of those in my year had taken an A-level in Religious Education. I hadn't, although I had come quite close with Philosophy after my teacher had said at the sixth form open evening, "If your child studies Philosophy at A-level be prepared for big arguments around the dinner table." My father grumpily replied, "We have those already."

Despite my interest in theology I wasn't a Christian. I didn't know what I believed in but was just looking forward to studying the Bible because one thing you can't argue about it is - it's fascinating. I had at my disposal world class professors and an amazing library and I soaked it all up. Slowly my studies also included time spent in analysing what I believed, if not the Word of a supposèd living God. Then I had to examine the Bible to find what was inconsistent with it. I could find nothing of any importance. I read extensively, working my way through many of the sixty thousand books in the library in the faculty as well as the university library. I talked, read, discussed and in the end I gave up! I held out my hands and said, "I believe!" I had a vision of a cross when I was alone at night in my bed and I knew that there was a living God who wanted me to submit my life to him. So I did. I was baptised in my last month at Cambridge and then went travelling for the summer before taking to the slopes in the winter months.

I have always loved skiing and so to spend the winter in a ski resort seemed a good way to get some runs in whilst also earning a bit of money. I thought that I may even find myself a lovely boyfriend. I went and worked as a live-in chalet girl in Les Gets which is one of the resorts in the vast Portes du Soleil ski area. It's a great place for intermediates; more advanced skiers can find other resorts nearby for the really challenging stuff. I was mostly waitressing and housekeeping for the around twelve guests that we had every week. It was certainly an eye-opener and an interesting lesson in how people behave together, and the different ways in which they interact, whilst on holiday.

One Saturday in particular will remain with me. Usually six couples, mostly adults, would appear but one evening in January this year twelve men in their early and mid twenties turned up. They were by and large charming. I didn't know if they had wives or girlfriends. I wasn't supposed to ask intrusive questions so didn't but there are ways of saying things that beg a response. This enables one to get an answer should you be wanting to be nosey. Things like, "If it wasn't for your partners would you stay out here for more than one week?"

On the Sunday the group had come back to the chalet after après ski. They had their showers, got changed, eaten dinner and gone out again. As I was also living in the chalet I sat in the sitting room area whilst they were out. When they returned, all very merry, one of them, I'll call him Ed, had brought a young lady back with him. I had to explain that there were very few rules, but one was that only the guests were allowed to sleep in the building. "She won't be sleeping!" Ed exclaimed. She then left and I had a short conversation with him as he wanted to know how I could sleep in the chalet but not be a guest. He was a bit cocky but I patiently explained that if he wanted looking after with bedding, clean rooms, and food during his stay then I needed to be there. He took this with good grace and went to bed. He was quite cute I thought but knew nothing about him and wasn't in any particular rush to find out.

The following evening all twelve had dinner early and then went out. They asked me along and I agreed as this wasn't against the rules, in fact it was encouraged. I took them to a lively bar and we had a good time. Everyone got split up and I ended up walking back to the chalet with Ed. On the way back he told me that he fancied me like mad and was I allowed to go for a drink with him the following evening? I said that I was and so I did. My cute thoughts were now handsome thoughts but I was able to control myself and as for not knowing him at all well I was perfectly safe in a ski resort. However the evening did not finish as I expected.

I was looking forward to my date. After dinner on Tuesday we walked out of the chalet together and he said that he wanted to take me somewhere for a quiet drink. I knew just the place - quite, cosy and intimate. As a first date there was plenty of talking to be done but it wasn't the usual conversation that one would expect. It started out normally enough though with smiles and compliments and hand-holding on the way to the bar. He turned out to be a very unhappy person. He said that he was only "sort of" single as he had told me the day before (without being asked) and that he was separated from his wife of only three years. In his search for happiness he had had several relationships since separating and had been getting drunk every weekend and a couple of weekdays, every single week. "I didn't mean this to be a counselling session," he said, "but you always seem to be so happy. What's the secret?" I took a deep breath as I reckoned I could help with two of his issues.

"In short, in my humble opinion, you're chasing the desires of the flesh," I told him. "That may sound very dramatic but please hear me out seeing as how you've asked. You don't know when to stop. One drink is great, but it's great because it's just one. If you have more than one you think that will be greater. It may be a bit but then it's diminishing returns. Happiness doesn't increase by drinking more, drinking more just gets you drunk and gives you a hangover in the morning. Slowly your body and mind will also suffer. So I'm really happy having only a couple of drinks in the evening. As for relationships, in your case women - stick with one. You won't get happier chasing more. You'll just never have any sort of intimacy that a monogamous relationship brings. You will merely end up continually jumping over fences because you think the grass will be greener. It won't be." I recommended him a book, *Live no Lies* by John Mark Comer and quoted Ed one of the researched ideas from it with regard to oxytocin and vasopressin, "the two chemicals released by our body during sex that bring our attachment system online and cause us to bond to another person. It seems that the more sexual partners you have, the *less* capacity your body has for intimacy." Ed put down his drink and we left without him finishing it. I seemed to have got through to him on a level that he appeared not to have been on before.

We walked back to the chalet in silence. Ed was thinking and I was praying. Back at the chalet he asked if we could talk some more, so we did. I sat down with him at the dining table and he told me about how he had been thinking about getting divorced from his wife. Then he told me that he was on this trip to give him some time away to think about the situation. I said to him, "You'll be happier if you get a divorce," is a myth. "Many times the reason for divorcing is that one if not both of the parties feel that they will be happier as a consequence. Some might, especially if there is real abuse in the relationship but that's a small percentage. In the majority of cases the individuals just end up even unhappier with many regretting their actions to the day they die. There is some research that points to as many as fifteen percent of divorcees actually remarrying their ex spouse. Don't believe the lie about what will make you happy." "It's probably too late," he replied. I told him that it was never too late but that at that particular moment it was getting a bit late as I would need to get up and sort out breakfast for him and the others! I thought I had said enough and so I got up to go to bed, leaving him with his thoughts. I hadn't told him that I was a Christian but as I reached the door I turned to tell him that I would include him in my prayers that evening. I was surprised to see that he was gently weeping. I let go of the door handle and went and sat beside him. "What's your wife's name?" I asked. He told me. I didn't even ask if he minded, I just said out loud a prayer there and then for him and his wife, for Ed to make the right decision and for his wife to be responsive even though I had no reason to doubt that she would be. In bed I prayed for them both some more. He seemed so desperate to be happy but hadn't realised that that happiness was already there. He just had to acknowledge it and work on it.

The following day when I went to give the guys their dinner in the evening there was one missing. They told me that Ed had left after breakfast and had gone home - to his wife.

Gstaad

Accidental acquisition by an ageing aristocrat.

Every year my wife and I ski in Gstaad, Switzerland. We've done so for many years, staying at the same five, but more like six, star hotel.

My wife likes the finer things in life and who am I to disagree? Maybe that should be an exclamation mark! When she's had enough of skiing for the day it's a quick blast of après in a Jacuzzi or hot tub - there is a difference - followed by a spot of shopping. There's plenty of the latter to keep even my wife and also my bank account entertained for ten days.

For Christmas last year I bought her, among other items, a pair of black Prada, Gore-Tex leather and knit ski gloves complete with a red Prada stripe down each back. They cost over five hundred pounds but as she often complains that her hands are too cold, then too hot then sweaty and round again I was told by the sales assistant that not only are they Prada and therefore exceptionally well made but also that they are water-repellent. They comprise a seamless knit at the back, which is described as being like a second skin, and a leather palm. First class. She loves them.

In March this year, one day we both finished skiing early. We had been over to Schönried and had returned with time to spare so my wife implored me to, "...look in a few windows on the way back to the hotel." How could I say no? We left our skis with the hotel taxi that was standing by and began our stroll down the main street, only marginally hampered by our footwear. We weren't going to be running anywhere after all.

She walked directly into one of the larger upmarket shops. She was immediately to be seen wandering around poking this and that. The last time that I saw her inside she was heading for the jewellery counter which is always a pricey few steps. I went to look at some new jackets at the back of the store before getting rather bored and returning to the jewellery counter. Melissa was nowhere to be seen! In fact there was no one to be seen, not in that department at least. I looked around and was surprised to realise that she must have left in something of a hurry. Not only that but she had left her gloves on the counter - her beautiful Prada pride and joy. I picked them up and headed out. Fortunately I spotted her far down the road just about to turn the corner, so I quickly started after her waving her gloves in the air. Now, being a man of a certain age, I have an enlarged prostate. Nothing to worry about but apart from keeping it under review the only minor inconvenience is that it reacts badly to caffeine and alcohol, necessitating the need for a pee soon after having imbibed or merely starting to. We had had a couple of glasses of Champagne at the bottom of the piste not fifteen minutes earlier and it was already starting to kick in. I tucked the gloves into a pocket and zipped it up before popping into the hotel next door. I breezed past the concierge and located the facilities. I was at work longer than usual as my doctor had been lecturing me on the need to take my time with a shake at the end then to wait a bit and then have another shake. "Make sure you get that bladder as empty as you can Anthony otherwise you'll be back again within five minutes."

When I returned past the front desk one of the staff beckoned me over. "Pop yourself down there for a moment sir," he said, gesturing towards a sunken leather slipper chair. "There's a bit of a ruckus outside and we've locked the doors momentarily as a precaution." "If I sit down in that I'll never get up; I've got to go and find my wife and I've never used a back door in my life." "Then I would suggest the bar. Have a drink on the house sir."

I didn't need telling twice and so I clumped off to the members' lounge making the somewhat reasonable assumption that eyes would be more on the ruckus than a random gatecrasher. I was correct and was served a glass of Champagne from a newly opened bottle. "On the house," I confirmed. "Yes, sir, I know sir." You don't get this sort of service in any Commons bar. "What's going on outside?" I enquired from my high-backed stool in front of the bar. I wasn't intending on staying very long. "It's the police. They're on the ball around here. They wait and wait and then POUNCE!" "What sort of criminality?" "Believe or not drugs mostly, then escorts, then jewellery."

I had a very pleasant chat with Robert. He was from Essex which I think is a first for me and I informed him so. I told him about my second home in Suffolk. "Near enough," he replied graciously.

I took two more flutes of Champagne before Robert announced that life outside had returned to relative normality and I was able to leave which I did, via the gents, out then immediately back in again for a top up of the urinal.

I stomped back to our hotel and finally sat down in the lobby. I was rather exhausted. I had just finished removing my boots and swapping them with Derek for my bedroom footwear when Melissa came over in her stockinged, or more accurately thermalled, feet carrying her slippers. She was still in her ski jacket. "Darling, where have you been?" she enquired. "I thought something dreadful had happened.

You weren't in our room, I..." I held up my hand and she stopped. She took a couple of deep breaths then sat down beside me and went to put her slippers on. She then told me that after trying on a few pieces of jewellery she had glanced around the shop trying to find her paymaster, having decided that she adored two items, but as she couldn't see me decided that I had scarpered. "I told them I needed you to pay and that I would be back the same time tomorrow. Then I left. I walked down the road looking in the shop windows and then came back here and straight up to our room." "It's quite simple," I explained. "I went over to look at some clothing and when I returned you had gone. So I came out after you. I saw you in the distance but then I had a call of nature and so went next door to oblige myself. However I was then locked in because of some commotion to do with drugs, escorts or jewellery the three top suspects are. But all's well that ends well, but..." I lowered my voice, "...who was in a bit of a hurry to leave because..." I unbuttoned my jacket pocket and reached inside for the Prada gloves, "...they left their Christmas present on the jewellery counter?" I pulled out the gloves with a flourish as if I were producing a rabbit from a magician's hat, and waved them in the air.

"Not me my darling," said Melissa, without missing a beat, as she waved her hands in the air. "I'm still wearing my gloves. Look."

Many thoughts ran through my mind at that precise moment. Suffice to say Melissa didn't go back and purchase her jewellery the following day or any other day and next year we're booked in to St Moritz and my wife's had a very radical new haircut.

Heathrow

A worried wife on her wedding night.

I met my husband-to-be one August and by the following June we were married. I was in my late twenties and it just seemed the right thing to do. Many years later I am still married to the most loving man that I have ever met, but at the beginning I wondered whether my marriage to him was going to last much more than one solitary day.

One thing that we both had in common, and still have, is a love of skiing. I had always skied in the winter and am not one for lying on beaches although I love the sun, so what could be better than summer skiing? We booked to go to Canada for our honeymoon and we were to be staying in Whistler Blackcomb, the largest ski resort in North America that had summer skiing on the Hortsman glacier. I was very much looking forward to it in addition to getting married of course.

As we were going to be catching an earlyish flight my fiancé booked us in to the then Heathrow Penta hotel for our wedding night. After a busy day with wedding, reception and evening do we arrived at the hotel just before midnight, exhausted but well prepared for our flight in the morning.

We awoke to a loud knock on our door. I'll let Chris take up the story...

Jen prodded me in the arm. "There's someone at the door," she hissed. I had booked breakfast in the room and I presumed it was the waiter. I looked at the clock; the time was just as I had requested for our breakfast. I jumped out of bed. I was completely starkers but I felt I had to answer the knock. I thought that I could probably hide behind the door. The room was a P shape. From the door facing into the room there was a narrow corridor with doors to the toilet and bathroom on one side and a small wardrobe on the other. From the door one couldn't see the bed, as the corridor was so long, until one was further into the room. As I headed towards the door I pulled on one of the sliding doors of the wardrobe. I found a dressing gown hanging so I grabbed it and put it on. It was a bit short, very short in fact - cotton, colourful with vertical stripes and a matching belt that I quickly tied into a bow. I opened the door to be greeted by a waiter with a large tray holding several silver domes, plates, coffee cups and so on. "Room service breakfast," he announced looking me up and down with the slightest of frowns. "Very fetching sir," he continued with a seedy smile. "Come in and pop the tray on the bed," I requested as he shuffled past me and along the corridor.

I appeared back in my wife's sight just as the waiter was putting the tray on the bed. Now it was her turn to look me up and down. Her frown was slightly greater. I gave the waiter a small tip and showed him to the door. Back in the main room I said to my wife, "Tuck in," as I began to lift the domes to investigate what was underneath. "Stuff tucking in," she retorted. "I want to ask you a question." "Fire away," I said nonchalantly as I picked up a glass of orange juice. "Just tell me," she demanded, "why are you wearing my dress?"

It turns out she had hung it up when we arrived at the hotel so that she had something relatively uncreased to wear to the airport. How was I to know if she didn't tell me? I crept out of the hotel that morning. I've never worn any of her clothes, mistakenly or otherwise, since.

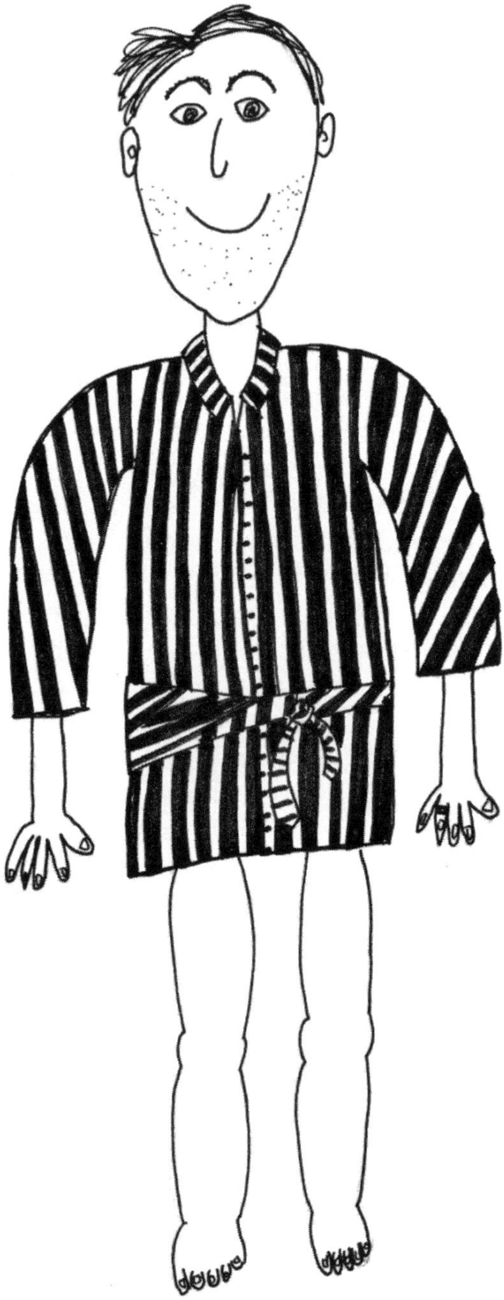

Les Houches

Four young guns meet their match with the Swedish ski bunnies.

Four of us married men have an annual week's skiing somewhere in the French Alps, usually in January. One year we decided to try Chamonix where the average skiing ability is far greater than ours but it's not all about the skiing.

We found a lively bar / restaurant in the centre of town called Moö. It's named after three Scandinavian friends called Morten, Oscar and Örjan who set it up and it was full of Scandinavians. As my ancestry is Danish I was naturally drawn to this wonderful place. The four of us are all happily married which means that we can chat to females without there being any ulterior motive on our part; we're just old blokes having fun and being friendly on our holiday.

One late afternoon we were back après skiing in Moö when we got chatting again to four beautiful Swedish girls that we had met the previous day in the bar and had spent this day skiing with. They had taken us down one of the blacks on the Grand Montets. They were very good! I say girls, they were at half our age - already in their early twenties but still with the friendliness that the young instinctively have. They were quite happy to talk to us oldies especially as we kept buying them drinks. They were on a mission to ski every run in Chamonix and Les Houches - twice, including all the blacks off the Grand Montets and the one above the Argentière glacier. They are some of the most challenging in the Alps. I had already skied Point de Vue with a guide, Tobias, and when we came to a long traverse I asked Tobias what would happen if I fell. "Here you do not fall," was his blunt response. We were getting on just fine with the

Swedes when one of them, Stina, said, "Those boys keep looking at us." We turned around and, sure enough, four lads, who looked no more than about twelve but, as it turned out, were all eighteen or nineteen, were staring at Stina and her friends with mouths open wide. "English," I said. "They're pink." The girls giggled.

When I was at the bar buying yet another round of drinks one of the lads sidled up beside me. "Bit old for those ski bunnies aren't you?" he suggested just a little too aggressive in tone and contemptuous in content for my liking. "Just friends," I said. "Why?" Then his big boy introduction rather crumbled when he asked pathetically, "Do you mind if we come and talk to them?" "That will be up to them," I replied, "but we're not going to cramp your style."

No sooner had I returned with the tray of drinks and told the girls that they had some admirers than the four lads sauntered over and started some very small talk. The girls were receptive in a typical Scandinavian way but the boys were so out of their depth and sinking further. "So, do you girls ski?" asked one of the boys. "Er, yes, a bit," said Pia, not letting on that they had all been skiing since before they could properly walk. "How about you?" Pia asked. "Oh yeah, I've skied for five years," said another. Pia realised that this actually meant five weeks. "Do you ski blacks?" she asked. Oh yes they did! The girls finished their drinks and it was my friend's turn to go to the bar. But before he got his round in he asked the four boys if they would like to buy the girls a drink. Cue much spluttering into their glasses. Chatting up evidently didn't extend to buying drinks for their crushes. "It's okay," one of the girls said with a wink in my direction. "The old men will buy our drinks," and off my friend tottered. "So, how do you fancy skiing with us tomorrow?" Pia asked. The boys looked up. "Us?" "Yes, you." They looked at my friends and me. "Don't look at us," I said. "We've had our ski lesson today and tomorrow we're doing the Vallée Blanche." "Yeah, sure," one of them scoffed. I stifled a smile.

The following late afternoon we were back in Moö when the girls walked in. They came up to the bar and greeted us warmly. "How was the Vallée Blanche?" they asked of the off-piste glacier run that mostly involves avoiding couloirs. "Easier than what you put us through on Tuesday," I replied. I looked around. "Where are your toy boys?" The girls looked at each other and smiled. "It's like this," said Stina. "Come and sit down. The thing is. We don't know. We met them this morning and they confirmed that they were okay with blacks. So we took them to the top of the Grands Montets and asked them if they fancied doing a bit of off-piste." (There's a horrendous off-piste on the other side of the black that we had already done with the girls.) "They said, 'Sure,' so we skied over to the start with them and looked down the mountain. 'Ready?' we asked. 'Yes,' they said so off we went, like we did with you, wuf, wuf, wuf." Stina had stood back up and was now in full demonstration mode in front of the bar. Basically these four girls ski synchronised, side by side; it's very impressive. "When we reached the first bend which is about three hundred metres down we stopped and looked up the mountain. The boys were still at the top. They were sort of scratching their heads. They hadn't moved so we continued on. And we haven't seen them since."

And none of us saw them again for the rest of the holiday although there was a sighting at the airport and no one was in a bandage so nothing was bruised or broken, apart from four young egos.

Ischgl

Teenage trauma with a black run adventure and a stand-in skier.

When I was about thirteen a few years ago we went on a family holiday to Ischgl. The ski area is huge but it's quite good because so long as you don't go over a ridge on a lift all pistes lead back into town. That said my dad was always trying to get me go on the reds, of which there are loads - it's not really a beginners' resort - even though at the time I wasn't a particularly good skier. One morning we met up with one of dad's friends. His name was Matt and he was an excellent skier. The weather was very misty but Matt said that if we just followed him we would be okay. He wasn't hard to lose as he had an all black ski suit and orange helmet. We might've been okay but I don't think anybody else thought that he was okay - from a distance he looked like a matchstick.

We went down one of the few blue runs and then we did a red. Matt said that red runs are the worst because they're full of (mostly English) skiers who should be on the blues and French skiers, both home and abroad, that are good enough for blacks and treat the reds as if they are practice slopes but still go as fast as if they were on a black. Then dad said that blacks are not allowed if you're young like I was because, "You don't see blood on black runs, just limbs." I had not been on a red run much before and I soon fell over. No one saw me and as my ski came off I had to put it back on and all by myself. It took ages! When I finally caught up with Matt he went down a black run that was really steep. Then it got even steeper and steeper and Matt was going faster and faster. Then I fell over again but I didn't stop this time and I just slid down and down and down. There was just no way that I could stop. I kept on going - sliding then rolling and going really fast and someone was screaming so loudly as I went past them. Then I hit a big softish bump and I took off then landed in some very deep snow and that slowed me down. When I finally did come to a halt at the bottom of a lift there was another run going across me with loads of people on it. Then Matt came over to me but didn't say anything, he just waved up the mountain but no one could see him because it was too foggy. Then more people came and stood round me and they were all talking to themselves but not in English. Then, and this is why I haven't given you my real name, I started to cry.

Fortunately my mum suddenly appeared, also crying, from out of the mist and through the crowd. She pushed everyone aside and as much as she was able to in ski boots she ran to me and lifted me up off the snow in an attempt to hug me. The first thing she said was, "Is anything broken?" I told her through my tears that I didn't know but if it was it was a bit late now. Then she asked me where I had been and I said, "Only following Matt." The word "only" is a good one to use in these sorts of situations. She picked me up in her arms and started to cry some more. She asked me where I had skied from and I pointed up the mountain and I said, "From up there," and Matt gasped and said that that was the blackest of black runs in Ischgl and he sounded all squeaky! Mum asked me why I had gone down it and I said that I was following Matt. Then I looked over as Matt took off his helmet and he was a "her"! "Oh dear," I said and mum hugged me some more. Then she asked me where my skis were. By now the real Matt had appeared. There were two matchsticks! He pointed up the black run and said, "Up there probably." Mum started to get very cross and told me that I knew that they were hire skis and that she would probably have to pay a big fine. I said that I didn't do it on purpose. Matt said that it would be fine because the skis would reappear at the bottom of the run when the snow melted but mum said that she wasn't going to stay in Ischgl until May just for a pair of skis. Then she just skied off and left me with Matt so Matt said, "We might as well do the black now, and do it properly, if it's okay with your mum and dad." I said to him that the only way that I could do it at present would be by walking down. Then we went and found mum and decided that it was time for lunch.

After lunch Matt disappeared for half an hour with one of my boots and came back with a pair of skis for me that looked just like the ones that were on the black run somewhere. He told mum that he had hired them from his local shop and I should return them at the end of tomorrow and told her where it was. We didn't do the black run again though and mum skied next to me for the rest of the day and the day after.

The following morning we skied before packing and starting the long drive home. I only found out recently that mum had scraped the barcode labels off my new skis from Matt's hire shop then she took them back to our hire shop and told the ski technician that the labels had peeled off by themselves. The technician explained that the labels do not peel off as they are heat-glued on but apparently he took the skis anyway and didn't say anything else so mum was happy. She told me that if Matt had been bothered by what she hadn't done then that wasn't her concern, it was his and the other hire shop's problem and that if he was so concerned HE could have gone back in May to retrieve my skis.

We never skied with Matt again.

Lenk

The day the lights went out. Two Swiss saviours.

In 1999 I went on holiday to this Swiss resort. It's great for beginners and early intermediates as nearly all the slopes are blue or red whilst advanced skiers can ski over to Adelboden where there are a few more blacks.

I was there with my wife and her sister and her husband Mark. We also had between us five very young children so we had chosen a hotel with family-friendly facilities, which we arrived at mid-afternoon after our long drive down from Calais and an overnight stop.

1999 is a year that will not be forgotten for those that were skiing around Christmas time. We had been in the resort for a couple of days when there was a massive freak storm with hurricane-force winds that roared in from the English Channel. In Versailles the wind toppled ten thousand trees on its path of destruction. It continued into the Alps across all eight countries. In Lenk it took out the electricity pylons up to our resort. There was no electricity in the resort at all. There was none in the hotels and, even worse, the ski lifts stopped working. The only saving grace, so far as our stay in the hotel was concerned, was that it had mains gas. We were therefore able to have hot food although it was cooked and eaten by candlelight. There were open fires everywhere. This lasted for four days. We survived! We are very grateful to all those who worked so hard to get the power back on and who looked after us beyond the call of duty when it was off.

Our head waitress was called Elisabeth which sounded, when pronounced with a Swiss accent, as "hell's breath."

This became her nickname which she loved! She went round with a powerful head torch that she even had on when serving our evening meals. We always thought that it looked as though we were being served by a coal miner or were on some weird sort of scout camp when at our table.

After a couple of days we were getting very bored indeed. We just went with the flow but it has to be said that there were others in our hotel who were having major acceptance of situation failure as if the hotel managers could somehow repair the pylons all the way to the resort simply by clicking their fingers. One man in the bar on the night that the storm hit said that he was going to sue. When I asked him what for he replied, "Too much snow." Some people! "Good luck with that," I suggested. About the only way to do any skiing was to walk up the pistes which is, as anyone who has ever tried it knows, very slow and laborious with bulky clothing, equipment and thin air even without young children, so we didn't bother. We stayed at the bottom of the slopes and resigned ourselves to a bit of tobogganing. At least the kids were enjoying themselves.

We decided on day three of no electricity that rather than eat in the hotel we could drive somewhere for a late lunchtime meal and make it into a bit of an adventure. We asked around and soon found out about one of the restaurants high up in the mountains on one of the pistes that had remained opened as it too had gas. One of the locals pointed out the narrow route to us between a couple of buildings although it didn't look much like a road as it was completely covered in snow. He told us just to drive over the smooth snow with trees on one side and the mountainside on the other. "Take care on the hairpins; you'll need a run-up at each one," he cautioned, "and make sure that your chains are firmly on." For some reason we rang up to make a reservation even though we didn't think it would be very busy. At least someone answered the 'phone and took our booking so we knew that we weren't to be going on a wild goose chase.

We gingerly set off in our two cars as it began to snow again and headed towards this apparent road that was more of a track. We were climbing up the mountain behind the town. At the time I had a Mercedes estate and Mark and his wife, Joey, had their Volvo estate. Mark didn't have any snow chains but did have front wheel drive which apparently can be quite good for driving in snow, certainly better than rear wheel drive although being low down can be a problem due to the lack of ground clearance. How were we to know? I did have chains on my Mercedes but I was somewhat weighed down by a large roof box that I had added before we had driven down and wasn't going to bother taking off.

The track was getting steeper and steeper. Not too much fazes me but it was becoming quite terrifying! Mark's car was sliding all over the place on the virgin snow and we only managed the hairpins on a wing and a prayer. Fortunately they were so tight that they were very steep. This meant that not so much snow could collect actually on the bend but it did mean driving through even deeper snow on each run up but it was going okay. After the first bend I thought that we should turn round and return back to the town but there was no room to turn. All the passing and reversing places were full of snow so we had no choice but to keep going. After we had negotiated a few more of these bends with the snow falling thicker and thicker the mountain wall suddenly disappeared and we found ourselves on the side of a piste. We couldn't see where the track went on its upward trajectory but there was a flattish ridge with a short, steep kink in the middle that crossed the wide piste to our restaurant that we could now see. The first part was actually going downhill a bit. Judging by the lack of any tyre marks no one had crossed this piste in a vehicle for at least several hours or maybe just a few minutes. We could have turned round at this point but we decided that having come so far we might as well try to reach our destination. My wife suggested we leave the cars where they were and walk the last bit but that was easier said than done without skis or snow boots on everyone plus small children so we agreed that we would continue the drive.

Mark started off first but was soon totally out of control. His car started to snake a bit but then mysteriously spun round. He actually went down onto the piste but miraculously his car managed to find its way back onto the level ground. A thought of him careering down the blue run made my blood run cold. It was only a blue but even a blue is too steep for a car when there's snow on it I reckon. I was too close behind him and so jammed on the brakes. I managed to stop and not hit him but it was close. Mark was now facing me and as there was no space to turn back round he decided to continue the journey in reverse! As I started off I heard this rather worrying VVVRRRRRRR-DUFF! sound and so braked. However, instead of the car stopping it veered to one side and imbedded the bonnet in a snow drift on the piste above us. I jumped out of the car and made my way round to the back. I know I should have stopped after a couple of bends and tightened the chains but I didn't bother and now I was confronted with one of the chains that had come loose, spun round the inside of the wheel and severed the brake cable. Mark, meanwhile, had continued his drive in reverse and had then driven backwards into another part of the snow drift a few yards in front of me. Neither of us could then move our cars an inch. They were both completely stuck. We had wives and five youngsters in the cars and Mark and I are standing outside in the snow scratching our heads as to what to do. We revisited the option of leaving the cars and attempting to walk now that the restaurant was a bit nearer but common sense told us that wasn't an option. It wasn't quite an emergency and we thought trying to walk to the restaurant could easily have resulted in someone falling, probably down the piste with broken bones as a result. There was also the risk that some of the children might have mistaken the blue for a giant toboggan run and just jumped onto it.

After about five minutes of frantic pondering and not getting very far we spotted a VW Golf coming towards us from the direction we had just come in. The car had studded winter tyres and inside were two young, spunky Swiss guys. They didn't need us to wave them down. They stopped and got out to see if they could assist. I explained that I needed to jack my car up to get the wheel off so that I could get to the snow chain but every time I started to lift the car up it slid further into the snow. "No problem," one of them said in perfect English. "We can drive our car over the snow and get in front of your front bumper with the snow acting as a cushion. That will stop your car slipping so that you can lift the car up on the jack and get the wheel off. Then we can dig your car out; we have a shovel." And this is what we started to do.

Picture the scene: Three cars on the piste, two of them, a Volvo and a Mercedes, stuck. Skiers coming down past us having set up a skidoo relay system from the town and up the slope. Some were from a few of the mountain chalets dotted around and were just skiing little bits of the slope. A few people tobogganing. Two distraught wives. Two frustrated husbands. Five screaming kids. Added to all this it was starting to get dark. Just as I had got the wheel off my

Mercedes and the Swiss guys were tackling the snow chain I could hear a sound familiar to anyone who lives on a farm or central London. I looked up just in time to see a Land Rover Defender with big knobbly winter tyres careering across the piste towards us. Just before it reached us it effortlessly pulled off the track, onto the piste, past us and back onto the track. Only then did it stop. The driver, another Swiss guy but somewhat older than our two saviours, wound down his window, stuck his head out, looked behind him, and surveyed the chaos. Then, gesticulating wildly, shouted, "'Ello! Let me giv view som advice! You need to git yourselfs a decent BRITISH car!" And then he drove off. Just like that. Charming.

We did eventually get to the restaurant, "Sorry we're a bit late," and there were people in it and we did get back to town with less difficulty as it was downhill so we mostly slid. We did consider taking the piste but Land Rover man who at least came over and bought us a drink said that that was an option reserved for him. Braking was fortunately veering the correct way round the hairpins and as it was dark what we couldn't see we couldn't fear. I got the brake cable fixed the next day because they do have garages in the mountains and all was well.

What didn't end so well was the effects of the storm elsewhere in Europe. Nearly one hundred people were killed including two who were crushed in Crans Montana by a falling ski gondola they were travelling in, with another three injured. A tree had uprooted and crashed into the lift cable sending the gondola plummeting to the ground. And all we had was a dodgy snow chain and an incompetent operator. I wonder who I could have sued? Myself? The snow?

***

Scooby-Doo saviour on the slope.

One year we were stuck in Lenk in a hotel halfway up a mountain. There had been a storm and all the electricity had gone off so none of the lifts worked. Fortunately we had gas in the hotel.

One afternoon we were out on the blue piste that ran past our hotel. We were taking our two young children on a plastic sledge up and down a short stretch of the slope. It was quite steep so I was going down at a forty-five degree angle so that I could effect a controlled stop by turning upwards instead of speeding down the rest of the run.

My husband had been watching on but then decided that he wanted a go. He sat on the sledge, rested his feet on the front and tucked our two children in front of him between his long legs. I told him that he needed to have his feet free to slow and turn in the snow but he wasn't having any of it. "If I lean I can stop," he said with far too much authority when he actually had no idea what he was doing. I just let him get on with it.

He started off perfectly well but soon he discovered that he couldn't turn by leaning and so went straight across the diagonal gathering speed all the while. He had taken the precaution of checking up the piste for skiers and sledgers but there were none. What he hadn't bargained for was a large dog that decided to cross the piste diagonally from the other direction. This Great Dane came bounding down the piste getting closer and closer to my husband's out-of-control sledge. It was on a collision course and I had a gut feeling that someone/thing was about to get horribly hurt.

The present went into slow motion as the moment of impact approached. I wasn't sure when the Great Dane became aware of the sledge and its passengers but it must have been late on because it made no effort to stop. Instead it attempted a very ambitious leap that was so early it was doomed to failure. My husband screamed as his lap took a direct hit. The dog didn't move and my husband instinctively grabbed it as he continued to career across the piste resembling something out of an episode of Scooby-Doo.

The weight of the dog was so great and so much to the upward side of the sledge that the sledge suddenly turned to the right and it came to a very gentle stop just feet from the hard snowy bank that would otherwise have resulted in multiple broken bones. As I slid down the slope to reassure my children, kick my husband and thank the Great Dane the dog bounded off. I said to my husband that he was very lucky to have such an intelligent dog looking out for him. He was genuinely shocked but after he had recovered he said that he was totally in control and the dog was just frightened.

Early evening we went into the hotel restaurant for dinner with the children. When we sat down there weren't many people around and it was fairly quiet. Suddenly my husband asked, "Can you hear that low rumbling sound?" It was a sort of throaty, "ggggrrrrrrrr." We looked all around and then we saw the source. My husband's new friend was tucked under a table staring at him. "Oh my goodness, look," I said. "It's that Great Dane." My husband jumped up to go and tell its owners what a great job it had done - by mistake. "No mistake," was the reply. "He's a mountain search and rescue dog. His been fully trained." My husband bent down to give it a stroke and got his arm bitten.

Le Lioran

Teenage translation trip-up when trying to be considerate.

Le Lioran is a small ski resort in the Massif Central. I went there once with my school. We were mostly beginners so this resort was great because you could ski from the highest point to the bottom on blues and greens.

All those on this week were studying A-level French so there was an educative element to the trip. We all stayed with French families in and around the area. I stayed with a girl called Pascale with whom I had been corresponding for several months. She wasn't very like me at all, I don't think most French girls are. We got along well enough though. On our first excursion into town after skiing the first thing she did was buy a packet of cigarettes. She offered me one but I refused.

One late afternoon I was sitting in a café with Pascale and her friends. I could speak fairly good French but was always keen to learn more. I carried my vocab. book with me into which I wrote new words and phrases along with the translation. The things that Pascale said kept me busy! One expression that kept coming up in the café was, "Je m'en fou." I had no idea, so I asked her. Pascale and her friends smiled and in a Frenchy sort of way said, "It means something like, er, 'It doesn't matter.'" That was good enough for me. It probably meant more like, "I don't mind," but either would be about right I thought. Both phrases made sense in the context of what they were saying. What I hadn't appreciated though was that some phrases are a little bit too colloquial to easily be translated. I was soon to learn a very important lesson and that is - check with someone!

We left the café and went back to Pascale's house. Her mother was busy getting dinner ready. In French she said that we had a choice. This seemed to me not unusual as the French often cook several dishes at the same time then save a couple for later in the week. This is especially true for casseroles and stews as they love letting the flavours develop. Pascale's mum asked me in French as she spoke no English, "What would you like for dinner tonight?" I didn't mind, not at all. It didn't matter to me as I'm not a fussy eater and was happy just to eat what was put in front of me. I was searching around for the right sentence which isn't always that easy as so many words and phrases can have slightly different nuances, let alone be outright rude, when I remembered the café. I had my answer. Perfect! "Je m'en fou," I answered brightly. At this point, unexpectedly and without warning, all hell broke out. "PARDON?!" screamed my normally placid host. What had I said? Pascale went bright red. "You must not zay it to my muzzer. It is bad; it is not good." What had I said? "But I don't mind what I have for dinner," I said rather feebly. No reply.

We had stew for dinner and it was taken in silence. I tried to look up the phrase that had caused so much offense in my phrase dictionary when we had finished but it wasn't there. I went to bed confused and sad. What had I done?

The following day we met our teachers at the top of the main lift. "How's it going?" miss asked cheerfully. She could tell from my expression what the answer was. "What's the matter Amanda?" She put her hand on my shoulder. "I'm *in loco parentis*. Tell me, I won't be cross but I need to know so I can sort it out." Then I started to cry. I hadn't seen that coming. It was probably the shock of what was about to be revealed, even though I hadn't wilfully done anything wrong. "Pascale's mother simply asked me in French what I would like to eat for dinner and I said, 'Je m'en fou' because Pascale said it meant..." I stopped: miss was smiling. "Why's it funny?" I sobbed. I went to quite a progressive school so, although swearing wasn't encouraged, if it formed part of the substance of a situation it was tolerated. This went for the teachers as well. Miss said, "You've told Pascale's mother, in answer to her question, that you don't give a f**k what you have for dinner." Pascale was now smiling. She understood. She would.

Miss came to Pascale's house that evening and explained the misunderstanding so after that all was well. The only problem was that Pascale's mother wanted to know where I had learnt such an expression. Miss explained that at our school we read some quite immersive contemporary French literature and that I had probably guessed at the meaning and guessed wrong. Pascale nodded knowingly, as well she might.

I've forgotten quite a bit of my French over the years but "je m'en fou" will stay with me forever. I've used it a few more times since, mostly on purpose.

Mayrhofen

A steep learning curve for a group of first-time skiers that takes in clothes, travel, accommodation, food, skiing with no lessons, chair lifts and a hotel spa, with a few lessons learned for the following year.

Mayrhofen will always hold a very special place in my heart as it was the first ski holiday that I ever went on and nearly my last.

We were four twenty-something couples in the mid 1980s - all friends, and mostly still are, that were always hanging around together. One day during the summer months we were discussing which was our least favourite month and I said, "October." It still is! It's the month when the clocks go back and the weather starts to get cold, wet and windy - sometimes all three together. At least November has Bonfire Night and December, after Advent, is one big party, then there's New Year's Eve. January runs a very close second place. No one has any money but at least the days are once more getting longer. The majority view was that, actually, January was the worst month. "So what can we do in January to liven it up?" I asked. Someone suggested skiing. Not one of us had ever been on a ski holiday before, not even in school so we had absolutely no idea what to expect but we did a bit of research, found that that the price wasn't prohibitively expensive and so booked up. My friend Jimmy was put in control of the budget and he was charged with keeping the overall cost as low as possible.

Preparations seemed to be very similar to any other foreign holiday; the only minor difference was in the additional clothes required - ski suit, gloves and goggles. I went into Bromley one Saturday morning in September and came out of C & A, a shop that at the time was a major presence on most UK high streets selling cheap clothing, with all that I needed.

I then decided to go one better and buy a pair of skis and boots. However I soon learnt that these were prohibitively expensive to buy new - together they would have cost nearly as much as the holiday - so I looked around for a cheaper option. At the time Exchange and Mart was the go-to place for mostly second-hand goods. It was a fat, tabloid-sized newspaper that was stuffed full of classified advertisements, a bit like a print version of Ebay, that was published weekly. I purchased a copy and sat down to work my way through the ski boots section. I soon found a pair that seemed to be perfect. They were black leather, my size and had hardly been worn. They were for sale for eight pounds and the seller lived only a few miles away. Soon they were in my possession. I also researched some second-hand skis but I decided not to push my luck as I decided that a degree of technical expertise may have been necessary that wasn't needed for a pair of boots. I proudly showed off my new purchase to my admiring friends and they were all in agreement that they looked very fine indeed. Jimmy commented that it looked as though I could go ice skating in them but what did he know, there were no blades attached after all. I bought some shoe polish for them and by the time that we were ready to go on our holiday they were so shiny they would have passed a parade ground inspection.

No flights from Gatwick or Heathrow with this holiday. Jimmy had booked the holiday with Ski-Plan and we were to be flying from Lydd airport, which is tucked away on the Kent coast not far from Dungeness. We drove down the motorway before exiting and onto the Romney Road. We arrived very early and so decided to have a quick pint in the pub opposite Lydd airport's approach road. Once we were tucking into our drinks the landlord asked us if we were going to the airport. When we said that we were he offered us the use of his car park for the week. "If you buy two more drinks each it will be free. I'll drive you all up to the airport myself and you'll avoid the ridiculous costs that you will incur parking in the airport's field." We readily agreed.

The airport itself appeared to be very much a family affair with the sales assistant in the small shop reappearing to check our boarding passes. Our aeroplane was a Dart Herald turboprop. It was very noisy. We had pairs of seats that faced each other across a table, a bit like on some trains. We sat and munched on our sandwiches that we had been advised to buy in advance at the airport as there was no onboard food. I am surprised that the pub landlord hadn't tried to sell us some.

We only flew as far as Ostend in Belgium. From there we were transferred onto a coach for the long drive to Austria. The trip was made longer due to the driver taking a detour through Holland because, as he explained, "The fuel's a bit cheaper."

We finally arrived at our accommodation very late at night but were greeted warmly by the owner. She was an old lady called Anna and she always walked around with a wooden spoon in her hand. I felt as if I was back at school. She looked like a farmer's wife, dressed as she was in faded warm woollen clothing including a pinny that never came off. I thought that she had come straight from tending some cows. It was a tiny guest house with rooms over two floors. We had all four bedrooms on the first floor and our party comprised the majority of the guests. There were no *en suite* facilities as such although there was one (locked) shower on the landing. To gain access we had to go and obtain the key from Anna and pay her two schillings (then about ten pence) each. The shower was only available in the evenings. It was such a performance! One of us would have to get the key then go back to their room to find a towel, then use the shower then return to their room, get dried and dressed before returning the key. This was per person so you can imagine how long getting ready in the evening took with eight of us! By the second day we were sending one person down to get the key, quick showering as couples and then the first person returning with the key half an hour later. Anna soon grew very suspicious at our apparent lack of cleanliness as we all appeared for dinner looking as though a miraculous transformation had taken place from the eight smelly, sweaty individuals that traipsed in through the back door after a lively après ski session an hour earlier. We shouldn't have been surprised that the following day she would come up the stairs and catch Guy and Bev emerging together from the shower room not least because Jimmy had been the one to request the key. Anna caused a commotion that was excessively disproportionate to the crimes committed but as our German was restricted to Bev's O-level and she recognised none of Anna's words we had no idea what she was saying so we merely nodded and gave the appearance of having been chastised. We didn't get the wooden spoon though. The following evening when Guy went to get the key he had to pay twenty schillings.

Breakfast was meagre. Bread roll and jam plus tea or coffee. (The rolls were artisan though, like mini cottage loaves.) Jimmy was much troubled by this. He was used to a full English at home and was going to try his best to get the same out of Anna. "Full English please!" he announced when she emerged with a pot of coffee on the first morning.

"Bitte?" she enquired and wandered back out of the dining room. "We'll just have to break it down," I suggested. Having read too many war comics during my youth I knew that "schweinhund" was a pig-dog. "It's very offensive to a German as a form of abuse but if you use one half of it you may get some bacon." "Or a slice of dog," Guy unhelpfully suggested. Bev had confessed to a German O-level qualification and informed us that an egg is an "eye." So when Anna returned to check on us all Jimmy put up his hand and confidently requested, "Schwein and eye bitter." "Ya, schwein und ei, schwein und ei," Anna repeated and left the room. "Cracked it," said Jimmy and rubbed his hands together in gleeful expectation. A few minutes later and Anna was back. She was holding a plate that had on it a slice of ham and a hard-boiled egg in its shell that she placed before Jimmy with a smile and a bill. Once Anna had once more left the room Jimmy said, totally unfazed, "All we have to do now is find out what 'fried' is in German." By the end of the week seven of us were still on roll and jam whilst Jimmy was tucking into a full Austrian English.

The guest house was a short distance from the lifts of Mayrhofen and so, on the first morning, a minibus collected us to take us to the main lift via the ski hire shop. On board to meet us was our rep., Julie. We were all wearing our brand new or borrowed ski gear and I had my boots tied together by their long leather laces slung over a shoulder. "Oh, I say," she purred, "are you going to do a spot of langlaufen?" "Er, yes, skiing," I suggested. "Yes, but langlaufen, cross country?" "Er, no," I replied. "Down like on a slope." "In cross country boots?" "Er, yes." "Whatever," she replied as if to put an end to the conversation and it worked. She handed out the lift passes that we had pre-ordered. "How many of you have booked ski lessons?" she enquired. "Oh, we're not having lessons," one of my other friends, Jackie, breezily informed Julie. "You've skied before?" "No, none of us." Julie had evidently been told not only not to prolong awkward conversations but also not to cause an argument. So she merely shrugged her shoulders.

Once we had been fitted for skis and boots and I had a pair of cross-country skis, we decided not to head up the main lift but to walk out of town a short distance to practice our turns on a small snowy hill at the side of the main road. It wasn't actually too bad. We managed to ski across rather than down the hill, the only difficulty came with stopping. This was mostly achieved by attempting to turn back up the hill or by simply falling over. After an hour of walking a few yards up the hill and then skiing down / across it, Jimmy announced that he was going to attempt a schuss. We had no idea what he was talking about and we watched in horror as he descended the hill in a straight line, gathering speed all the while. He was going far too fast to attempt even one of our homemade stops. I was witness to Jimmy skiing through the broken fence of the garden of a chalet that fortunately was positioned sideways alongside the main road, across the garden, through the broken fence on the other side, and across the road before coming to a halt on a very flat piece of snow-covered land that we assumed was a frozen lake but which was probably nothing more sinister than a playing field or a putting green. A coach coming along the road passed by so close to Jimmy that the driver felt obliged to give him a loud toot on his horn. Quite what he expected Jimmy to do none of us to this day has any idea. His epitaph could have been interesting.

It was time for lunch so we walked back into town.

Perhaps fuelled by the addition of a couple of pints of Alpine ale with our gulaschsuppe, we decided to try our luck on a ski lift in the afternoon. The first was easy as it was a gondola so all we had to do was sit down clutching our skis. Once we had disembarked, in order to put off having to tackle a real piste Jimmy, who had already almost lost one life on this first day, decided that we should "have a go" on a chair lift. We copied the other skiers and put on our skis before joining the queue. Looking back I am surprised that no one tried to stop me getting on with my cross country skis but things were a little more relaxed in those days and once I had been shouted at by the bottom life attendant, not for my skis but for the fact that there was a sort of bar that I had to pull down to stop me from simply jumping, or more likely falling, off that no one had bothered to tell me about as with my choice of footwear, I sat back and enjoyed the view. As I approached disembarkation I took a look at where I was supposed to go and decided to stay where I was. Cue more shouting, this time from the top lift attendant, as I failed to lift the restraining bar. The foot rest scraped across the snow and now I was heading for a large wheel that the cable was wrapped round. "Good," I thought, "I can go back down the easy way." No such luck. My chair went round the wheel on the cable and when I arrived back at the raised slope where I was meant to have alighted twenty seconds earlier the chair lift suddenly stopped. The attendant gestured to me to lift up the bar and get off which I did. I shuffled over to where I was supposed to have disembarked and looked down the very short slope, probably no more than about twenty yards, at the end of which, being Austria, there was an open air bar. Skiers were standing all around enjoying their refreshments at tall, round tables that were scattered about, the idea being that those who wanted to go and do a run without stopping could simply ski around or to one side of them. As I stood contemplating my next move the chair lifts suddenly sprung back into life and a few seconds later Jimmy was shouting at me, "Go, Johnnie, go!" I turned and was horrified to see that he was heading straight for me, restraining bar up and preparing to touch down. I looked at him and then the drinkers. They looked so calm; they had no idea what was just about to happen but I had an inkling. It was them or the chair lift / Jimmy combo crashing into me. I knew which I preferred. I shuffled off the landing / launch pad and flew down the short run. "Err, excuse me, EXCUSE ME!" I cried as I literally piled into the imbibers taking them down like nine pins in a skittles' alley. A perfect strike. Then Jimmy followed backed up by the other three pairs. Carnage and confusion reigned. We extracted ourselves from the drinkers, picked ourselves up, promised that we would go and buy everyone a beverage from the bar and proceeded to leg it or whatever the skiing equivalent is. We skied, shuffled, took our skis off and walked around the other side of the building and regrouped.

All dressed (and kitted) up and nowhere to go. Kamikaze Jimmy on the far left

We would not be allowed to go back down the chair lift so the alternative was to take off our skis and walk down the side of one of the pistes, "but it could take some time," said Bev - something of an understatement. There were signs pointing to blue and black runs but as we had no idea of which was the easiest and which was the hardest we decided to go down the red. This was only because the start of it was directly in front of us and so we could see it, unlike the other two. It was just like our hill from the morning in as much as it was wide; unlike our hill it was fairly steep but we approached it in much the same way. From the top we all traversed to one side then, such was the negligible angle we were on, ground to a halt. Once we were together Jimmy asked, as we faced a bank of snow, "How do we turn?" "I don't know," I said, "but even if I try I'm going to end up dead." I looked down the slope - it seemed to be getting steeper. In the end there was nothing else for it but for us all to take off our skis, turn them round so that they were facing back across the piste and pointing slightly down, put our boots back into them and gently push off. By the time we were back on the side we had started from we had descended about a yard. We took off our skis and repeated the procedure. It was in this way that we skied or cross-countried the piste in its entirety, at least until we reached the top of the gondola station and were allowed to use it to descend. And that was our first day's skiing. We had no lessons for the rest of the holiday and contented ourselves with wandering around the town with our skis slung over our shoulders and occasionally going up in one of the lifts that we could walk on and off and having elevenses or lunch or on one day both, one leading straight into the other then getting the lift back down.

On the way up and down the road to and from our guest house we would pass a largish hotel that had a sign outside that read,

HOTEL SPA - NON-RESIDENTS VELCOME

Jimmy decided one afternoon at après ski that he was going to pop in on the way back to Anna's and find out how the land lay. He reported back that for five schillings each we could make full use of the velcoming spa facilities. "Everything is provided," he was told.

The following evening we eschewed après in favour of the hotel spa. We changed out of our ski gear and headed down the road with swimming costume and a five schilling coin each. For all Anna knew, it was going to be very pongy at dinner. At the reception we handed over our cash and the Fräulein, Emily, who was about my age and beautiful, gave us a towel each once I had filled in some sort of registration form on everyone's behalf. She was immaculately dressed in a black starched skirt, white blouse and white apron, a far cry from what we had been experiencing up the road. We were pointed in the direction of the stairs. "Down zere please. You haf as long as you like." They weren't stupid, they knew we would have to eat and drink at some point, I thought. We descended the stairs and walked along a narrow corridor. At the end there was a door, "SPA". We pushed it open and entered. We looked around and took in the various delights through the fog: a huge Jacuzzi, sauna room, steam room, that sort of thing. It was very quiet. We headed for the changing rooms and arranged to meet in the sauna. We had only been seated in the large sauna for a minute or two when the door opened and in walked a late middle-aged couple and a young boy - starkers! Ignoring our open mouths they introduced themselves and sat down among us. The man said his name was Jean-Paul and he was with his wife and grandson. His grandson was twelve years old and didn't appear the slightest bit fazed walking around the spa naked and with his naked grandparents. Jean-Paul then proceeded to tell us that wearing swimming costumes wasn't really the done thing in Austrian spas whatever one's age or sex. Us boys didn't need telling twice. We pulled off our trunks and went with the flow. The girls preserved their dignity until we all jumped in the giant Jacuzzi and Jean-Paul and his grandson followed, turning the heating up. We had been lounging in the Jacuzzi for a few minutes when J-P stood up and announced that he was going to the steam room if anyone would like to follow. We didn't. As we sat in the bubbling water Guy noticed a small sign on the wall opposite. It read BAR and underneath there was a button. "What's BAR in English Bev?" he asked. "I don't know," she replied. "Bar probably." "Press it Bev," Guy demanded. "I'm not getting out," said Bev as she slunk further down amongst the foam. "You do it." It was left to me as usual. I climbed out of the Jacuzzi, went over to the button and prodded it just in case it wasn't earthed I told the others. The reality was I didn't want to have to have a conversation with the first aid person or housekeeping. "Bar. Bitte?" came the sound of our sweet Fräulein Emily. "Er, it's us down here. Four lagers please and four gin and tonics. We're in the, um, spa," I added, waiting for her to say, "Sorry, no drinks in the spa." Instead she said, "Yes, I know who you are and where you are John. I will be down in a minute." Someone had been looking at the registration card! I ran back over to the Jacuzzi and jumped back in. I didn't really mind my good friends seeing me naked (the one that did mind wasn't looking) but I wasn't going to impose myself on poor Emily who was only doing her job. As it happened I had no choice.

Soon Emily appeared with a large tray holding four enormous beers in glass glasses plus the other drinks. "Just down there," I commanded, pointing to the floor. "No you must take zem from me," she replied. I have never received a satisfactory explanation as to why this should have been, suffice to say I found myself out of the Jacuzzi taking the drinks, one at a time, from Emily and passing them with one hand to the recipients and with the other trying to somehow shield my manhood. Jean-Paul reappeared and knelt down by the Jacuzzi chuckling. "Pay when you leave," Emily informed us and disappeared into the mist but not before she had given me the sweetest of smiles and then topped it off with a wink. It was some time before I felt able to emerge back out of the Jacuzzi without anyone staring or calling the police.

In the Jacuzzi with Jean-Paul, his grandson, beer and not much else

We had two more sessions at the hotel spa during the rest of the week and on our last evening I went out for a drink with Emily after she asked me out. We went to a lovely little bar that I hadn't known about and I ordered myself a lager.

As we sat chatting she said to me, "The last time I saw you holding a beer..." I vowed to return to Mayrhofen but sadly I never did. We returned home by the same somewhat convoluted route that we had taken to get to the resort. We were met by the pub landlord at Lydd airport and ferried back to his hostelry. We were allowed to go on our way once we had bought several drinks each.

The next year we went skiing together again apart from my and Jimmy's girlfriends, and a new couple. I had a beautiful new girlfriend, Elaine, since Mayrhofen and had bought her a ski suit from Marks & Spencer for her Christmas present. The intention was that she was coming skiing with us. Then I had a funny turn and took Jimmy instead. He wasn't going to come but then this spare place became available and so he flew on Elaine's ticket. No one batted an eyelid at the airport when checking in as a female. This time we all had lessons. We went to St Johann in Tirol and had Eva as our ski instructor. We all fell in love with her - all eight of us. There didn't appear to be many mountains in St Johann, just hills, so we soon got the hang of skiing, including stopping, now we had some expert tuition. At the end of the week Eva presented me with a certificate that stated that I had achieved level 5. Not bad for a week. The year before, had she been there, I think I would have been on level minus 5. As it is, I think I'm still working on level 6.

Returning home, one evening I bumped into my ex, the lovely Elaine, in a local pub. "How was your ski trip?" she asked. "It was fine," I replied, "but I realise now that it would have been better with you." "That's too bad. Do you know what I did with the ski suit? I took it back to Marks and exchanged it for a heap of really sexy underwear. And do you know what the best bit is?" "Er, no." "You're not going to see any of it."

Now ski experts, the following year we took ourselves off, with another slight change of personnel, to Zell am See to stay in a hotel with its own spa, plus swimming pool. On the second evening we all less one who was late and who shall remain nameless, ventured down. We went in the changing rooms and found families - mothers, young children - and decided that the wearing of swimming costumes most definitely was the done thing in this particular spa, probably because of the fact that it had a pool and was catering for all ages. We met back up at the poolside and found no one doing a Jean-Paul. We had been in the water for twenty minutes or so when we heard a loud scream. A woman came running out from the changing room area and jumped straight into the pool with her young daughter. The mother still had all her clothes on. She waded through the pool and got out the other side before pulling her daughter out and putting her behind her back. Then our latecomer appeared. He wasn't wearing a stitch. With the woman watching on he jumped into the pool. He then swam over and suggested we go and take over the Jacuzzi and find the BAR button. The woman had already disappeared with her child. Our friend's wife climbed out of the pool and went into the changing room, returning waving a pair of trunks that she threw at her husband. "Put these on," she commanded. "We're not in Mayrhofen now and there's no BAR button. Our friend did as instructed and just in time. The soaking wet woman reappeared without child but with a man immaculately dressed in a suit and tie. The woman pointed at our friend. She appeared to be hysterical. Her finger, in fact her whole body, was shaking. The man came over and commanded our friend to get out of the pool. He duly obliged. As he was doing so the woman turned round and faced away. It was just as well as the man's face was a picture. He apologised and said to our friend to get back in the pool. He then led the woman away. As soon as they were out of sight there was, to put it mildly, much merriment. Nobody seemed to care after all, bar one. The only person who was put out was our friend when we pointed out to him that no one present was offended because he didn't have much to offend with. He got the last laugh though. As we were leaving suit reappeared at reception and handed our friend a magnum of rosé. Totally unfazed he turned to us and said, "The best BAR - a free BAR!" and, having graciously thanked the suit, we left, some of us wondering what Jean-Paul and his grandson would have made of it all.

Méribel

Ski chalet shenanigans.

Aka Merry Hell. A very British resort but live with it! There is extensive skiing thanks to it being part of the Three Valleys. It's also the middle valley so you can guess what the first question is every morning.

Three couples plus my wife and I took a catered chalet for the week and managed to have quite a riotous time thank you Méribel. On the first night we found ourselves in a pizzeria that slowly morphed into a bar with a band, a Beatles tribute band no less. It had two lead singers so the music was literally non-stop: when one of the singers needed a breather the other one took over, sometimes mid-song. After they had finished we went downstairs and found ourselves in a cavernous bar / nightclub. As the evening wore on various members of our group drifted back to our chalet. I was left with Lynne - not my wife.

Eventually we made our way back. Indoors it was pitch black. We sat on the sofa together in the dark and worked our way slowly through the remainder of a bottle of red that was left over from dinner. It seemed as if I was in a dream at first. A door opened and then someone appeared in the open-plan kitchen. It was Lynne's husband. He didn't put a light on - he just made his way to the fridge and opened the door. It was stuffed full of food that we had been told by the chef not to touch. We felt like voyeurs in the shadows. "What's he doing?" I muttered to Lynne. "He'll be looking for the orange juice," she replied. And he was. He found an opened carton and took a long swig before ejecting it all from his mouth and over the floor. "Sssshhhh****t!" he exclaimed. Dramatic but almost a whisper. He replaced the carton and disappeared off to bed. Ten minutes later so did we, separately.

In the morning my wife and I came down to breakfast to find the chef mopping the floor. "Oh dear," said my wife. "Someone been sick?" "I'm not sure," said the chef, "but I seem to be very low on pumpkin stock."

***

Wednesday was chef's day off so we had to fend for ourselves. We were given options and we decided on authentic French bistro in the middle of nowhere. We arrived at our venue - small, intimate and very French. The trouble started with our token vegetarian - all he could eat was a green salad. "Vegetarian? Comment?"

On the very French menu (no English translation) was *le pigeon entier*, whole pigeon. I imagined a, well, whole pigeon - something like a whole chicken only smaller, a mini *poussin* perhaps - gutted, trussed and roasted in a rich red wine sauce with plenty of garlic.

I was to be disappointed.

The presentation was superb but I had in mind a block of meat. Instead I was served two small breasts that had been further sliced although they had been coated with an excellent fruit, possibly plum, sauce. The vegetables comprised a golf ball sized ball of cabbage and a similar sized filo pastry ball shaped like one of those checked picnic cloths that one would place one's packed lunch on before pulling up the corners, tying them together and attaching to a long stick that would be held over a shoulder like something out of Snow White and the Seven Dwarfs or Dick

Whittington. "Not very *entier* I complained to my wife as I cut into the cabbage ball. "Oh." Inside I found the innards - a liver, the kidneys, a heart, that sort of thing. "Am I supposed to eat it?" I asked my friends. No one had an answer. "What's in the filo pastry thing?" Lynne asked, poking it with her fork. "I hate to think," I replied. "Just pop it whole into your mouth and chew," she commanded. "No way!" I said. I picked up a spoon and with the back of it tapped at the parcel. It fell apart and inside I found a beak, the legs and claws, the eyes.... "I don't know whether to eat it or try to rebuild it," I said as I tucked in. I took the view that they wouldn't put on my plate something that would poison me but it was fine. I simply washed each mouthful down with a glug of claret. I got through two bottles (they didn't sell lager) only to be told by our waitress as she collected our plates that whilst the cabbage and filo pastry was meant to be eaten, the contents were presented, albeit hiding, just to show that the pigeon was fresh and indeed whole. "I don't expect I'm the first," I suggested. "No, not the first Englishman," she replied. I still think they did it as a joke.

They could have just said not to eat it all. Still, I got my own back. I put on a restaurant review site after I returned home, "The pigeon was crunchy."

Méribel Les Allues

If you ski down near the woods today, you're sure of a big surprise,
'Cause there you will see a lady fair, who wished she was in disguise.

This is one place my family went to and to where we can never return unless we have all had plastic facial surgery and changed our names.

Méribel is a great resort, and what's more the bit below it - Les Allues - was founded by a British man, Peter Lindsay, who was born to a Scottish father and Irish mother. He started out in the 1930s with the building of a lift and then the first hotels and chalets. What you see today in this delightful village has flowed from these small beginnings. By the amount of times you hear English spoken in the resort you would be forgiven for thinking that most of the residents have flowed from him as well.

There's a great run off the Olympic chair lift above Méribel. Don't take the blue, go to the black called Face. Face goes into a red run called Village which is great fun and never very busy. It's a ski trail; it doesn't get bashed. It can get quite narrow and although isn't very steep it seems to get loads of snow so you need to be good at off-pisting if you go down it soon after a snowfall - which my husband and I did the last time.

Village runs above Méribel Village and ends up in Les Allues from where you get the long gondola back into Méribel.

On this particular morning we were at the top of the lift looking down Face. There was no one on it and there were no ski tracks. We decided to go. It was just the two of us. We crossed our fingers and off we went.

As we got further down we picked up a ski school that had come down the blue. We stopped to let them go first. We waited a couple of minutes before following where they had gone on Village. It's a fairly long run with no restaurants which is relevant because I really needed to have a wee. I had needed one at the top of the chair lift but hadn't said anything. Now I confided in my husband that I could do with going at that precise moment onwards but sooner rather than later. It was something to do with the cold, I was sure of it.

"We're a bit exposed," he said. "What happens if someone skis round the corner? Let's go a bit further down where there are some trees." This is what we did and fairly quickly. We were soon well past the ski school. I skied over to the right hand side of the piste and disappeared into the woods. I turned round so that I was pointing down in the direction of the piste and pushed my skis into a bit of a snowplough. When I learnt to ski I was told under no circumstances should you take your skis off when on or off piste as you will either sink or not be able to get them back on again - so I didn't. I wedged my skis in the snow as best I could and undid my salopettes. I pulled them down as far as they would go and then did the same with my knickers. Immediately I got a very cold blast on my bum and I knew that I had to be quick otherwise I thought I would get frostbite. At the very least I would start manufacturing a few stalactites. As I started to wee I pushed my heels out slightly to avoid peeing on the skis, not that I should have worried as they were hire ones. In any case any wee that hadn't frozen on exit would soon be wiped off when skiing through the powder. Unfortunately, the action of moving my heels and the fact that I was almost sitting on the backs resulted in my skis, oh horror of horrors! - starting to move! As I picked up speed through the trees I tried to stop but I couldn't as there was nowhere to turn and there were so many trees that I couldn't do a snow plough. I couldn't stand up because the wind resistance was against me and I couldn't use my ski poles because I had left them straddling my little yellow puddle.

Fortunately it was a straight path out of the trees. Unfortunately I was still weeing. The shame, the embarrassment - there were people on the slope, not just my husband! Loads of them, waiting as if anticipating the arrival of the village idiot. They were all looking at me! I screamed...

***

I can honestly say I have seen a few sights on ski holidays but this one took the biscuit! I was standing patiently at the side of the slope taking in the view when I heard a little scream. Then a big scream. Suddenly my wife whooshed out from the woods with her bum almost touching the snow, salopettes and knickers round her ankles and arms outstretched like she was getting ready for a prostrate crucifixion. Although I hate to say it this wasn't the worst of it. That honour was reserved for the fact that she was leaving the excretal equivalent of a Red Arrows' vapour trail. "What the..." I muttered but the best was yet to come. She shot across the slope heading straight for the ski school children that were neatly lined up on the other side. She wiped one poor lad clean out with a direct hit. "Sorry, sorry," she muttered as she picked herself up, pulled up her knickers and salopettes and put her skis back on. She then skied quickly off leaving the young lad screaming and me still standing, rooted to the spot. Thank goodness she hadn't removed her helmet or goggles so she remained quite anonymous and they didn't know that I was with her. I side-stepped into the trees to retrieve her poles. I found them soon enough, I just followed the trail.

I skied back onto the slope and left the ski school in a huddle at the side where my wife had crashed. They didn't notice me because they were all gathered round my wife's victim who was still sitting down in the snow. I schussed down to Les Allues where I found my wife standing by the lift looking very, very sheepish. Without saying a word we jumped on the gondola together for the slow ride back up to Méribel Centre. Then my wife said that her shoulder really hurt and couldn't move her arm so then we went straight to the hospital...

***

I went back to the hospital the following day and was x-rayed again. Thank goodness we had taken out insurance! When the doctor asked me how I was feeling I said, "Bored! Very bored! Ski resorts aren't designed for invalids." He then told me about a drop-in centre where injured skiers could go and get a free drink and have a chat with one another. I decided to give it a go. I found the building easily enough. Inside it was like an A and E recovery room only with carpet and soft music playing.

It was quite busy and so I made my way to the nearest available seat. I found myself next to a teenage lad from Lyon although he lived mostly in Liverpool with his English mother. We were soon comparing injuries. I told him that the reason for the plaster on my arm was a bit embarrassing and so he could go first with what happened to him. He said that he had broken his leg in three places, including a compound fracture, and he wasn't even skiing at the time. He told me that he was just standing on the side of a piste with his ski school when this person on skis came flying out of the woods like a prostrate polar bear on a skidoo, hurtled across the slope leaving a trail of orange pee like their fuel tank had burst, took out the ski school before imbedding themselves in his knee. Then they took off down the slope and were never seen again.

He didn't see me again either. I scarpered back off to the hotel where I remained for the remainder of the holiday - a bit like lockdown with attitude.

Morillon

A very sharp shooter in the ski chalet.

A large group of my friends and I met up with another group of friends and rented a huge chalet for a week. To make the cost as manageable as possible we made sure that the chalet was filled to capacity. As a single man I was given a bunk bed with another single man, Andy, whom I hadn't met before but we got on fine - to start with. I had the top bunk and he had the bottom.

Andy had a new pair of moulded ski boots. This was when they first became popular and they were his pride and joy. They were ridiculously expensive he told me but said that they were worth it as they were a perfect fit. He told me with his eyes misting over that a cast is made from your foot and inserted into the boot. Any gaps are then filled with a sort of foam that hardens. He said that the foam is not at all forgiving but once you have your feet in them the comfort is unsurpassed. Well you could have fooled me.

At the end of the first day's skiing we met back in the boot room. We all leant our skis against the wall and hung our boots on heated metal pegs that went inside the boots. All except Andy that is. He was fine with his skis but his boots were going upstairs with him. "I know there's not much chance of them being stolen but I don't want to run the risk. There's no other boot that I could ever wear now and there's no way that anyone's going to get the chance." "Whereas I've left mine in the boot room hoping that they will be stolen. I've had them for years and I would love to be able to afford a new pair," I replied. "Sorry old chap and all that," said Andy not sounding at all sorry. "But you really do need to get yours replaced," and then gave them a little kick. I was going off him rapidly.

That first proper night was party night. Music and booze, so much booze. I was quite content with drinking a couple of beers but we had all been implored to buy a bottle of spirits from Duty Free and donate them to the cause. There were so many bottles and no lager. I told Andy I didn't drink spirits but he started to get a bit agitated and told me to join in with the fun and not be a wimp. "Be a party animal!" he said with a big grin. Then someone decided to start making cocktails. This mostly involved mixing a large glug of this spirit and a large glug of that, a large glug of this, a large glug of that. I had the same conversation with Andy again. Then it was time for forfeit games. Every time I lost it was Andy right next to me shouting, "Swallow! Swallow! Swallow!" like a demented doctor trying to get me to take my pills. He was being quite obnoxious and I wasn't the only one to notice it. I finally crawled up into bed at about 2.30am. Party animal Andy had already gone to bed and was fast asleep so I didn't turn the light on.

At some point in the night I woke with a start. I felt sick. I was going to be sick. No warning. Now! In the good old days my mother would send me to bed with a towel and a bucket. "Just make sure that it goes in the bucket," she said. "I don't want it all over the bed." "And neither did I. I leant over the side of the bed and was sick, very sick. Then again. And again. My stomach muscles contracted and up it all came as lumpy liquid. Then I fell back to sleep. It must have been almost instantaneous after all that strenuous effort.

In the morning I awoke to a strange howling, as if a wolf was being strangled. I didn't move and I kept my eyes shut. Soon there were several people in our room. "Look at my boots," Andy howled. "They're full of sick!" I had scored a direct hit - each of the three times. "What am I going to do?" "Perhaps give Freddie lager tonight as he wanted," someone suggested. Strangely no one was sympathising with Andy.

We all went off skiing and left Andy to sort out his boots by himself. (He subsequently tried to claim on insurance but found that damage through sick wasn't covered.) He spent much of the morning washing them and rinsing them out, washing them and rinsing them out. He had them drying on the heated metal pegs for the rest of the day and then the following day, bringing them up to our room and putting them under his bed each evening. He didn't realise for two days that the pegs only heated up overnight. He refused to ski with his feet in anything else. What at idiot! On the third night, once he had worked it out for himself, he left his boots downstairs on a couple of pegs so that they would finish drying out completely. Someone stole them.

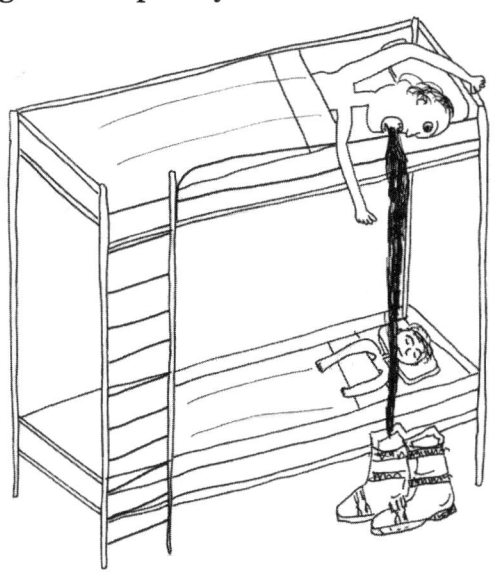

Obergurgl

If you think skiing's expensive spare a thought for someone whose bill could have been more than most.

A group of eight of us (four couples) usually go skiing together. In the past we have used a travel agent but one year we had a DIY ski holiday. That is to say we booked the flights, transfers and hotels ourselves in order to give us as much flexibility as possible. It worked so well that we decided to do the same the following year. During the summer we agreed that we would go to Obergurgl, a very high Tyrolean village so has a very good snow record compared to other Austrian resorts. We settled on Hotel Edelweiss & Gurgl; it's in the centre of the village with ski-in ski-out. Just what we wanted. Fantastic!

The previous year we found that the hotel that we booked wanted paying up front but this Obergurgl hotel didn't appear too concerned. My friend's husband, Paul, is an investment banker with one of the large American banks that has an office in London which is where he works. He's professional, slick and organised. This is of course mostly possible because he has a team of people around him who enable him to do what he does best - making money - by being as productive as possible. He has people who make his coffee, get his lunch, run errands, that sort of thing. Last year the only matter that was a bit of a faff was getting everyone to make separate payments for everything so for our coming trip our investment banker friend said that it would be easier for all concerned if he made just one payment on our individual behalves and we reimbursed him. This made absolute sense.

I had heard of personal bankers but Paul's bank took this to another level. Forget the customers, he had his own private banking personal banker within his own bank! Top marks!

After a few weeks had elapsed he updated us. We were now in September. Everything was under control we were told. We had to make a few payments upfront and Paul said that he had asked his personal banker whether he could use the department's services to buy the Euros in order for him to pay the hotel deposit. He was told that of course he could. He even told us that his personal banker had said that that sort of thing was, "what we do." "The beauty of doing it this way," Paul purred, "is that, as well as being just one payment to the hotel, I'll be able to get the best Euro exchange rate so we will all benefit. I'll pass the benefit of the advantageous exchange rate onto all of you. It's not a problem; I'm just happy to play my part in saving you a few pounds and no commission either." The seven of us readily agreed. I was pleased to have such a helpful friend.

Then it all went very quiet, too quiet. We knew that we would have to cough up eventually for the hotel but we didn't know why Mr Organised had been quite so silent. Naturally no one was in any hurry to chase him up and we knew that had there been any problem he would have let us know. We did know that we would have to pay eventually and we were ready with our money for when Paul asked for it. We had already paid him for the flights so we assumed something was happening in the background.

A few more weeks elapsed and then Christmas was around the corner. It was at this point that one of my friends broke the silence. She had obviously been thinking the same thing as me and requested a pre-ski gathering for us all. We got together a few days later to iron out any last minute issues.

All I had on my mind was the accommodation and was the first to mention the deposit and our preferential exchange rate for the payment. At the mention of the word "payment" Paul went very red. Had he stolen the money I wondered. But no, we hadn't given him any yet so what was wrong? "It's all a bit embarrassing," he said. "When the hotel emailed the invoice for the deposit a few weeks ago I printed it off then took it up to my personal banker straight away and put it in front of her. I said to her that I would like it paid and to let me know what the exchange rate was that she was going to use to debit my account. She picked up the sheet of paper and examined it closely. 'It's quite legit.,' I told her. 'I'm dealing direct with the hotel.' Then she spoke. 'What is it?' she asked. 'It's the deposit for the hotel,' I replied. 'Don't you remember? We had a chat about it a while ago. You said that it would be okay.' At this she put down the invoice, took off her glasses and sighed. 'Paul,' she said. 'I can't use the personal banker services of our bank to get the foreign exchange to pay this piddling little amount.' 'But you said that you would,' I told her. She sighed again. 'Paul. We are a big bank. We deal with big money in big numbers. When you said that you wanted me to get some Euros to pay a deposit on a hotel in Austria I didn't think it was for a ski holiday.' 'In that case, what did you think it was for?' I asked. 'I thought you meant that you wanted to pay a deposit because you were buying the hotel,' she replied a bit too brusquely for my liking." Then he added hurriedly, "So I've paid the deposit out of my own account with no preferential rate. Sorry but that's the way it is. I was just putting off having to tell you."

We had a great time in Obergurgl but I often wonder how much my friend's husband actually owned for his personal banker not to bat an eyelid at his misunderstood suggestion that he was buying a hotel in an Austrian ski resort.

On the Motorway

The feeding of the five thousand - almost.

Some years ago, to keep costs down, we travelled to the Alps by coach. It was a long and arduous journey leaving very early in the morning and arriving very late in resort. However everyone was in good spirits; that is until my dozy husband, Derek, screwed up the itinerary and everything else with it. Derek had decided before the trip that he wanted to brush up his French. He had studied it a little as a child but had done nothing since then. Rather than let me teach him - I am a French teacher after all - he said that he was going to buy a large phrase book just before we left home. It should have helped him get by in most situations that he might reasonability have been expected to find himself in but it didn't help him at all, it just caused grief and embarrassment.

We caught the coach as arranged and crossed over the Channel to Calais without incident. I should have known everything was going too smoothly. The other passengers on the coach were very friendly and Derek had fallen asleep so that was good. Our first big stop was at lunchtime at a service station that was far better than most in the UK. Although many French service stations aren't too bad at all, this one was the best I had ever visited. It was quite small and had a very regional feel to it. There was local food and drinks, hand-knitted clothes, artisan pottery - that sort of thing. Sandwiches could be made to order. Derek had woken up and staggered off the coach telling me that he was going to order us a couple of ham sandwiches. "Can you do that in French?" I asked. "Yeees," he replied sarcastically so I went off to the toilet and left him to it, telling him that I would meet him back at the coach.

We had been given twenty minutes which was more than enough time for everyone to go to the loo and get some food but when I returned to the coach there was no Derek. Everyone else was back except my husband. "Hurry," said the driver so I did, back to the sandwich counter where I found him looking a little flustered. "What have you ordered?" I asked. "Just two ham sandwiches, um, in French." "What did you say?" "I said, 'deux san, er, sandwiches a jambon s'il vous plait, madame.'" "The thing is Derek, everyone's back on the coach and they're waiting for us. Well you actually." Without asking my husband if I could get involved I said to one of the cashiers, "Madame, mon fou mari a commandé des sandwiches de jambon. It sont prêt bientot?" "Presque madame."

I sent Derek back to the coach while I waited for the sandwiches that I had been told were nearly ready. And waited. When they did finally arrive - in a large cardboard box - I asked what was in it. "Deux cent sandwiches - comme il a été commandé."

I paid an extortionate amount and rushed back as quickly as I was able. I climbed the stairs and put down the box. The door shut and the driver pulled away without waiting for me to sit down. I picked up the microphone and coughed into it: it was on. "Ladies and gentlemen," I announced. "I'm sorry for the delay but my dozy husband who is brushing up his French but doing a gentle sweep rather than anything more strenuous has somehow managed not to order two ham sandwiches but two friggin' hundred..."

It was ham sandwiches all round after that, four each in fact. When we arrived in resort Derek threw his phrase book away.

Passo Tonale

Schoolgirl skiing crush that ended up with a broken heart and more besides.

Oh how I fell in love with my ski instructor on my second school trip. His name was Leonardo and was twenty years old. I was fifteen but I decided the age difference didn't matter on holiday. Looking back now I realise that he didn't pay me any more attention than any of the others in my class but at the time I felt that whenever he spoke he was speaking just to me and when he was doing a demonstration he was doing it just for me. I'm going weak at the knees thinking about him right now. It's just as well I'm sitting down. He was medium height, tanned, brown eyes. He spoke Italian English which means that he went up on every last syllable. On my second night I had a dream about him but that dream will remain in my memory for ever and not be put down on paper, except to say that we had three children together and although I wasn't very up on Italian boys' names at that age, some years later, when recalling the dream for the umpteenth time, I decided it was time to give my chimerical children, two boys and a girl, names. Funnily enough, I still have dreams about Leonardo but we've moved on and our children now have their names in my dreams. How bizarre is that? You will understand why I have not given my name; I don't think my lovely (real) husband would completely understand.

After day one I was confiding in my unilateral love for Leonardo with Ollie, who was one of my best friends at school. "How can I stick out amongst the ten pupils?" I asked him. "Five are boys so I would imagine they're not going to get a look-in. You know what Italian men are like." I didn't and that was half the problem but I wasn't sure what to say so I just listened on. "Then you have Mary and no one ever looks at her, then there's Tina and she's got a boyfriend, well two actually although I haven't told you that so that leaves only three. In the old days there was no going up to a girl and asking them out to the cinema or maybe to go round his mum's for tea so ladies used to wait until the object of their affection was within speaking distance and then they would drop their handkerchief. Then the man would pick it up and give it to the lady and say, 'Excuse me, but I think you may have dropped this,' and the lady would act all innocent and say, 'Oh deary me, how very silly of me. Thank you very much.'" "And then what?" I asked. "And then he would ask her back to his mum's for tea or out to the cinema or whatever they had before films."

I told Ollie that there was no way that I was going to drop a dirty paper handkerchief in front of Leonardo so he suggested a twenty-first century equivalent, "like a ski pole." It didn't work. The following day when we were waiting for everyone at the top of the chair lift I skied in front of Leonardo and when I thought that he was looking I dropped my pole. He said nothing. "Oh dear, I've dropped my pole," I said. "Oh dear, pick it up," he said as he turned away. So that didn't work. Git.

I had a debrief with Ollie in the evening and discussed more advanced forms of attention grabbing. "Don't drop something," he suggested, "drop yourself. Then he will have to do something. He may tell you to get up but if you wail, 'I can't' then he will have to touch you and once he's touched you you're halfway there. They're allowed to touch if it's an emergency," he added helpfully.

Have you any idea how difficult it is to fall over on purpose when you're wearing skis? It's easy to do it accidently when going down a run but you try doing it standing still on a flat bit of snow in front of someone whom you need to have looking at you. As we stood waiting at the top of the chair lift again I positioned myself in front of Leonardo. I couldn't go forward over my skis and I couldn't go backwards over them either. It would have to be sideways. But it was a long way down to the ground and I needed to fall on my hands which I couldn't do whilst holding my ski poles. I had to ditch them first. So I dropped them - both of them. As I was preparing my accidental slip Leonardo said, "Oh, for goodness sake Jen: one pole yesterday, two today. I'm going to have to take them away from you tomorrow," and then he skied off calling out, "Follow!" I took solace from the fact that at least he must have been looking at me.

By day four I knew what to do but it unfortunately worked rather too well. On the first run of the day we were once more waiting for everyone outside the gondola station. I stood behind Leonardo and quietly unclipped my ski boots. I laid down my poles and prepared to make a small noise to attract Leonardo's attention before falling on my hands and lying on the snow whimpering. How was I to know how icy it was going to be? No wonder we were told to always keep our boots on whilst skiing. As I lifted my second boot out of its binding and prepared to fall, I slipped - a proper big slip like someone had coated the ground with banana skins only it was, er, ice. My small noise became a scream followed by silence. I had fallen flat on my nose and I can tell you one thing - icy snow is very, very hard. Like concrete in fact. As I lay there, even then wondering if I might be touched by my potential paramour, I could feel blood coming out of my nose. At this point Leonardo uttered a command that I had never dreamt I would hear coming from his mouth,

"Don't touch her!"

I wanted to scream, "No it's okay - please touch me!" but I couldn't because I then passed out.

I had sort of fainted but only for a couple of minutes. When I came to I was lying down with my back in some medical person's lap. Ollie was holding my legs upright. There was blood everywhere. A great pool of it had slowly crept across the ice and snow and then seeped into it. There was no doubting the location of the "crime" scene. "Would you like a handkerchief?" Leonardo asked, waving a large paper napkin in my face. "It's a bit f*****g late now!" I screamed. "But you know what I really want you blind pig - YOU!" I don't think he understood (or maybe he did) because he just blinked.

I found out at the hospital that I had in fact broken my nose and later on that day I had huge bruising around my red, swollen eyes. That was the end of my skiing for one year and guess who didn't even visit. My nose is a permanent reminder of my schoolgirl skiing crush - that and my dreams. My husband doesn't know; he thinks I broke my nose playing netball.

Le Péage

Le péage: noun / a bottleneck on French motorways where vehicles play bumper cars when approaching and practice drag racing when departing.

The bane of all drivers on French motorways. Everyone has to stop to take a ticket, and at the other end stop to pay, at a toll booth unless you have an electronic pass, which most drivers don't seem to have, that lets you use the Télépéage lane. Sometimes there are the most horrendous queues despite there possibly being about twenty toll booths open. With two lanes of motorway opening into twenty lanes much pushing and shoving, without actually much touching, of cars is in evidence as drivers try to get in the shortest queue even if this means cutting up a load of other drivers. Once at the booth it's an unwritten rule that you will complete the transaction as quickly as possible. The husband of one of my girlfriends aims to discharge the formalities at every péage without the car wheels actually stopping turning. This means that sometimes my friend has to insert the ticket from the front passenger seat and one of the children has to tap the debit card from the back passenger seat as the car creeps along. No wonder he has a large horizontal dent on his bonnet.

Every single motorway junction has several exit toll booths that I assume are all manned. Goodness knows how many people are employed in France simply to keep an eye on them and to sort out problems with English drivers.

At one particularly busy péage my husband spotted a gap! He drove to the booth at the far end. The queue was a bit shorter and that was the reason for his mad dash. Even though there were loads of lorries around us there were fewer actual vehicles so all he could say was, "Result!" He repeated "Result!" several times as he gloated at the cars alongside us that had been waiting in their queues for considerably longer.

The machines don't allow for right-hand drive vehicles so from the passenger seat I was in charge of pressing the button to get the ticket but nothing came out. Then we didn't know what to do. To be stuck behind a car, especially an English one, can cause all sorts of problems. Drivers began bibbing their horns very aggressively as I very methodically pressed all the buttons, one after the other, including a bright red one. This resulted in someone speaking to us from probably miles away. My French is okay but I had no idea what this person was saying so all I could do was shout so that everyone behind me could at least hear if not understand, "Your ******* machine has not given me a ******* ticket!" The person behind the red button replied what I later realised was, "En haut! En haut!" but it sounded like she was saying, "Oh no!" Then my husband stormed out of the driver's seat, went to the lorry driver behind who was English and who actually hadn't been tooting and said, "You'll have to ******* reverse as the ******* machine won't give me a ******* ticket! Sadly my husband didn't quite realise that it would be impossible for the guy behind us to reverse his artic. any more than about one inch.

My husband then went to the next lorry and stretched his head up as far as he could at the driver but there was no one there. Once he realised that he had to go to the wrong side he had calmed down a bit but he was still shouting. "NO TICKET!" he said when the French driver leant out of the window. The man said what my husband thought was "Oh no!" also. However, he was able to be at least a little bit more helpful. He pointed at the machine, about two metres up. There, sticking out of another slot was - a ticket. "That's very clever," I said to my husband once he had retrieved the ticket and jumped back in the car. "The machine has a ticket height for cars and another for lorries." "Not if it thinks I'm a lorry," he said crossly. It's our fault for having a four-wheel drive with a roof box. We're going to leave it at home next year. That or get a Télépéage account.

***

We had had enough of having to negotiate airports during February half term and so decided to drive the following year. It was a breeze by comparison. The only niggle was at the several péages that you have to negotiate on the motorway. My husband sat in one queue muttering to himself that next year we needed to get whatever it was to enable us to sail through without having to stop and work our way through our debit / credit / FEx cards to find one that actually decided that we had money.

Back home I did some investigation and found that it was possible to buy a Télépéage pass from the U K. It only cost a couple of Euros for each month that you use it in. I applied and this little box soon arrived in the post. It was then that my husband took over. He said he read all the instructions.

This year we avoided the scrum and took the furthest booth where there was no one waiting. My husband was approaching a bit too fast. "It's fine," he said, "The barrier will lift in time so long as I go no faster than thirty mph." "I think you mean kph," I replied as the barrier didn't lift and my husband took the arm clean off and was then arrested.

Back to Gatwick queuing next year I reckon.

La Rivière Enverse

Mealtime miscarriages.

A hamlet nestling in the foothills near Morillon in the Haute-Savoie, above the Giffre river, is home to Ferme Sterveda, a two-hundred-year-old farmhouse that was once owned by a builder of my acquaintance, David Thomas, who, along with his girlfriend Corinne, had converted it into several individual residences. They lived on-site with their large Alsatian dog called Biscuit. A large group of us drove down there one winter and took the place over for a week. The building's highlight was a subterranean dining room called The Den that was witness to a number of amazing evening meals. It was atmospheric, intimate and candlelit with a large open log fire. The irrepressible Corinne used to bring out the cheese after dessert and we had to learn the names of some of these obscure local *fromages* before she would serve them to us. It was all great fun and every day we looked forward to our evening trips down below.

One summer we took our mountain bikes. I had a new, top of the range branded bike with ceramic brakes. David was beside himself with excitement when he saw what was attached to my roof rack. It had hardly touched the ground and he was taking hold of it, sitting on it, putting his feet on the pedals and squeezing the brakes. "I would love to have a go," he enthused. "Take it for a bit of a spin." I was in no way precious about it and was happy that someone was taking such an interest as my wife certainly wasn't. I told him that I needed to check all the adjustments though after the long drive down. Then Corinne suggested that David wait until the following day and take it in the morning, instead of his old bone-shaker, to the boulangerie to fetch the bread, croissants and Danish pastries for the guests' breakfast. This I agreed to.

In the morning I watched David set off, rucksack on his back. I told him that the brakes were fierce. "When you want to stop you will stop," I told him. "Very suddenly. Pull on the levers gently and always the back brake first." "I know, I know," he replied impatiently and off he went once I had given him a little shove up the track. He had to climb a steep hill for a short distance then cycle along a narrow path for a couple of kilometres before descending a gentle slope into a neighbouring village, Le Plan. I went back inside and waited. When finally I saw him returning along the top path I went out to greet him. He saw me, waved and wobbled, then he began his final descent. He was going far too fast. "Brake!" I shouted and he did, putting the bicycle into a noisy skid as the tyres ripped up the gravel. I covered my eyes and peered through my fingers. At least he had slowed down a little. Then he released the brakes and once more gathered speed. He levelled off on the tarmac and once more I shouted, "Brake!" This time he panicked as he was going too fast again and rapidly running out of ground. A sheer drop beyond the car park was looming large and far too quickly. Momentarily he pulled on the front brake first but that was enough. The bike came to effectively an immediate stop. The back of the bicycle shot straight up like a bucking bronco throwing David into the air. He somersaulted over the handlebars and landed rucksack first on his back. "Are you alright?" I asked although I was more concerned about my bike than my winded host. Corinne rushed out and pulled David up by the two rucksack straps at the front until he was sitting. I prayed that he didn't have any broken bones. Then she unzipped the rucksack and peered inside before pulling a croissant out still in its paper bag. It was flatter than a slice of bread. She had no sympathy. "Back you go," she commanded. "And this time take your own bicycle."

Back to the winter. One evening *La Fondue Savoyarde* was on the menu, nothing else. It consisted several local cheeses that had been slowly melted in a heavy, enamel, cast iron pot over a low flame, to which had been added loads of local white wine and not much else. We were given copious quantities of stale bread (also part of the tradition) which we were supposed to spear with a fork, dip in the cheese sauce and swirl around until sufficient of the mixture was clinging to the bread. Then we had to pop it all in the mouth and take a slug of red presumably to take the taste away.

There were six of us at our table and once Corinne had disappeared we all decided that it was, and there's no *gentille* way of putting this, disgusting even with the addition of so much wine. What a waste! We each wondered what we should do. There were various options. The men mostly agreed that we should simply tell Corinne. "Sorry, we tried, but it's not really our thing." Someone thought of putting it on the fire but we decided that that could go horribly wrong. As to the just telling Corinne the ladies thought that she would be very disappointed after she had gone to so much trouble preparing the fondue. As well she might but we didn't need to lie. In the end we decided on the food equivalent of pouring the glass of rank wine into a flowerpot. My wife went to our room and found a plastic carrier bag. She returned and surreptitiously (it was a candlelit room so wasn't too difficult) poured the stinking mixture into the bag and disappeared outside. When Corinne returned to see how we were getting on the ladies pronounced the fondue, "very good" whilst the men sat quietly, grinning like simpletons. Corinne complemented us on having eaten all of it. "Would you like some more?" she enquired solicitously.

Eventually we wobbled upstairs to bed and quickly fell fast asleep, starved of protein but overdosed on *Savoie Jongieux*.

In the morning, when I had come to, I asked my wife what she had done with the fondue. I thought that she may have thrown it to the edge of the car park. "I'm sure they'ld be some wild animal that would have eaten it," I suggested. "I don't think the local population would be very pleased with us for intoxicating a bear or a wolf or whatever else roams around here at night," she replied, rubbing her head. "If it had eaten that lot it probably would have been plastered and then hurled itself off the edge. She said that she had used her initiative and put it under the bed. Indeed she had! I should have known as the smell was now obvious. I hooked it out with a ski pole. The fondue was still in its plastic bag but had now congealed into a light yellow rubbery blob. There was no time to dispose of it so I pushed it back under our bed and went out for a day's skiing.

That evening was a DIY dinner. It was David and Corinne's night off and so we had to partially fend for ourselves. We were left with all the food that had been pre-cooked; we just had to serve ourselves and clear up. It was a roast leg of lamb and after the evening before it was a vast and welcome improvement. We ate the lot! When clearing up my wife put the bone in a large wheelie bin that she found outside the back door to the kitchen. Then she had a brainwave - she went and retrieved the previous evening's gloop and added it to the bin, covering it up with the empty wine bottles and other detritus from the meal.

The following evening we complimented Corinne on the fabulous roast but we knew something was wrong straightaway. She wasn't her usual smiling self and didn't look very happy. "It's not good that you put the bone in the bin," she complained, "because this morning Biscuit found it. He tipped the bin over because he knew there was something in there that he would like. He could smell it. Lamb bone is particularly bad because it can splinter and harm him. He also found..."

Corinne's voice trailed off. We all knew what she wanted to say. "...a plastic bag full of my wonderful Savoyarde fondue." But she didn't. She just said, "...um, other bits among the rubbish." Then my witless wife spoilt it. She said, "Did Biscuit have a bit of a hangover around lunchtime?"

We never returned.

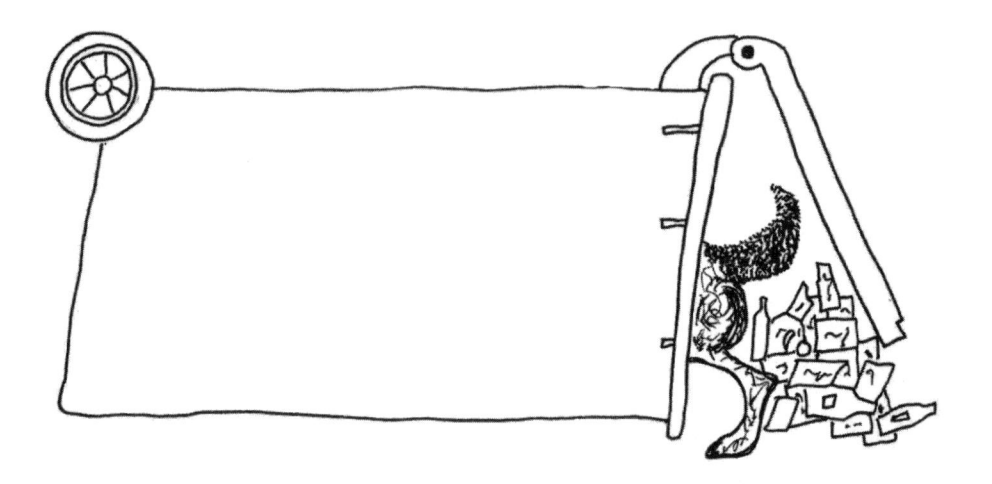

La Rosière

Skier gets exactly what she bargained for, possibly, on a button lift.

"A great resort for beginners," is how a work colleague described La Rosière in France so it sounded just right for my friend and our respective wives. We could go and do the long reds in La Thuile in Italy all morning and our wives could stick to the blues on the French side and have as many coffee stops as they wanted.

Having said that, on the Monday which was our second day we all skied together around La Rosière, almost. My friend and I and his wife went up the long chair to Roc Noir and skied the blue underneath several times. My wife decided that she wanted to perfect getting on, staying on then off a button lift for some reason. It was one that she had been on the day before with her friend and was in another part of the resort. I thought it couldn't be that she was that bad on them. Then she said she liked the blue run next to it so in the end we left her to it. She might have been getting plenty of lift practice but her friend told me that the run was but a fraction of the length of the one we were doing so I thought she would soon get bored and come and find us. However she kept going until lunchtime when we met up in a restaurant at the bottom of the button.

It was quite busy in the smallish restaurant and so the four of us ended up sharing a table with another similar group of four who were English and naturally we all got chatting together. Then my wife stood up and headed for the toilet. The other two couples were over for the season and they asked us where we had been skiing that morning. I said that we had been going up and down Roc Noir: up on the chair and down the blue.

"Very sensible," said one of the women. "You don't want to be going on that lift over there, Poletta, especially if you're female." She waved in the general direction of the lift that the females had been on yesterday and my wife had been going up all morning. "Oh, why's that?" I asked. "Because it's known as Poletta Pervert. More than likely that you'll find a hand from Henri between you and the button as the pole is handed to you," said one of the women and we all giggled like imbeciles. "That's the lift my wife has been doing all morning," I said and we all laughed again.

When my wife returned from the toilet no one said anything or as much as smirked. We had a very pleasant lunch but when it was time to get back on our skis my wife said that she was going on the button lift again just to really get the hang of it. However my friend couldn't stop himself saying, "Be careful otherwise you'll have a very red bum by this evening and it won't be sunburn!" She then gave my friend and then me and finally my friend's wife a very strange look. At that point I thought I ought to rescue my wife from the claws of temptation. I told her that I had missed not skiing with her in the morning and to nearly quote Gladys Knight on *Midnight Train to Georgia*, said, "I would rather live in your world than live without you in mine - if only for the afternoon. I will join you on the button and the blue." My wife then had a rapid change of mind. She said that she felt much happier on button lifts all of a sudden and no longer needed extra practice. "I'll come and ski with you three. Let's go and do some reds.

I hope Henri wasn't too disappointed.

Saint-Dizier

A hotel in town with rooms that come complete with guests already installed...

There was a time, before the children reached school age, that we could go skiing in January or March and not February when the French are on holiday, and specifically the week that includes Valentine's Day when it's half-term across most of England and hotel prices double. In those far off days we didn't need to book hotels and flights months in advance and cross our fingers that there would be some snow; we would wait until a few weeks before we had planned to go then check the weather, check the snow, book the ferry (always room), book the accommodation (always space) and off we would go. I didn't bother to book a hotel for the overnight stop as there was always space somewhere. France is so easy and relatively cheap for overnight motorway stops.

One year my wife and I, with another couple, were coming back from the Alps and we found ourselves early evening in Saint-Dizier. We should already have stopped and found somewhere to stay the night but we had been a bit late leaving the resort. By now we were getting just ever-so-slightly nervous about finding somewhere as it wasn't the time of year for sleeping in the car and I told the others so. "It would be a bit cramped," said my friend's wife without totally rejecting the idea. We must have been getting a little bit desperate. We pulled off the motorway and headed for the centre of town. Not being the greatest of French speakers we wasted a fair bit of time following the signs for the first hotel we could find, Hôtel de Ville. We finally reached it only to discover that it was closed. How bizarre! Then it dawned on us that Hôtel de Ville wasn't a hotel at all but the town hall. Then we found a couple of hotels but they were both full. We were now getting worried. I suggested that we find somewhere that maybe wasn't quite so appealing and thus not so full. In the distance I could see a garish neon sign flashing over the rooftops. We decided to investigate.

A few minutes later we drew up outside Hôtel de Champagne, an old but stylish building on three floors. Attached to the wall on the first floor was our beacon - a large neon Champagne bottle sign that flickered primary colours. I wouldn't want to sleep with that outside my bedroom window I thought. Unless it had blackout curtains I would probably have had a seizure.

I was going through a bit of a louche period at the time. I was in the habit of wandering into hotels and upon ascertaining that there was availability would insist on having a look at the room before taking it. If the receptionist demurred I would say that I had had bad experiences in the past and I just wanted to sniff the sheets and check for cockroaches, that sort of thing. I was ever-so-slightly affected for I wouldn't have bothered to look at a room and then reject it unless it were terrible and I wouldn't look at a room unless I was needing to stay somewhere. I had never, ever turned down a room and I wasn't expecting to do so this evening even though the interior of the building was a little tired. After all, so were we.

We parked the car and I jumped out. As our wives started to gather the overnight bags I commanded them to wait a few minutes whilst I went and inspected the rooms if they had availability. I left them in the car and I slowly walked up to the entrance, having a good look around as I did. As I pushed at the large glass door I realised that my friend, David, was behind me. He's a few years younger than me and I like to think that he considered me his mentor although he probably didn't; he just didn't want not to be part of the action.

There was an old boy at the desk and a young lady. He was a bit scruffy, a little unkempt but it suited the look of the hotel so I wasn't too bothered. She was smartly dressed. "Monsieur," I said to the man, primarily to warn David indirectly that this was only going to be a two-way conversation. His French was minimal, mine only slightly better, but I had cultivated quite an impressive accent. It sounded very French and was let down only by the language that was coming out of my mouth and the fact that I hardly ever understood what a proper French-speaker's reply was. "Vous êtes le patron?" (You are the boss?) I don't know why I asked this. I expect it was so that he knew that I was to be taken seriously as I was wanting to deal with the top level of the hotel hierarchy. "Oui," he replied. "Je voudrais deux chambres, chaque pour deux personnes pour le nuit s'il vous plait. C'est possible?" (I would like two rooms, each for two people for the night. Is it possible?) The patron nodded and gave me the price. I had no idea how much it was. I turned to David. "Is that okay - the price?" David nodded. Now it could be David's fault if the bill was too high. "You said it was fine." "Ça c'est bon monsieur mais je voudrais avant voir une chambre s'il vous plait." (That's fine sir but before I would like to see a room please.) The patron, who was reaching behind him for a couple of keys, then stopped. After a second he reached for a third key which he handed to me saying that that was okay and I would find room 168 on the first floor. As I climbed the stair David said, "Did you see how he gave you another key when you said that you wanted to take a look?" "Yes I did. He's given us the best room. A great trick to get the best room. That often happens," I lied. It had never happened to me before as far as I was aware. Oh, I was such a puffed up prat in those days.

We reached room 168, unlocked the door and entered. The room was fine if a little dated but that was the least of our worries. There was an opened bottle of Perrier on a table along with a glass. "Oh look, complimentary slippers," said David pointing at a pair sticking out from under the bed. "It's like Goldilocks," I said. "But what's that noise?" "It's the shower." Then it stopped. David and I were rooted to the spot. Better to be caught standing still than be seen trying to beat a retreat as if we were on the way out after "breaking and entering" with the intention to steal.

All of a sudden from the bathroom emerged a man, fortunately wearing a pair of underpants. "Hallo," he said. "Can I help you?" There was no need to explain. The patron was all at once behind us and speaking in English. "I yam sorry. No, no. Not this room. There has been a terrible mistake," he said, looking very flustered and waving his arms about. "I am so sorry monsieur," he said to the man. "No need to apologise," said the man. "I thought things were just about to start getting interesting. It could be a great way to solving a full hotel - shove the newcomers in with someone else. I'ld be up for that!" The patron had already taken the key from the lock and ushered us out shutting the door behind him. "We'll just confer with our wives," I said in English. He understood perfectly. That is to say he nodded. "The car's starting to look more attractive," I whispered to David.

Downstairs we found our wives in the bar, tucking into a bottle of rosé. Also on the table were a couple of keys. "I think we ought to stay here," I suggested. "I'll just get our room keys." "Too late," said our wives. "We've checked in already." "Can I just look at your keys?" I requested, holding out my hand. "I've ascertained that the room to avoid is 168." "Oh look," said my wife. "We have 167 and 169. That should be interesting."

And it was.

Saint-Dizier outskirts

...whilst out of town bring your own commune.

We stayed in a hotel on the outskirts of Saint-Dizier, a city on the edge of Champagne country, on the way down to the Alps for our annual skiing holiday. My husband was in the habit of booking us all (four couples) into either a minus star motel of the sort that had a bedroom with a moulded bathroom in one corner or a bed and breakfast that would often be on a working farm where the day started with a bleeding co-co-ricoing cockerel kicking off at silly o'clock. This year I was in charge. I told my husband that he had saved so much money over the years putting us in grotty grot that he could jolly well spend it all this year on something more acceptable to me and everyone else we were travelling with. Then I said that if he didn't put me in charge I wouldn't go. And that was that ladies.

I found a reassuringly expensive hotel that looked like an old manor house. It boasted *lits à baldaquin* (four poster beds) in every one of its enormous rooms. That was enough for me. My female friends had stipulated somewhere nice and romantic in the countryside and this place was just the ticket. When we arrived we wandered into a charming reception area. The walls were lined with dark wood panels; small but very atmospheric. There was a wide staircase at one end that accessed all floors. The very genial *propriétaire* enquired after our journey and then asked, in French, whether we would like to eat in the restaurant. So often this can be a bad move as one can find oneself, in my experience, as the lone diner in a cavernous *salle* where last orders are at about seven-thirty in the evening. However, seeing as how it would otherwise have meant a drive into the city and then time wasted trying to park, before even starting the chore of finding a restaurant I took it upon myself to say thank you and that, yes, we would all eat in. The lady beamed and decided to make more small talk with me. I was happy to oblige. In the meantime, my husband and non French-speaking friends had been scooped up by an enthusiastic and friendly porter who was busy whisking overnight bags towards and up the stairs, gesturing for my husband and friends to follow.

The owner was in full flow, explaining how the building had been in her family since whenever when there was a bit of a commotion on the staircase. "Don", whom we nicknamed after Quixote, the eponymous romantic hero of the book, appeared at the bottom of the stairs. "Come quickly Jane," he commanded. "Something terrible has happened!" His furrowed brow gave sufficient gravitas to the, as yet for me at least, unknown situation. Don was one of those people who spoke not a word of French believing that if one used English loudly enough and repeated oneself several times the interlocutor would eventually understand. Don turned on his heels and made for the staircase, with me following on behind, whereupon he took the stairs two at a time until he reached a door that actually opened off the staircase. He went through and I followed into the room. There I found my husband and friends standing around looking perplexed; everyone was silent, except Don. The room was huge. Both of the two corners facing me had a large four poster bed in them. "Look!" Don blustered. "Yes?" I calmly asked. "What's the problem?" "It's a great room," he said, "but Lynne and I are not sharing with you and Graham or any of the others. No way! I want a room with Lynne and no one else!" "Madame," the porter interrupted and I turned to face him; Don was staring blankly at one of the beds, "c'est pour deux personnes seulement." (It's for two people only.) Yes, it was a bedroom for four but we were only expected to take one of the beds; there were three more double rooms for our group the porter explained in French. I looked at my friends and stuck two fingers in the air. They smiled and so did the porter. I then asked him in French what the weather forecast was for the following day and he told me. "What's he saying?" Don demanded. "He says that there's been a big mistake. We only have three rooms booked and he's sorry but two couples must share," I replied. "I'm not sharing!" Don almost shouted but before he could suggest that maybe two other couples shared, his wife, Lynne, piped up, "I don't mind sharing; it could be rather fun!" Don, who hadn't been married a year was less than impressed. He was very much a man, a man's man and there was no way he was sharing with another man - and his wife. "I simply can't believe....this is not...oh, how can you screw up big time Jane?" "It's not my fault," I complained. "I booked four rooms." "I can't believe it," Don sighed. "I need some fresh air." He pushed past me and descended the stairs. The rest of us managed to give it a few more seconds before bursting into fits of laughter. "We'll take this room," said Sally. The rest of us trudged further up the stairs to find the other three rooms.

Graham had the first bath, quick but luxurious, then got dressed for dinner. I had an hour left to get ready and I was going to make the most of it. "Go and find Don," I told him, "and tell him we've agreed to take the broom cupboard." "No chance!" he replied. "I'm going to go and find Don to tell him that he can go and use the facilities in Sally's room because they've bathed and pampered and are now going out for a walk. That will confuse him further." Don refused to play though. When Graham found him he was complaining to the landlady in reception. He was still demanding his own room. "Il n'y en a pas," (There are none) she said. Graham took him into the bar where Don drowned his sorrows for an hour.

We had a fine meal in the restaurant which was an adventure in itself. As was often the case, it was almost empty. Don, unshowered and smelly, enquired as to why it was so when all the rooms were taken and was told that there was a coach party on its way. That's what I told him anyway by way of translation when I was actually discussing the breakfast options with the waiter. Don turned his attention to the food. He said that the wine should be reasonably priced seeing as how most of it only had to be driven down the road from the bottling plant but he was mistaken in this also. It was one of those places where you could select the vineyard and then decide on a vintage from around five years ago up to and even beyond fifty. The wine list was as big as a book with prices that started from where I would normally stop looking. The green salads were typically French. I had one as a starter and it came looking like a Brobdingnagian caterpillar that had exploded. It tasted divine though, helped by a special ingredient that I discovered that evening and have been using ever since - walnut oil.

As we sat in the bar with our coffees and *digestifs* talk turned once more to the bedroom problem. Don's wound-up spring started to uncurl once more. "I can't believe any of you are happy to share," he complained. "I suppose I can understand a few blokes on the floor together but not couples. That's almost..." "Old-fashioned?" Lynne suggested. How she didn't wet herself there and then I've no idea given the look she received. It was only when we were making noises about retiring and suggesting that Don could sleep in the bath that things suddenly took an even more dramatic turn. The owner came over to inform us /

me that she had found somewhere for Don to sleep. "It's outside but very comfortable," she explained. When I translated he smelt a rat. "She didn't say that!" he challenged but this time she actually had. She nodded her head and told us to follow her. We all went out of the front door and around the building to the back. We then took a narrow winding path that led down to a river. We turned a corner and in front of us, at the side of the path, was a caravan - small but new looking; it appeared well cared for. Madame pointed to the door. "Come on Lynne," said Don as he took his wife's hand. "This may well do. Finally." Gingerly they opened the door and peered inside. It was very neat but was evidently someone's home, albeit temporarily, with food on the table and beer on the side, a few photos in frames and clothes hanging, that sort of thing. We all crowded inside and sat down where we could. Just then our friendly porter appeared with what looked like more food, his supper on a plate, covered in foil. "What's he doing here?" Don demanded. The man rambled on for a bit gesticulating wildly. "What's he saying?" Don asked, not for the first time that day. "He's saying that Lynne can sleep on the pull-out bed up that end because it's a single and you Don can sleep on the double at the other end. You have to pull out the seat..." "Stuff all that," Don interrupted. "Ask him why I can't share the double bed with my wife." "Because zat iz my bed az well," said the porter in almost perfect English. No one said a thing. Don put his head to his hands. "I'm having a bad friggin' dream," he lamented. "A nightmare of epic proportions. What in the name of Riley is wrong with you all? You're supposed to be my friends!" "Better come to bed then darling," Lynne said, jangling a set of room keys at him. "I AM NOT SHAR..." he began before he looked up and saw me jangling another set of keys at him and then Sally and the other couple doing the same. He blinked, confused after a few too many drinks as to what was now going on.

It was the faintest of smiles from the other couple but it was enough to get us all going. We could hold it in no longer. The laughter coming from that caravan was so loud we would have woken all the other guests, if there were any. "YOU B*****DS!" Don screamed. Who said the French don't have a sense of humour?

When we reached the ski resort the following day and we were walking down the main road Don disappeared into a bookshop to reappear a few minutes later. In his hand he had *Linguaphone French Complete Course*.

Five years on and he's speaking French, apart from the accent, like a native. I could never pull the same trick again with Don but I have other friends. Maybe one day we will take them to the four poster bed hotel.

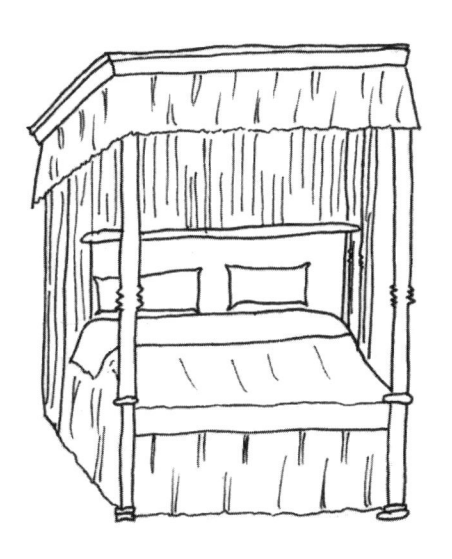

Sainte Foy

In France most understand French and many understand English; a fair number understand both. In the Val d'Isère region not everyone understands French - but everyone understands English. You have been warned.

Or more accurately Sainte-Foy-en-Tarentaise (what's it all about - the French and hyphens in place names all over the show?) is a small village that one passes through on the road from Bourg-Saint-Maurice to Val d'Isère. There's not much skiing to be had there, for that you have to turn off the road at La Thuile, which is further on, and ascend via several hairpins for about four kilometres.

Three of my friends and I were staying in Val d'Isère for a week's skiing and, without our wives to keep us in check, had been spending more time participating in après-ski than just ski. (We had all been to Val d'Isère the year before with our better halves and young children so they knew that we were perfectly safe going by ourselves as we would spend most of our time in Moris Pub (sadly no longer there) listening and bopping to some of the best bands in the Alps. The previous year we had been much taken by Mike and Richie, a guitar and sax-trumpet-flute duo, accomplished musicians whom we had said "Hello" to after the gig as was our want. In any case we had been chatting to Mike's girlfriend who had been beside us jigging along to the music so we thought the least we could do was introduce ourselves as seasoned groupies. I seem to remember that I put in a request for Led Zeppelin's *Whole Lotta Love*, with its distinctive guitar and drum intro, but was turned down because, "We don't play that.")

Halfway through the week we decided that we ought to do a bit of skiing if only to be able to produce some proof when we returned home other than broken something. As a scout leader I knew all the tricks: boys who whittle down bars of soap with their penknives to make it look as though they had had at least one wash, or rubbing a bit of chocolate in a strategic place on each pair of underpants - you get the idea. We needed to get on the slopes if only to take a few photos. We also decided that the following day we would try out Sainte Foy. We had been told that it was the resort that the local ski instructors go to on their day off so we felt that we would be in good company. We would be able to get transport from the bus station to the resort. That evening we pushed the boat out just a little bit too much. It was lunch, après-ski, dinner, après-après-ski and club. Some of my group would have been quite happy to remain in bed until lunchtime, but we had made an agreement and so most of us made it to breakfast at 8.59am, one minute before it closed. None of us was feeling particularly well to say the least and the thought of a bus ride down the hill was not at all appealing. Nevertheless we made it, sort of, to the bus station and then wondered what to do. It was all rather intimidating with buses big and small, coaches and taxis coming and going but I was satisfied that I had sufficiently understood that we were to get onto a specific fifty-two seater that I confidently told my friends to follow me as I jumped on the coach that had "Bourg-Saint-Maurice" on the front of it. I told the driver that we wished to alight at Sainte Foy. He pointed me down the coach with a few incomprehensible words. "Okay," I said although it wasn't had it been important. My friends joined me and Will reached for a sick bag. Our skis went in a large cupboard-like box that was attached to the back of the bus.

We didn't move for twenty minutes but when we did, with no one else on board, we experienced a new white-knuckle theme park ride called "Shake Your Passengers' Guts Up!" as we flew down the valley at impossible and probably illegal speeds.

We drove past the sign that pointed up to the ski resort station "à 5 mn" and through La Thuile. I jumped up and made my way to the front of the coach whereupon I tried to explain to the driver that we wanted to go to Sainte Foy and needed to get off and Will really need to get off like, um, now please. The driver beckoned for me to sit back down which of course I did. At the next village the coach finally pulled over and indicated that we now should get off. "Er, where's the snow?" I asked in my best French and he pointed up the side of the valley. We alighted and stood in the small car park that we found ourselves in at the side of the road. Opposite there was a restaurant. "I feel so sick," Billy moaned. "I don't think I can go on!"

Having already gone well past the five minute drive sign there was no way that any of us was going to walk anywhere so we stood silently for a couple of minutes, wondering what to do next. We were on the verge of going into the restaurant to ask for a taxi back up the hill when a large minibus pulled up. I went over to the driver's side and said, "Sainte Foy?" with a hangdog expression. Once again we were beckoned on and we sat down, skis in hand. At least this time we weren't alone. A couple of other skiers were in the back row. They were ready for action with their goggles down and gloves on. He was in the corner seat and she was next to him cuddled up in one arm. "Hallo, bonjour," I said with a smile. No response. This I considered very odd indeed. No one in a French ski resort speaks neither French nor English so I felt I should take an instant dislike to this stand-offish pair. However I gave them the benefit of the doubt and assumed that they may have simply been deaf.

By now we felt that we might start to be able to muster / mutter a few words. The four of us were slouched over the minibus seats like car-crash victims and, as the minibus turned round and started back up the road, I pondered aloud whether we were going back to Val d'Isère. However we were somewhat relieved when we arrived back in La Thuile and the driver took a left-hand turn past the "à 5 mn" sign. Now a bit less concerned, we started to relive out loud the excesses of the previous evening. "I feel so ill," Will complained as he opened a window and tried to stick his head through. "How many of those stupid B52s did I drink?" "Too many Will." "Why was Billy pole dancing with that pillar?" "Why did Webbo dip his frogs' legs in his beer?" "He said they had too much garlic on them and he was seeing if they could swim without a body." "I feel so ill," Will repeated. After the driver had slung the minibus round a few hairpins he drove into a small yard with a garage. He then got out and wandered off towards the building. "Are we there yet?" "I don't think so, the other couple haven't moved." "Maybe he's going for a pee." "Let's just wait and see what happens." Eventually the driver appeared, got back in the minibus and continued up the hill. "I feel that going up this high is making me feel worse," groaned Billy. He asked Will for a sick bag but he hadn't any left. An interim assessment: we were a disgrace to our families.

Looking back on that trip up the mountain to the ski resort I can understand why we might have appeared to the outsider to be our own little comedy routine but at the time such a thing was not at all in our minds. We were only concerned with survival that day. We reached the ski area, bought our day tickets and made our way up the first lift.

Sainte Foy is a charming resort, far too good for the likes of us. Originally a tiny hamlet, much sympathetic building has taken place in recent years. You could be in the middle of nowhere with minimal crazy après-ski, the emphasis being on good food, quiet bars and spas. At the top of one of the runs I felt as if I had forgotten how to ski. I charged down a red and took out a "SLOW DOWN" banner that was slung across the piste. We discovered an eco toilet that intrigued us more than was wholesome. We eventually decided to try and ski all the pistes that afternoon. We managed most of them. At one point we skied round a corner and to the side we espied an enormous snowy jump. As we looked at the powdery landing area we realised that we were being watched. The couple from the minibus were sitting on the steps of a mountain refuge and they had a perfect view of what I was considering doing. "Go on, jump!" the man cried. "Go on!" the woman squealed. They may have been English, there was definitely a bit of an accent present; they certainly could speak and understand the language. They weren't deaf. "Er, no, not yet. I don't feel too good at the moment. Maybe another time." "Coward!" the man shouted. I was sorely tempted, very tempted indeed but my friends weren't egging me on because they would have to have followed if only to pick up the pieces. "Another day," I rather lamely replied and we continued down the piste. I didn't care; we would never see them again. Then we took some photos.

It was a great day's skiing and I felt that the next time I went to Sainte Foy I would bring my wife and family.

Après-ski was calling. We took a taxi back to Val d'Isère and by five o'clock we were feeling a slightly better. We should have drunk nothing that evening but the body clock was telling us that it was time for a pint or two.

We headed straight out to Moris Pub. The Val d'Isère gig guide had informed us that Mike and Richie were playing and we certainly weren't going to miss that. We trudged up the steps and through the double doors. The party was already in full swing.

There is something very self-satisfying in walking past the band on your way to the bar and giving the musicians a little wave or a knowing nod. It's even better if they reciprocate. It's as if you're part of the band just by being known by one, or even better, all of the members. The only thing you don't want them to do is frown as if to say, "Who's that?" Punters are watching and they're thinking, "I wonder what they play? They're cool. I wonder who they are?" and that's the idea. I had already seen Mike's girlfriend through the sea of people and waved. She had reciprocated with a big smile and an even bigger shrug of the shoulders. She had remembered us! We were part of the band. As we walked across the front of the crowd, in the respectful one metre space you get at the beginning of such gigs, when everyone's not yet fuelled and filling every spare centimetre space with dancing, I caught Mike's eye and gave him my oh-so-cool little wave and a nod. As he strummed his guitar at the end of the song they were playing he nodded back! Oh yes! He remembers us also! Then he stopped playing. Then he spoke. "Ah, my old friends!" boomed out of the speakers. Oh my goodness! He remembers us enough to vocally acknowledge us and I was at the front! Everyone was staring at us. I felt that I should have, at that moment, jumped on the stage, grabbed a guitar and taken over the microphone before shouting, "Allll-right! Who wants to hear some rock 'n' roll?" before launching into *Whole Lotta Love* in front of my adoring, screaming fans apart from the fact that I'm not Robert Plant, nor Jimmy Page, I don't have fans, I can't play and I can't sing. So I didn't.

"How are you feeling?" he asked. "Allll-right!" I replied.

And then the bombshell: "And Will? Is he feeling any better?" It was now me who was frowning. I turned and looked at Will at the back of our short line. He shrugged his shoulders but he wasn't smiling, he was frowning also. He was still feeling quite ill. Mike strummed a chord.

"Ladies and gentleman. This morning I was on a minibus with my girlfriend. We were minding our own business, going up to Sainte Foy when these four lads got on..." He then told the whole friggin' story to my now no longer fans.

That was at least fifteen years ago. This year I went into the best bar in Val d'Isère, Le Petit Danois, with my wife and Will and twenty-one year old daughter, Zoë, my son Charles and his friend Marco. By chance Mike and Richie were playing and they were in the middle of their set. They were playing with another pair of great musicians, guitarists, Karen and Andreas. As I slunk round the back of the crowd to get a drink Mike stopped playing. "Hey! Sainte Foy!" Then he addressed the crowd.

"Ladies and gentleman. Some years ago I was on a minibus with my girlfriend going up to Sainte Foy when these four lads got on..."

Apparently Mike has been dining out on this story for fifteen years! "Come on John," he cried when he had finished. "Come up the front like you do when your family's not with you and put in a request. We can play anything you want." I fought my way to the front.

"I would like *Whole Lotta Love* please Mike."

Sestriere

The novice skier who started on a black.

When I was a teenager I went on a school trip for four days to Sestriere. Goodness knows why as it's mostly intermediate and difficult runs and quite a few of us had never skied before. I had been on a nursery slope in England near where I lived but it was dry plastic stuff that had so much friction in it that you could easily stop without wanting to whilst at the same time doing a passable impression of a Van de Graaff generator guinea pig.

On the first day we were divided into three groups: beginners, intermediates and advanced. My dad was forever telling me to push myself and I figured I wasn't a beginner beginner so I said that I was an intermediate. Then we had too many intermediates so I said that I would go into advanced. I thought to myself, "How hard can skiing on snow actually be?"

How was I to know what our instructor would then do to us? We were put on a chair lift and then a drag lift. I had been on a drag lift at the dry slope but it was only about thirty feet long; this one went on for miles! I managed to get off okay but then our instructor Matteo showed us what we were going to ski down. It was a black! I took one look at it (it looked like I was being asked to jump off a cliff) and told him, "There's no way that I'm going down there." He said that it got easier because the rest of the way was "just" a red. When I still refused he told me to wait whilst he took the others down and back up again. I watched them disappear off the side of this cliff. I removed my skis and sat in the snow. To anyone who asked I said that I was waiting for someone.

When they finally reappeared I said that I would go back down on the drag lift but he said, "It doesn't work like that." He told me that there was no way down and that I was selfish and he would come back and sort me out later. I sat there for hours! Eventually three old men who were English saw me crying and came over. I told them what had happened and said that I was going to die. They said that no piste is unreachable by the piste patrollers and that I would be able to get down to the town even if it didn't involve any skiing. In short they said that I could be rescued and that they could 'phone a number and get out a stretcher or a skidoo or a helicopter. "But I haven't broken anything!" I wailed. "I don't want to be an imposition. I'm not an emergency." "Don't worry," one of them said. "This isn't like the NHS. It's private. Do you have insurance?" "I don't know!" I sobbed. "Well if you haven't the only thing that will be broken is your bank account!" "Or your parents'!" added another. I knew that my mum would not be able to afford to have her bank account broken. She had scrimped and saved to send me on this trip and I was going to have to get down the cheapest way possible, even if it meant a hospital bill at the end when I jumped off the cliff or tripped and tumbled all the way to the bottom. When one of them asked if I could snow plough I told them the whole story about the nursery slope and how I had volunteered to be "advanced." "We can do this," they said eventually. They showed me how to place my skis behind one of the men in a snow plough, put my arms around him and not to make any sudden movements. "Try not to touch my skis," he instructed. "I can't bend down that far!" I exclaimed and they all laughed.

It was in this manner that I conquered that black slope in little traverses all the way down. When we reached the top of the chair lift the men said that I could take it back down the slope but I said that I would rather ski some more if it was okay with them. The men took it in turns and we went down the quickest route which was the black, naturally! It's only now that I am older that I am beginning to understand how difficult it must have been for these three men to take me down a black run like that, but they did! I didn't fall over once.

I was hooked! I couldn't believe that I had made so much fuss at the top of the drag and that I could probably have snowploughed all the way down on my own had I had to but as one of the men said, "The only real difference between a red and a black is that on a red if you fall you will eventually, generally come to a halt on the piste whereas on a black you may well go over the edge," so I'm glad I didn't try. I was just cross that I had spent the best part of a quarter of my skiing holiday refusing to go down a poxy black.

I bumped into my fellow "advanced" skiers at the bottom of the chair lift. They excitedly told me that Matteo had gone all the way back up to the top to find me. "That should be interesting," I muttered.

There was a load of activity between the teachers when we finally arrived back at the hostel and Miss Gibbs took me to one side and asked for, "a full oral report of the day. I just need to know."

The following day the advanced group had a new instructor and no one saw Matteo again but I expect he lived. I was put in the beginner group and we did a blue. I snow ploughed it perfectly but not before I had fallen over twice: once off the chair lift and again on the first turn. My new instructor asked me if I had skied on snow before. "Yes," I replied, "But only blacks." "Don't you mean greens?" she asked.

I'm still skiing and to this day I have never met anyone who ever skied a black before a green, blue and / or red.

Shorts

Shorter stories and anonymous resorts in no particular order.

Chair lift trauma.

I love skiing but have never got used to chair lifts. Funnily enough getting on and off them isn't a problem. What I hate about them is the height of them. Why do they have to be so stupidly high? No one on the ground is more than about seven feet tall at most so why do they make the lifts go any higher than this? I realise that sometimes they have to get up and over sheer edges but they could place the pylons so that the lifts go up on the hypotenuse instead of starting a few hundred yards back. Then there's the bouncing. Whenever a chair lift stops, and they stop too often and too quickly, the chairs bounce as if they're trying to detach themselves. As I sit there, hundreds of feet up, my only thought is, "When the cable snaps will I survive?" Through one eye I glance at the ground far below and pick the spot that I'm going to aim for when I fall. Then I have a look for the nearest pylon: is it behind me or in front? If I reach out could I grab it? And forget a bit of wind when they start to gently rock to and fro. By the time I'm getting off at the top I'm a nervous wreck. I'ld rather walk thank you.

***

Mama Do (Uh Oh, Uh Oh).

This year at Easter I was in Avoriaz, skiing with my fifteen year old son and a few of his too-cool-for-ski-school friends. Skiing to my mind is a mostly very relaxed sport. Sure there's a bit of work to be done but up in the mountains it's calm, atmospheric and quiet. At least it used to be until my boy came along. I would prefer it if he concentrated on his skiing but if he's going to have music blaring it's probably best that he doesn't have it blasting through an earpiece resulting in him being a danger to himself and those around him. The only alternative (really?) is some ghastly speaker dangling from his rucksack that belts out some dirge that can be heard at the bottom of the piste from the top. We (they) were skiing behind four young ladies dressed in the most amazing ski suits - I was a few ski lengths behind - obviously trying to impress with their appalling music choice, but getting nowhere as the ladies were continuing their stylish skiing with not one backward glance. I stopped my son and told him that if he and his friends were looking to dazzle he needed something a bit more mainstream and upbeat. "Like what dad?" he asked. "Like, show me your playlist and I'll choose." I landed on Pixie Lott's first, and seminal, hit single and we again took off down the piste with, "What would my mama do?" blasting out. We were on a Pixie loop, listening to more of her fabulous songs but by now the four ladies were nowhere to be seen. We went round a corner and were nearly at the bottom when we finally saw them. They had stopped! As we skied slowly past one of them waved and so the lads all stopped too. "This could be interesting," I thought. "I wonder what they're going to say?" It wasn't what either my son or I was expecting. One of them turned out to be soul singer Jocee. One of the others, who was dressed in the most florescent of florescent orange all-in-ones with thick black lines down the sides, came over to us, smiled, and said,

"Wow, you're playing my music."

Unbelievable but true. We were being spoken to by no other than the amazing Pixie Lott herself, who was out on the slopes getting in a bit of skiing before her marriage a couple of months later. So my son had no chance!

Most of the time when you're skiing you have no idea who you may be overtaking, brushing past, sitting on a chair lift with but that day we did find out and I'm so glad we did. Pixie didn't need to stop and speak, she could have just let us ski straight past but she didn't - she had a word with us and let us take her photo. What a coincidence though, and what a great sport. Thank you Pixie Lott!

***

A lesson learnt from the chair lift.

Youngsters today don't remember the days not that long ago when adults never wore a helmet, but go back a few decades to when I was a youngster skiing in the States and there were no safety bars on the chair lifts. One thing some American resorts used to do - I've never seen it in Europe - and some still do, is have different queues depending on whether you're one, two, three or four skiers in a group. This avoids all that shuffling about just behind the gates. Invariably there's a seat or two that's not taken on each chair which can make the difference between no queue and a short queue, or between a short queue and a long queue.

Some lifts have / had someone directing the skiers. "Two twos, one three and a single, one four..." and everyone would get into position. In such queues one could work the system as a single and zip through the queue very quickly.

All those years ago I was in a queue for a two-man, no restraining bar, chair lift. At this particular resort if you were a single it was considered "good form" to raise a pole in the air if you were on your own and just about to get on the chair, so that another single could join you but for no other reason than to keep the queue moving. A beautiful young woman was just about to get on on her own. She raised her pole in the air and shouted, "Single!" I didn't need telling twice. I was in love! I fair pushed a few other singles over in my sole mission at that point to get on her lift. I succeeded. She was stunning. I looked at her, smiled and then started to gabble. All I let her tell me was her name and what she was reading at university. On and on I went - asking her questions, answering them myself, just being a complete dick as I prattled away all the while thinking I was God's gift. I was waving my skis backwards and forwards, doing a passable imitation of a cross-country skier in the air, when the snow took me. I hadn't realised that it was a lift with a middle station for disembarkation, where the golden rule was to lift one's tips in order to get onto the platform in one piece whether you were staying on or not. I was getting off but I hadn't intended to. I hadn't read the signs, I was too busy. Both my skis dug deep into the snowy bank and suddenly there was nowhere for me to go except off. With my skis wedged my body stopped but the chair kept going as it sort of flattened me but best of all face-planted me into the icy platform. As I lifted my head, ignoring the command to "DUCK!" from the chair coming up behind, I realised that I had broken my goggles and blood was pouring from my nose. I had also grazed a cheek. Cindy turned round in her chair and shouted, "We could have made a great couple if you had allowed ME TO SPEAK!" Then she turned back round again. "See you at the top?" I squealed. Then the second chair ran over me.

By the time the chairs had stopped, I had been extracted, been put on a free seat and got to the top, Cindy had disappeared. "Probably got fed up waiting," I thought to myself then spent the rest of the day going up the same lift and down all the runs that went to the bottom. I never saw her again. But at least I'm a better listener now.

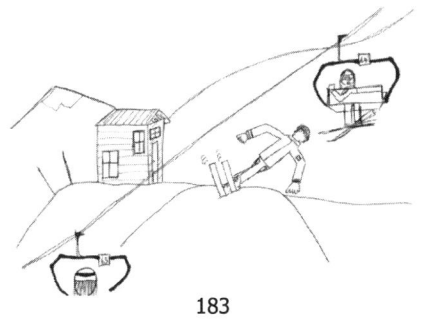

***

The longest skis.

Back in the 1980s skiing wasn't about style or grace, in fact it wasn't about skiing at all. It was to some extent about who had the coolest face paint but mostly it was about who had the longest skis. Of course, longer skis meant higher speeds and less control but for us six days a year skiers it was about how we looked, and never more important than in the lift queue apart from those lifts for which you had to have your skis on your feet and not in your hand. Carving skis had yet to catch on, it was all about the length. The actual length of ski wasn't important; it was the length relative to one's height. We would stand in a lift queue and shake our heads at those whose skis were shorter than their owners. If skis were roughly the same height as the person who was holding them that was okay but it was far better to have skis that were longer than one's height. That always gained kudos in the ski lift queue. There was much talk amongst my friends who were around the six foot mark of one eight fours or one eight sixes. Respect was given to those friends who had longer skis than their height whether or not they could actually go down a blue slope wearing them. I found a new trick in order to gain admiring glances - I started to hold my skis about a foot off the ground in crowded lift queues, that always got people staring, "Gosh look at him! He must be good!" It soon became a habit. Fast forward to last year when I was away with my and another family. Ali wanted a photo taken of the group after lunch. Instinctively I went to the back of the group and held my skis a foot in the air. Though I say so myself, the picture does look impressive and Ali did remark when she saw it, "You have some serious skis there; I didn't realise they were so long!" "Neither did he," my wife responded gruffly.

Holding my skis over a foot off the ground

***

Never take a short cut.

My wife and I were staying in Solden with another couple. One evening we decided to try a new restaurant and went on a bit of a route march trying to find somewhere that had been recommended and that we had booked. It was up the piste a bit and we found the footpath that we had been told about but somehow took a wrong turning. We had been walking for far too long when one of my friends saw it. It wasn't far away but it was the other side of some houses. The correct route was to go further up or back down the path and follow it round to the other side of the houses and this is what three of us did. My wife, however, was having none of it. "I'm not walking a step more that I have to!" she complained. "It's raining and I don't want to get wet. In Austria it's perfectly acceptable, in the mountains, to walk across back gardens of houses if they're covered in snow." She spoke with authority and no one bothered to argue. There had not, however, been much snow in the resort. It was early on in the season and was not even particularly cold. We three set off walking the long way but when we arrived at the restaurant my wife was nowhere to be seen. Then she appeared - bedraggled, make-up running, soaking wet and shivering. "What happened?" I asked, incredulous. "I feel in a f**king fish pond, that's what happened," she replied. "So you've ended up wetter than the rest of us put together," was what my friend really should not have said at that particular moment, but he did. We went into the restaurant while my wife went home to change, but she didn't reappear. It was probably just as well. My friend ordered fish.

***

We don't need our passports now - we're in the E U.

A few years after the U K joined the E U my sister took her first holiday abroad in many years. She went to Megève with her husband and they drove. They went down to Dover, then over on the ferry. They had a fabulous week but when they returned they hit a spot of bother. Going through U K passport control at Dover they were asked for their passports. Steve produced his but Linda couldn't. She said to the official, "We're in the E U now. We don't need our passports." "Oh yes you do," said the official. "How did you get to France?" "No one asked for it either at Dover or Calais on the way out. And not on the way back either until now," my sister replied. "I can assure you madam, that even though your passport was not checked on the way out or on the way back, until now, you still need to carry it." "What did you do?" I asked Linda, incredulous. "I just told him,

'It's a bit late now. What are you going to do about it - send me back to Calais?' I looked at Steve and I'm sure I saw a little nod but then they let me past saying, 'Next time make sure you bring your passport.' And I replied as Steve sped off, 'And next time make sure you remember to check it.'"

***

Mullit merchandise.

Many years ago I heard Mullit, a rocking four-piece in Dick's Tea Bar, Val d'Isère. They were superb! I bought a t-shirt. Their lead singer / guitarist, Ed, is still going with drummer Jamie as Mullit and the Machine. I see them every year. The guy selling the t-shirts was possibly Ed's dad or uncle, I can't remember. It was one design, one colour - black and red on white. A few years later they were playing at another venue. They had a new t-shirt out. You could have it in different colour shirts, different sizes, different colour logos. I told my wife that I would like blue on red. Dad / uncle was missing so Ed was in charge of the large holdall. He delved deep inside it during the half-time interval. Wrong colour t-shirt, right size. Right colour t-shirt, wrong colour logo. Right colour logo, right colour t-shirt, wrong size. Shirts were flying everywhere. Finally, with his head deep inside the holdall even I could hear Ed scream, from the other side of the venue, "I'm a rock and roller not a friggin' t-shirt salesman!" He must have got his act together though. This season they sold three hundred!

***

The perils of owning more than one ski jacket.

We were staying in Verbier in a chalet-hotel. The skiing was great but the hike up the road every morning to the lift was a real effort as our accommodation was some way down on quite a steep hill. In our party we had a woman who was a real pain. She had so many clothes. She would finish skiing, go for a drink then leave the rest of us in the bar while she went back to the hotel to get changed because she said she felt sweaty. Then, when we all went back she would have a shower and get changed into another outfit before coming down to dinner. Then, before we went out for another drink, she would go upstairs and get changed again. She was a nightmare. Skiing was no different. Everyone knows that you should only have one ski jacket so that you can see and identify people from afar when you're on the piste. Not this woman. She had a different jacket for each day. What a poseur! It all unravelled on the Wednesday. We had just trekked up our hill having endured listening to this woman going on and on about how, but not why, she had not just one ski jacket for each day but two. Our group had all beeped its way bar one through the automated barriers when the woman said a word that I thought she had probably never uttered before. It turned out that in her haste to put on yet another different jacket she had forgotten to transfer her lift pass that was safely zipped up back at the hotel in one of the previous day's outfits. She pleaded with the lift attendant but to no avail; she had to trudge all the way back down the road and all the way back up. Even her husband was smiling as she plodded off back down the road. That was the end of different jackets every day although we did then have a big discussion about, if she was only going to wear the same one every day for the rest of the week, which one should it be? "The one with the lift pass in it," was my rather flippant suggestion.

***

The ski hotel with a dinner dress code and its own tie.

Ah, The Grand Hotel Zermatterhof. Five star luxury in the heart of Zermatt. Host to royalty, Hollywood stars, my family and friends and me! When we came down to breakfast on our first morning we were surprised to find that our little group was the only one wearing ski gear. There were plenty of fur coats, leather trousers and leather boots floating around but not one ski jacket, pair of salopettes or any Moon Boots. We soon discovered that this hotel was not just for skiers but for those Swiss residents and beyond who would go there just to take in the snow or whatever the expression is. We felt a little underdressed but worse was to come. When we went down to dinner we were told that the men had to wear a jacket and tie. My husband said, "I have no jacket." He was then shown a whole rack of jackets from which he had to pick one that fitted, which he did. He was told that he should wear it in the restaurant and return it after his meal. He was so paranoid that he was going to drop some food on it that as soon as he was given a napkin, a huge cotton job, he opened it up and tucked one corner into his collar. This looked infinitely worse than sitting at a table in an open-necked shirt. But rules are rules. Then the front-desk said, "You have no tie." He was then shown a tie, but not any old tie. This was a Grand Hotel Zermatterhof tie - dark blue with an embroidered edelweiss flower - that he was obliged to buy. Since then he has worn it on every occasion back home when the wearing of a tie has been demanded. It doesn't matter what the occasion - weddings, interviews, funerals, it seems to fit in with every occasion but all it is is a pretentious hotel tie. (A great place to stay nevertheless!)

***

The secret is not only knowing when to turn but actually to turn.

I'm quite a good skier but my problem is turning. I know that sounds stupid like I can't just go straight down, I realise that. One of my friends had her first lessons on holiday. Just before lunch and after her lessons on the second day she said that she wanted to do a blue because she had done one earlier in the morning. We took her on this chair lift and then down one. At the bottom there was a restaurant with loads of people outside. Off she went going faster and faster in tighter and tighter snowploughs. We thought, "Impressive!" but then it dawned on us that she was going too fast and was skiing as if she were preparing for an Eddie the Eagle ski jump but with the ability of Angry Birds. Straight into all the accoutrements she went; deckchairs, little plastic tables, coffee, ashtrays, Aperol spritzes, helmets went everywhere and that was without the people. With that amount of cushioning she fairly rapidly came to a halt. After we had said "Sorry" to everyone and limped (mentally not physically) away Sally said to us, by way of excuse, "Our instructor said we were okay on blues but I haven't learnt how to stop properly yet. The blue we were on this morning had a long flat bit at the end where we could slow down. He said that even if you're out of control you will always be able to stop at the bottom." "Well you did," I said. "Yeah, but into people," she complained. "I feel such a fool! If I can use people to stop me what's the difference between a blue and a black?" "On a black you won't be skiing into people, you'll be skiing onto them, possibly from a height of several hundred feet. The good news is, you probably won't remember." We went off to lunch.

So Sally can't, or couldn't stop, and I can but don't like turning. When I'm going down a run I know when I should turn but I hate that bit of staring straight down the mountain so I put it off for a second or two, continuing to kind of ski sideways, and then I find an icy bit so I can't turn there and then I'm getting a bit too near the side so I point my skis up the slope a bit and now I have no room left to turn and next thing I know I've imbedded my skis and sometimes also myself into a huge snowy bank. This is exactly what I did straight after lunch with Sally following. She, on the other hand, put in an excellent snow plough turn and stopped. Then she swivelled round to face me and said, "Oh, so that's how you stop! I think I've found a better way." I didn't talk to her for two days after that.

[Diagram: hand-drawn skiing lines labeled "THE LINE I WOULD BE HAPPY TAKING", "THE LINE I WANT TO TAKE", "THE LINE I ALWAYS END UP TAKING", "THE LINE I EXPECT TO TAKE"]

***

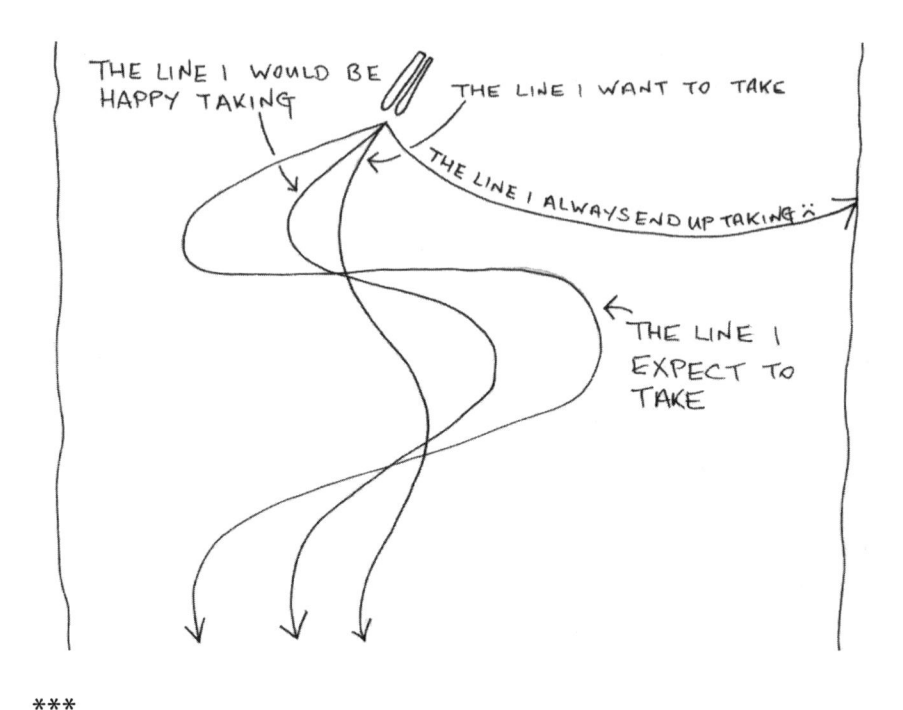

How to turn on a steep black.

I was going down a black run once that was far too steep for my liking. There was no way I was going to turn. Fortunately it was wide with trees on both sides. I skied into the trees and my husband thought I was out of control. I emerged a few seconds later coming out from the trees and skied across the piste then repeated the exercise as my husband watched in disbelief. "I thought you had crashed," he said when he caught me up. "Nothing of the sort," I told him. "I needed to turn so I held out my arm as I went into the woods at full pelt, grabbed a tree and in one fell swoop swung one hundred and eighty degrees round the trunk and out again. Sorted."

***

"I thought I heard you say that you could ski with only one ski."

I was on a chair lift with an American husband and wife and their very annoying kid. First the kid was saying in a loud voice what a good skier she was and how she could ski on one ski and on either foot if she wanted to. Then she was whinging about how her bindings were too tight and her boots were hurting. She was fiddling non-stop. At one point we went over a rock peak that was jagged and so steep there was no snow on it. It was totally inaccessible. By this stage the kid had taken one ski off the foot rest and was bent under the restraining rail trying to loosen the leg binding on her boot. (Giving her a quick shove did cross my mind.) She succeeded only too well for, as we went over the jagged peak, not only did her ski come off but so did one boot with the ski still attached. The ski fell back end down and embedded itself in a crack. Brilliant! Now it was the turn of the parents to have a moan and they were good at it. The top of the lift was approaching so the girl said, "Pop, you've gotta stop the lift!" Before I could stop myself I told her that that wasn't really the done thing in Europe. Kid glares at me. "Well how the hell am I goin' get off with only one ski?" she demanded. "I thought I heard you say that you could ski with only one ski," I replied. "Yeah, but I still need the other ski and boot on for y'know, balance." "Oh, I see," I replied as I lifted up the restraining bar and managed to stay on the chair just long enough to see kid stand up, get shoved a few feet forward by the chair before collapsing to the ground wailing like a piglet being slaughtered. I went up on the lift on my last day. Kid's ski was still there, wedged into the rock with boot still attached.

***

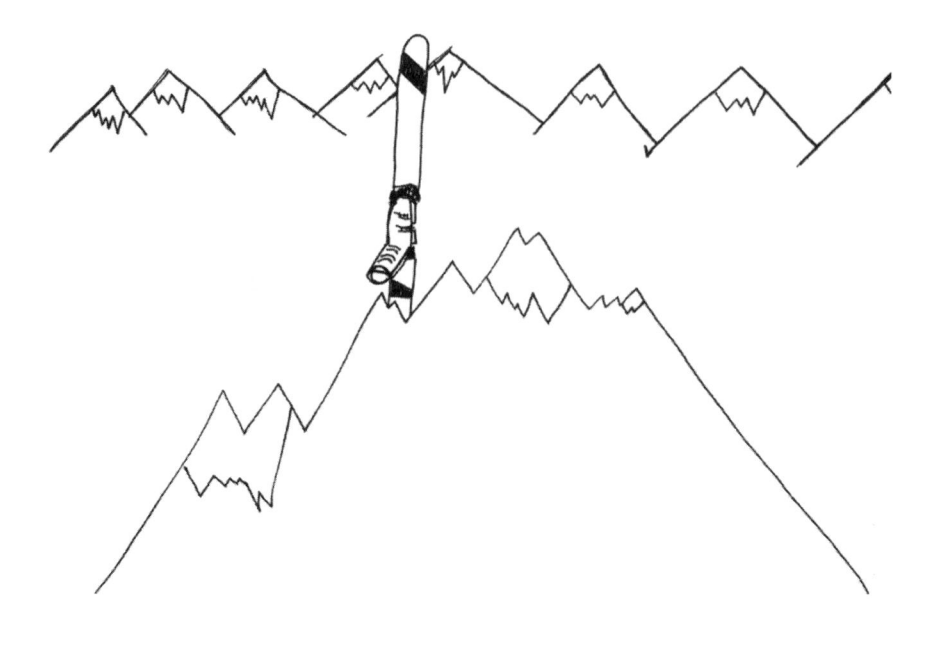

Never dangle your ski poles on a chair lift.

On my first ski holiday with my new skis and poles I thought it terribly rakish to sit on a chair lift with my poles dangling in contravention of the little picture at the embarkation point clearly showing a skier holding their poles in the air as if they're just about to strike someone. We were approaching a halfway getting on / off point when the lift attendant began shouting something at me that was impossible to understand. As the ground came up to meet us I realised what when I heard a slight crack. I pulled up a pole and found it bent into an L shape. I tried to bend it back but snapped the end off. I hadn't even managed one holiday with them.

***

A sparkle in the snow.

Several years ago one of my glamorous, female friends went to Aspen for ten days' skiing. She has loads of money although even she admitted that the trip would make a bit of a dent in her finances. She was, after all, going to be staying in one of the top hotels etc, etc.

One evening she was walking along a pavement that was separated from the road by a long and high bank of snow, when she saw something glistening in the snow under the blaze of the street lamps and shop lights. She didn't know exactly what it was but it was sparkling so she picked it up and put it in a leather glove that she was wearing. During the course of the evening as she travelled from bar to restaurant to club she regularly checked on the small item to make sure it was still there. She had a minor freak out when she couldn't find it but then discovered that it had gone underneath the inner lining of her glove.

When she got back to her hotel she took a closer look at the item and convinced herself that it was a diamond but probably not of much value. She packed it away in her suitcase and tried to forget about it. When she arrived back home she took it to a diamond merchant in Hatton Garden, London who confirmed that it was a cut diamond.

"Did you get it valued?" I asked. "Valued then I sold it to the merchant," my friend replied. I let out a little gasp. "If it's not too rude to ask, how much did you get for it?" "It is too rude to ask, but I'll tell you this much. The amount I sold it for more than paid for the holiday."

Alright for some, as they say.

***

Like father, like son.

I recently told my fifteen year old son about when I used to work part-time in a pub. I was an impoverished bank clerk and so, to make a bit of cash to see me through to the end of the month, I would pull pints at my local. I never used to ask young people how old they were, even if they were probably well under eighteen, but the landlord did. As I was taking a lager order from a young lad one evening my boss's head appeared over my shoulder. "Have you asked him how old he is?" "Er, no." "How old are you son?" "Eighteen." "When's your birthday?" "Um, er, fourth of April." "Which year?" "Two thousand and two, no one no um two thousand, er, twenty this year." "OUT!"

I told my son that if ever people are going to lie convincingly they have to get their facts ready in advance otherwise they will be caught out by the slightest hesitation when asked a question.

In Avoriaz this year I was at La Folie Douce for a spot of après. I had booked our group into Le Balcon which is the VIP area. It wasn't particularly V or I but it was a great experience as we got a bird's eye view of what was going on. I left the kids, including my looks-older-than-fifteen year old, to fend for themselves with the masses and got stuck into the Champagne. The drinks and the conversation was flowing when I decided to have a quick breather. I went and stood at the side of the balcony and surveyed the scene below. I could not believe it! My fifteen year old appeared to have one hand round an Aperol spritz (he assured me later that it was nothing of the sort although I never did get a straight answer from him as to what it actually was) and the other round a gorgeous looking young lady, but when I say young I thought she must have been in her mid-twenties. My little lad! I shouted at him but, well, that wasn't going to work. I would have needed an industrial grade fire alarm to sound but I didn't have one of those in my pocket. I had a dilemma: should I stay where I was and let him get on with it or should I go and rescue him? I had paid one hundred Euros to go into VIP. I stayed.

Several hours later when I scooped him up to ski the last bit of the run back into town I asked him what on earth he had been playing at. "Chatting up a lawyer dad," he replied. "How old was she?" I asked. "Twenty-five," he replied. "How on earth did you pull that off?" I demanded to know. Then I learnt a new lesson in life: if the children want to remember something you've told them then they will. "Remember when you said about getting your facts right in advance? Well that's what I did. I just put myself in [his twenty-four year old brother] Dan's shoes. I told her that I had a law degree from Cambridge and I was in M and A at Slight and May. I had a flat in Clapham and drove a Porsche 911." "Just as well you're not seeing her again," I replied. "I am," he said. "Tomorrow. Here."

I spoilt his fun the following afternoon. I told him I was going into the VIP area again but I didn't, I just went for a pee. Then I went and found him and her, sniffed his drank, downed it in one for him then said it was time to go because he needed to finish his GCSE revision that he hadn't done the evening before due to his mysterious hangover after two lemonades.

He still hasn't forgiven me.

***

Fun with the face paint.

You never see it these days but back in the day face paint was all the rage. Florescent all-in-one ski suits and matching or complimenting coloured lines of paint flicked diagonally across the cheeks. One lunchtime in Hochsölden my friend fell immediately in love with one of the young waitresses in a very posh hotel where we had stopped for lunch. She was attired in the distinctive form of dress that is worn in those parts. This revolves around a structured bodice that is tightly tied and embroidered. Her name was Heidi and she was paying my friend no attention whatsoever. After a few pints he decided that what he was missing was a bit of face paint. Some of us were carrying a tube or two in our pockets so we combined them with the sole aim of making our Casanova a smidgen more appealing. We had such fun! It was as if a primary school full of children had been let loose on him. When Heidi came over to take another drinks order my friend could contain himself no longer. "I love you Heidi," he purred. Heidi smiled. "Thank you. Would you like some more drinks?" My friend was none too impressed with this perceived rejection. "But Heidi, look at me. I've made an effort. What do you think? Adam Ant?" Heidi thought for a moment. "No, I don't sink so. Less Adam Ant, more Coco the Clown." She wasn't far wrong. My friend put his own face paint on after that.

***

Stop staring at my mum!

A group of us were in Moris Pub in Val d'Isère with Mullit performing. It was a late-evening gig and the place was packed to the rafters. The Mullit lads had even erected crash barriers around the front of the stage. The crowd was mainly twenties with plenty of seasonaires who had finished work for the evening. Then there was us lot; forty somethings, some with children of the same age as most of the clientele. We had secured our favourite spot in front of a square, wooden panelled pillar with shelf that could take four pint glasses. Perfect!

Pogoing, moshing or whatever it's called these days was in full swing when in walked a couple that looked distinctly out of place. They looked in their forties also, smartly and expensively casual, dressed to wound if not kill, but I quickly somehow gained the impression that they were a couple that had been forced into the bar but for some reason couldn't leave. I imagined them an hour ago in one of the many fine four or five star restaurants knocking back the white Burgundy with their out-of-season Dover soles, followed by, "No dessert for me darling," cappuccinos and *digestifs* in the piano bar for three hours, saying nothing to each other before retiring to bed and she now has a headache. They just appeared so uncomfortable. They didn't seem to be interacting with each other at all. It was impossible to hear what anyone was saying unless they were bellowing in your ear but there are other ways of communicating: nods, winks, smiles and so on. Then I noticed a child. He looked as though he was more the crowd's average age and fitted in with the dress code but he looked distinctly unhappy also. I wondered what was going on. He obviously wasn't the reason the three of them were there. They were standing about twenty feet away from us and further back from the stage amongst punters who were swaying more than jumping up and down and colliding. The man forced his way to the bar and came back with two small glasses of red wine. Their child didn't seem to be given a drink. I looked at my friend Adam and nodded in their direction whilst they were sipping their drinks. Adam glanced at them then looked at me and shrugged his shoulders. He was obviously having the same thoughts. We continued with our drinking and swaying.

After a short while I was surprised to see the man work his way over to Adam and say something in his ear. Adam looked at him bemusedly as he returned to his place. I was slightly separated from Adam by this stage so didn't bother to try to find out what was said.

Another ten minutes passed and then the child came over to Adam and had a quick but fairly animated conversation before he too went back over to where he had come from. A few more minutes elapsed and then the trio left. I was intrigued. As soon as the interval came I was straight over to Adam. "What was going on there?" I asked.

"Crazy, man, crazy," was Adam's reply. "I was just standing there, minding my own business when the bloke came over to me. I thought he was going to ask me where the Audi car showroom was but instead he said, 'Please stop staring at my wife.' I said, 'I'm not staring at your wife.' He said, 'She thinks you are.' I said that I was not staring at his wife nor anybody else and I should know. I said that I've got to look somewhere and our eyes may have momentarily met but staring is pushing it. I told him that if I was staring at anyone I was staring at Ed [the guitarist] to which he replied, 'Who's Ed?' then off he went. It was bizarre. A few minutes later and the boy's by my side. 'Stop staring at my mum!' he commanded. 'I'm not,' I replied. 'She says you are.' It was then that I have to admit I lost it. I said to him, 'There is no way that I am staring at your mum. I am staring at the band and she is in the other direction. I may be looking over your way to see when I can get to the bar but that's it. I've no desire to glance at let alone look at let alone stare at an ice queen. I don't know what your family's problem is but I've had it up to the neck with you three, well two at least. You're standing over there like you're at a wake instead of watching one of the best bands in the Alps but more than that you're dad's been over already and he's been going on about the same thing and now you are just p**sing me off.' Then I think I got to the crux of it. The kid said, 'Well don't stare, don't look and don't glance and just so's you know - he's not my dad so you can f**k right off.' Then the kid did, back to his mum and not his dad and then they all f**ked off themselves and I think there may be multiple secondary reasons but the primary issue I reckon, by that conversation, I've identified."

This incident happened twenty years ago and I still remember it as if it were yesterday. I often think about that young, now middle-aged man. I hope he's okay.

***

A little misunderstanding in conversation with Spacey, Saalbach's infamous Spitzbub DJ.

We were at Spitzbub in Saalbach that had a great DJ called Spacey. We got chatting to this larger-than-life character who talks to everyone and anyone as if they're all old friends including my wife whom he had never met before. I prised her away eventually much to her annoyance. Spacey asked my teenage son Sam how we'd got to Saalbach. Sam looked a bit simple. "What do you mean?" "Have you driven or flown?" Spacey clarified. Sam told him that we had flown. Then Spacey asked him, "Who did you fly with?" and ignoramus Sam replied with that tone of indignation in his voice that only fourteen-year-old boys can manage, "How am I supposed to know the names of all the other passengers?"

***

Manfred makes sure of his customers' skiing ability.

In Kitzbühel we had a charming ski instructor / guide called Manfred. On the first day he asked the three of us if we could ski reds. "Yes," we all said nonchalantly as we could ski anything. "Sure?" he asked. "Yes," we replied again. We went up a gondola and found ourselves at the top of a fairly steep but perfectly manageable red. "Is this okay?" he asked. "Yes, of course," we replied. "We can take a short lift down that misses out this first bit if you like seeing as it's..." "Manfred," I said, "what's the problem?" He then told us that the previous week he had had a one-on-one lesson with an Englishman. He was an airline pilot. When Manfred asked him if he could ski reds he just said, "Yes." Manfred took him down the slope we were now staring at but instead of skiing it he slid, fell and rolled down. It turned out he had never skied before in his life. "I thought I would soon pick it up," he said rather lamely once Manfred had gathered up his skis and poles and rejoined him, now imbedded in a snowdrift, at the bottom of the piste.

***

Possibly the best café gourmand in the world.

Café gourmand - not a coffee plus one mini dessert that you sometimes get in London, but a load of little desserts. Heaven! In Tignes-les-Brevières which is the furthest you can piste ski in one direction in the Espace Killy there is Restaurant l'Armailly. Inside it's all wood beams but it's outside where you need to be. Get there at noon and sit in the sun for the duration of your meal. Their café gourmand is a must. When we visited recently it comprised a coffee and no fewer than seven little puds. I think that's a record as well as being the best I've ever tasted!

***

Patience is a virtue.

On the way down to the Alps one year we stopped overnight in Morey-Saint-Denis in Burgundy country. Before we recommenced our journey in the morning my friend and I had a wander through the village with the intention of buying a bottle or two of wine to go with our first meal in our chalet. We stopped at a *cave* and decided to go in. We were placed immediately under the spell of a charming French lady who chatted through loads of wine with us nodding. We ended up buying six bottles of white and six red that she then oh so seductively put in a proper wooden wine box before nailing on the lid. "Combien de temps faut-il garder ce vin?" (How long should we keep the wine for) I asked. I was just being polite; I expected her to say that we could drink it straight away. "Trois ou quatre ans," came her reply. "Three or four years," I said to my friend. "No!" he gasped. "Yes!" she replied. Needless to say it lasted three or four days and by the end of the week it had all gone so we called in on the way home and got the box refilled, telling the seductress that we had given it all away. This time we managed it and some of it's still in my garage.

***

Pie eating competition.

I used to go skiing with a large group of friends, some of whom actually saw some snow and in the daylight. One day in Val d'Isère even the night owls couldn't avoid at least a bit of the white stuff as it snowed heavily non-stop for twenty-four hours. We gave up trying to ski after we went up Bellevarde Express and came down the steep bit of the black Face de Bellevarde. Normally, for the uninitiated, this is a seat of your pants ski slope but on this particular day it would have been easier going down in ski shoes. Every time we tried to turn we ended up in a snowdrift. Eventually we reached to bottom looking like abominable snowmen. It was time to look for something else to do for the rest of the day.

Over lunch a quite heated discussion broke out between Mark and Tom. Mark had said that he knew no one who could eat a pie quicker than he could. Tom rose to the challenge and was being very bullish about it in quite an annoying kind of way. Soon preparations were underway. There used to be a subterranean pub in Val d'Isère called Pacific Bar that sold hot Pukka pies. It always seemed to have snow banked up either side of the front door so it felt that entering it was like going into an igloo. David was sent off to see whether they had any pies left as we suspected that they would be in demand that particular day. He was then told to book a restaurant for us all for dinner. He returned to say that a restaurant was booked and the Pacific Bar had just ten pies left. He had had the foresight to pay for them and to have them put to one side to await our arrival.

We all trudged down to the bar at après time and sat around a large table away from the main crowd and the numerous plasma televisions that covered the walls. Mark and Tom faced each other and the pies were brought over; they were given five each. Someone blew a whistle and Tom was off. He lifted the first pie out of its silver foil tray and bit into it. His face immediately reddened but he didn't stop. Within about one minute he had the whole pie in his mouth and some of it he had already digested but he had started to sweat profusely. He picked up the second one whilst still chewing on the remains of the first but was going nowhere fast. In the meantime Mark had yet to put a pie near his mouth. What he had done was expertly poke through the crust of each pie six times with a finger so they all looked like the six on a dice. Steam started to emerge as Mark simply watched. When the steam had started to die down he removed the pastry lids. Only then did he start eating. Tom was on his third pie when Mark overtook him. From that moment there was no looking back and once Mark had eaten his five Tom was still only on number four. He didn't stop though, he just slowed down enough to enable him to blurt out, "Cheat" before taking another bite.

We waited for Tom to eat all his pies (no one ever told him that his were chicken balti) and then I announced that David had booked a table for dinner. To their credit Mark and Tom came along but whereas we all had cheese fondue they had a salad each.

***

A worrying encounter on the Trumpton lift.

There's a link lift in Flaine, France that is very short but steep and slow. It takes you up a rock face to join another lift in around four minutes. It's called a *télébenne* but we called it the Trumpton lift. Each lift is like the top of a cherry-picker or a rectangular hot-air balloon basket (only plastic) hanging from a cable like a chair lift. Each basket takes two people and you stand up in it. The lift comes round from behind and the back part of the lift that you are then facing opens. Next you have to chase it and jump on holding your skis. One day I was standing in a basket or pod / cubicle - whatever they're called - with a random bloke. Half way up I broke the silence. "Oh, I really feel like a fireman!" I announced in a far too camp a voice. "Don't we all love," came the unexpected reply. The voice was a higher pitch and melodious. The remainder of the journey was completed in silence and when we reached the top I made sure he disembarked first.

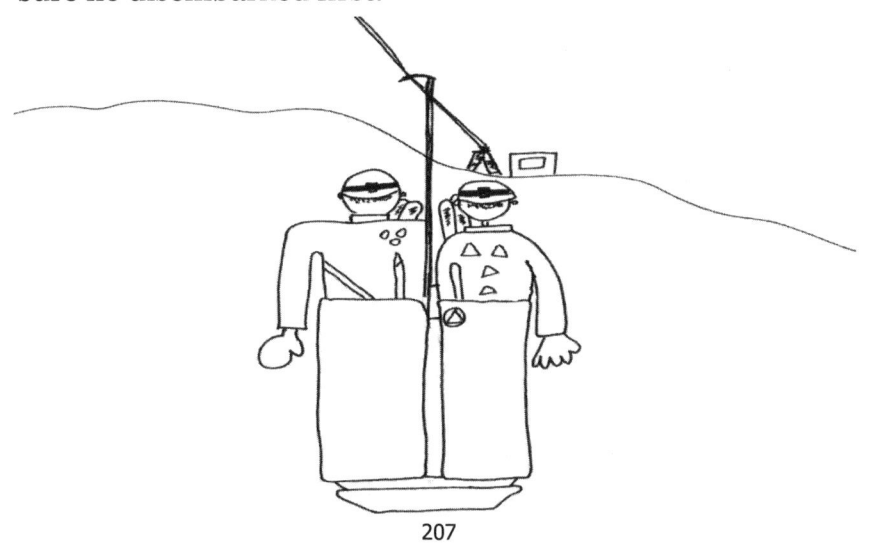

***

Don't lick the pole.

Last year we went on a school ski trip to somewhere in Italy. It was in January and freezing cold. I was thirteen at the time. As my three friends and I were considered "responsible" we were allowed on a four-man chair lift by ourselves. Once we had got going Henry said that it was possible to get your tongue stuck to the main metal pole by licking it. No one believed him but he said that he couldn't show us because he was in the middle so it was down to me or Danny. There was no way that I was going to do it whereas Danny was a bit stupid so he did. It was a proper lick as well and within a couple of seconds he was stuck. With the getting-off point fast approaching I turned round to sir who was behind us and shouted that Danny was stuck. Well, his tongue was. Fortunately sir had a whistle and so started to blow it. The lift attendant at the top saw that there was a problem and so gently slowed the lift right down. We came to a halt just before the ramp. Sir couldn't do anything so it was down to us to try to explain that Danny had got his tongue stuck. The lift attendant disappeared into his little hut then re-emerged with a mug of coffee that he carefully and slowly poured over Danny's tongue and fortunately it soon came off the pole. By this time quite a crowd had gathered and so when Danny finally got off he received a round of applause from everyone and he bowed with a big grin. He didn't get a round of applause from sir though; he got a detention and had to miss bowling.

***

Sportlov.

Standing at a busy snack bar on a terrace somewhere in Austria I was queuing behind some Swedish teenagers who asked me if I had any matches. Being an avuncular sort of guy we got talking. I said that smoking on a wooden platform probably wasn't the wisest move to which they told me that it was the only place where they could have a cigarette because their teachers were inside the restaurant. I then told them about the dangers of smoking and how carcinogenic cigarettes are but I got the impression they had switched off. I changed the subject. "Are you on half term?" I asked. They were all around fourteen and fifteen years of age and said that they were but in Sweden it was called, "Sportlov." "It means, 'sports holidays.'" "Oh cool," I said. "So you have to go skiing and curling and sledging and stuff like that?" "Yes," they said moving forward to the front of the queue. "We don't have that in England," I told them. "No you don't," one of them said. They spoke almost perfect English. "In Sweden we do sport, in England you just watch it." She then turned and asked the barman in French and German for a box of matches which he gave her. Then without a "goodbye" or a wave they were off. I should have gone and found their teachers but I didn't - I was a kid once. And I skied.

***

High-end cough medicine on the piste.

My mother always used to take a hip flask skiing and fill it daily with cherry brandy. From the age of about nine, after I had had my fill of each morning ski lesson, she used to allow me a sip or two, justifying her actions by saying to anyone who raised an eyebrow in the lift queue that it was just high-end cough medicine which is certainly what it tasted like.

***

Nearly everyone has a role in this group of four skiers, some more important than others.

I have an annual ski trip with three of my male friends while my wife and her girly friends go somewhere warmer. We have a few house rules that include one person ordering and another paying. We pay by cash. It's so much easier than four cards appearing every time we have a meal. That's reserved for the Dutch who are the bane of barmen apparently as they pay individually for everything. In bars we give one of our friends, the publican, our drinks' order that he then places. Another friend, the accountant, is banker and he pays from the cash kitty that is topped up at the start of each day and in between as is necessary. It's a very slick operation and comes into its own when it gets busy. We once went into a bar that had bar stools like mini bucking broncos, each seating two. We approached the bar and on one of these "bulls" there was a young lady, all on her own. I asked if I could talk to her and she said that I could. I introduced myself and had a little chat. Her name was Charlotte. "Aren't you going to drink anything?" she asked. "All organised," I replied as I could see the publican in action beside me. In due course a beer was put in front of me. "Don't you pay for that?" she asked. "All organised," I replied. "What's going on?" she asked with a slightly quizzical look. "Oh, it's easy," I said. "At the beginning of each day we all give one of my friends who's an accountant a bit of float and that's the kitty and he's in charge of that. Then my other friend does the ordering at the bar or wherever - he's in charge of that." "And what are you in charge of?" Charlotte asked. Without missing a beat my third friend, who had been listening in, stuck his head over Charlotte's shoulder from behind and said, "Oh he's in charge of the chatting up."

***

Gin and tonic margarita.

I have a friend who always took a hip flask skiing. The funny thing is, he hated the traditional spirit of choice, brandy, and so filled his up with gin and tonic. What was more of a problem was that he, quite sensibly, didn't wish to get intoxicated on the slopes so made up quite a weak mix. One time he thought it would be safer to put it in his rucksack but was alarmed to find, when we reached lunchtime and he fancied a tipple, that the drink had frozen solid. He never did that again and went back to, more accurately, tonic and gin. The only problem then was that he just got legless by elevenses.

***

Skiing is a rich person's sport.

When my husband and I go skiing my mother stays at our house to look after the cats. One year we had dug out a large amount of our front garden to turn into a place to park our car off the road. We had left the resultant large hole all over Christmas and it looked a bit of a mess waiting for the hardcore. The ground was very clayey and soon a large pond had appeared. Then it snowed a bit. Then we went on holiday. One morning my mother was in the front garden when an elderly neighbour passed on the pavement on the other side of the road. She was old, more like ancient, school who frowned on those who smoked, drank, or ate in the street, never called anyone by their first name and so on. She was posh, well-educated and terribly opinionated. Seeing my mother she stopped in her tracks then crossed over. Without introducing herself (presumably because there was no third party to introduce her) she called out, "When on earth are the Buckley-Smiths going to get their drive finished? It looks dreadful. Really spoils the area." My mother, who takes no prisoners, marched down the garden path and said in a similar tone of voice, "Show some compassion will you? Things are financially quite tight at the moment. I would expect that the reason, although they are too proud to admit it, is that they actually can't really afford it at present." My neighbour, instead of showing a bit of empathy, was not going to back down. "Can't afford it?" she spat out. "What nonsense. They've just gone SKI-ING!"

***

A Top Gun moment in Switzerland.

On a coach transfer from a ski resort in Switzerland, back to the airport, we had to stop on a busy main road to let a Mirage III interceptor aircraft cross over the road. I kid you not! The runway was on one side of the road and the hanger on the other. The plane taxied across the road and then turned a sharp left. It was only yards from where I was sitting, looking out of my window at this aeronautical beauty. The female pilot, who naturally had long blond hair (I think) looked out of her little cockpit window and I was sure she saw me. So I waved. And she waved back! I was in heaven. I still am. Whoever you are, that three second interaction many years ago is still with me. A real Top Gun moment.

***

No falling over.

Chamonix. Skiing for nutters. My husband and I were on an all-inclusive and that included a ski guide. One morning our guide took us up on the Grand Montets cable car. At the top we had a choice. Turn right and do the off-piste or go left and do the black. We chose the latter - down the Point de Vue piste. I don't know why we didn't just flip a coin. We first had to ski over steep corrugated ridges just to soften us up then we had to turn sharp left and do a long traverse. There were no trees and I couldn't see where the piste went to my right because it just disappeared it was that steep. "What's below that ridge?" I asked our guide. "The Argentière glacier," he replied. "Ohoh. What happens if I fall over?" "You don't," came his reassuring reply.

***

Jumping into skis failure with a happy ending for some.

I'm a female and I went skiing with a girlfriend, Anita. She came back from her first one-on-one ski lesson with her ski instructor to tell me that she fancied him like mad. Then she told me not about how she got on with her first ever ski lesson but waxed lyrical about what a dish he was and cool with it. She wouldn't stop. Anita had hardly ever skied before whereas I had so I had gone off for the morning whilst she went and worked out how to ski with a little expert tuition. "How do you put your skis on?" she then asked me. Humouring her I said, "I put the tip of one boot into the front of the binding and push down at the back. Then I repeat with the other foot." "Well," Anita said, "my ski instructor doesn't bother with all that. He just lines his skis up side by side then stands astride them before quickly jumping up and into them, both at the same time. It looks really impressive and I told him so so he showed me how to do it." I asked her if she had done it yet but she said, "No, not properly but I'll have a go. I'll show you after lunch. Then we can do a bit of skiing on the blue because that's where he's going to be this afternoon with another pupil and then we're meeting up for a drink, just the two of us if that's okay." I didn't answer. After lunch and a few too many glasses of rosé, as we both stood on the snow getting ready to do a bit of skiing Anita lined up her skis, standing astride them. Then she planted her poles in the snow, "...just to give me a bit more lift." She bent her knees and then, "One, two, three - up!" She jumped high into the air and as she came down attempted to plant her boots clean into her bindings. She failed. She went in at an angle, only partially succeeding before she lost her balance and fell over as the skis turned on their sides. Then she screamed. Fortunately we were near the bottom of the piste and so help was soon at hand. Turned out she had broken both of her ankles. That was the end of her skiing holiday. She sent me off to meet her ski instructor to tell him that she couldn't come out and to cancel her other lessons. I went out for a drink with him instead. One thing Anita did get right was that he was quite cool and a bit of a dish so then I told him what had really happened. He didn't refund Anita's lessons that she had paid for because he couldn't get anyone else at short notice so every morning I went skiing with him instead of being on my own. I didn't tell Anita, after all it wasn't my fault. Two years later we were married and still are. He's gorgeous! I've never tried jumping into my skis though. Anita no longer speaks to me.

***

Waterslalomskiing out of your boots.

I was skiing in Méribel with a group of friends. It was mid-March and by lunchtime the snow down to the resort was getting a bit slushy. Ralph, who was quite large, and I were on the last stretch down to the rond point when we found a small slalom course that no one was using. "I'm doing that," Ralph announced and off he went with me following on behind. I think it was something to do with the fact that we could see his girlfriend, Cindy, at the bottom who was waving up at us. Down he went wildly swaying from side to side as if he was dodging imaginary bullets being fired at him. He was totally out of control. As he went round the last bend the course straightened out. All he had to do was stop but he was going too fast for that. Instead he chose to ski through the huge puddle that had formed at the bottom of the slalom from barely melted snow. What he didn't realise was that there's a knack to skiing across water. It's called waterskiing and you need very fat skis and the technique is to lean back, not what you do when you're snow skiing.

Ralph started across the mini pond then all of a sudden his ski tips went under the water and stopped. Ralph didn't. The backs of his skis went straight up in the air with Ralph still attached and then, from a height of about three feet, he face-planted into the slush. Cindy turned and walked off which was a bit mean because we found out later that Ralph had broken his nose and lost two front teeth.

***

Foggy vision after an evening in the Krazy Kanguruh.

I was out skiing in St Anton and spent the first evening in the Krazy Kanguruh which is a very lively bar a little way up from town on a red run which can be reached by ski or on foot. The following day, despite it being just a little bit cloudy, my friend Eric kept complaining that he wasn't skiing very well because it was quite foggy. We couldn't agree with him but didn't say anything until lunchtime when we went into one of the restaurants and his contact lenses all steamed up. "Now I can't see at all," he complained. It then quickly became apparent what the problem was. Eric, in his rather inebriated state, had forgotten to take his contact lenses out when he went to bed the night before. Unfortunately he was on auto-pilot in the morning and inserted a second pair. No wonder he couldn't see. This was about the only time that I have skied with Eric when he skied better in the afternoon than in the morning.

***

Never trust a friend who speaks fluent French.

In Chamonix with a small group of very fussy eaters we stopped for lunch at a half-decent restaurant. One of the fussy eaters wanted to know whether the *faux filet* was horse. "I can't eat it if it is. Ask the waiter please," it was demanded of me being one of only two French speakers in the group. "No," I replied not wanting a fuss so they asked Mark to inquire. Mark had lived in France. He knew the game and was totally on the ball. When the waiter came over Mark asked, "Excusez-moi monsieur mais le faux filet - c'est le cheval?" (Excuse me sir but the steak, is it horse?) "Mais bien sûr," (But of course) the waiter replied. Mark turned to our friend. "No, it's not, it's prime sirloin," Mark informed him. Our friend ordered it and ate it. We never told him the truth.

***

French bevvie breakfast.

Stand in the main road looking towards the télècabine at La Daille and beyond the station there's one building that can be seen all by itself. It's an old farmhouse with stonewashed walls and very small windows that make it look like a tiny prison. This was my home for one week with a group of friends plus my wife. To the right there is an imposing block of flats and beyond that the *centre commercial,* home to a Spar supermarket and a few other shops.

As I was the only one in my group who seemed to want to get up in the morning I used to wander over to the centre and buy food for breakfast - croissants and pastries, that sort of thing. In the middle of the building there was a small bar. It was the size of a couple of telephone kiosks that had been plonked in the area around which were all the shop entrances. It is a weakness of mine to take my coffee in the morning like serious Frenchmen, that is to say an espresso with a brandy chaser, *un café cognac s'il vous plait.* I would sit in the company of mostly ski instructors for a short while knowing full well that when I returned with the groceries and pastries everyone else, apart from my wife, would still be tucked up in bed. After a couple of days I went from being referred to as *l'Anglais* to my Christian name by Anna, the lively barmaid who was there, bright and breezy, every morning. For all I knew she never slept.

It was not until the middle of the week that things began to unravel just ever so slightly. We had to go out for some emergency food shopping after après ski. I volunteered but my wife decided that she wanted to come along too. How was I to know that as I crept past the bar Anna would wave and shout, "Johnnie, would you like a glass of Mondeuse Avalanche on the 'ouse"? My wife looked at me and I shook my head. "Well I'm having one," my wife said defiantly and strode over to the bar. "And how exactly do you know my husband?" she asked of Anna once she had her drink in her hand and I then also had mine. "He is here every morning 'aving un café cognac with 'is friends whilst you are still in the bed." "Well he won't be tomorrow," my wife replied and she was right. The following morning and for the rest of the week all my holidaying friends and my wife were up and in the bar with me. The café cognacs flowed. One day we didn't even manage to do any skiing.

***

Formidables.

My French is not up to much but I can order a beer in the Frenchest of French ski resorts. It took me a bit of time to get to a pint of lager but over the years I've perfected it and more some! I used to often end up being served a bottled beer if I asked for *une bière*. I discovered that the phrase to use is *une bière pression* which then got me a draught beer. I still wasn't there though. It was one step forward and two steps back as I would be served a tiny beer - 25cl which is less than half a pint. Once I was served a 12.5cl drink, that's the sort of measure you'd get for a glass of wine. I was in a bar in a ski resort where they spoke a bit of English and they told me that if I wanted a really big beer I should ask for a *formidable* and see what happens. The next day at lunchtime I sat outside on a terrace and when the waiter came over I ordered *une bière formidable.* The waiter disappeared back past a load of Germans who were sitting by the door looking very unhappy with their piddling little glasses. When he returned and slapped down one litre of beer in an enormous thick glass jug with handle (thank goodness as I needed two hands to lift it) I was in heaven! I was amused to watch the Germans call the waiter over and, pointing, ask for six of what I was drinking. When the waiter served them *une formidable* each it was thumbs up all round. I tried my luck with one of my friends in another bar in the evening. "Watch this," I said as I ordered two formidables. "Non, pas de formidables," (No, no formidables) came the unexpected reply.

After all this comedy I have recently discovered that, actually, if you order *une pinte,* and order it through a scrunched up nose, you will get 50cl which is very nearly a pint - same as in the UK really without the froth. Got there in the end.

Le Snow Train

A costly brush with authority on the journey home.

In the days before the Euro was a pan-European currency I travelled to the Alps by train with two of my friends, Nick and Neil. Nick was almost perfectly normal but Neil was at one end of the scale, and mostly what many would consider the wrong end. We were only in our twenties yet he had already spent time in borstal, then a short spell in prison. His worst short-coming as far as it concerned me, although in reality there were many, was his complete lack of respect for authority.

From our respective family homes in north-west Kent we travelled on the train down to Dover. We alighted at Dover Priory station and with time to spare we crossed over the road and straight into the pub opposite where we stayed until our ferry was due. Once in Calais we jumped on a bus that took us to the train station at the top of the town. The train, which left at midnight, would take us into the heart of the Alps from where it was another shortish bus ride to our resort.

Nick, being a British Rail employee, had been in charge of booking the tickets and he was very keen to tell us on the way down to Dover that we had "sleeping accommodation." What this turned out to be was what we used to call a "dog carriage." It was an enclosed carriage, of which there were a few, within a longer carriage. We found our kennel and went in. There were seats to the left and right with double bunk beds (couchettes) above on both sides. The seats could also be turned into beds. Each had a little curtain that you could draw across. There was a vertical ladder over the window to enable a successful ascent to, and descent from, the top bunk. We dumped our stuff, Nick and Neil having bagged the top bunks with their suitcases on the bottom, and went in search of the bar as the train departed. We found it in half a carriage with the other half an open plan disco floor. It held about ten people. It would do for us. When we returned to our couchettes about an hour later, any longer would have been officially classed as torture, we found that we were not alone. "What are you doing here?" Neil asked the French couple and, probably, their daughter in a rather threatening way. They explained, in French, that they had booked three couchettes that just happened to be in "our" dog carriage. Neil then said something, in English, that was unrepeatable in either language, and still is, and climbed the ladder that we had discovered in the disco was known as, "the ladder of death." Neil then began to talk, and talk, and talk as I repositioned myself and three sets of luggage on a middle bunk.

After about half an hour of Neil's monologue the French guy asked Neil, basically, to shut up but when I translated Neil said, "Do you have a problem?" I wasn't sure whether Neil was asking me or the Frenchman but after Neil decided to tell the whole carriage, from the comfort of his bed, what he had been in prison for, our "gatecrashers" gathered themselves and their luggage and left. We never saw them again. They probably camped on the dance floor.

Although credit and debit cards, and travellers cheques existed at the time of this ski trip, Neil insisted on bringing all his spending money in cash. When we went out skiing he would put some francs in one jacket pocket, some in another jacket pocket, some in yet another jacket pocket and one note in his trouser pocket under his salopettes. He left the rest in the hotel under his pillow. Neil had a vivid imagination and thought that he might be mugged at any time, even on the slopes. He said that if someone threatened him he would offer the contents of his trouser pocket and thus lose just one note. "No one expects their victim to carry money in more than one pocket so I will just bring out a fifty franc note and say that that's all I've got." I told him that if anyone was going to be robbed on the slopes then he would be one of the last people to be picked on, mainly due to the scar across one cheek that even I never knew how it got there and it never seemed the right moment to ask.

We skied and après skied for England and so, by the time it came to depart, we had spent quite a bit of money. As we boarded the snow train back to Calais Neil was down to his last fifty francs. "Which pocket are you going to secrete that note in?" I asked him. "If you're mugged they won't take you telling them that you have no money; they'll search all your pockets." Neil said that he would take his shoe off and stuff it down his sock. "No one will think to look there," he assured me. "It's an old trick." "Not one I've ever heard of," I replied.

Nick had been very organised in getting the couchettes sorted out for our outward trip, less so for our return. We found another dog carriage but no couchettes. Neil was distraught. "I need to sleep!" he wailed. He sat back in his seat and spied the luggage rack above his head. It was made from sisal and criss-crossed together. No, not his head. It resembled a hammock, albeit a very skinny one, with a couple of metal bars in the way. "I'm not sleeping on the floor with my luggage up there," he complained, pointing at the hammock. "So what are you going to do?" Nick asked. "I'm going to put my luggage on the floor and I'm going to sleep up there," he replied, still pointing at the hammock. Suddenly he stood up, grabbed hold of the outer bar that was holding the luggage rack in place and pulled himself up and in as the train pulled away from the station.

Neil was just getting used to his new surroundings, wondering whether he really did want to spend the night with his nose not much more than six inches from the roof of the carriage with the constant risk that he may well fall out, when the decision was made for him. The carriage door was firmly slid open and in the doorway stood the train controller: ticket inspector, first aider, security guard... Basically there's no messing with the fat controller. "Billets messieurs s'il vous plait," he barked, holding out his hand. "Neil, ticket," I said. Neil tried to turn in his slimline bed so that he could get his hand into his trouser pocket. He let out a little groan. The controller looked up into the luggage rack. "Descend!" he barked. "Non!" said Neil defiantly using all the French he knew. The controller stepped into the carriage and gave Neil a mouthful in French. "He says you need to get down immediately Neil or you'll be fined," I told him. Then I turned to the controller. "Je m'excuse mon ami," I said with a shrug of the shoulders. The French understand a shrug of the shoulders. This one didn't. Neil understood one of the words. "I know what you're saying and I don't want to be excused. I decide whether I want to excuse myself and I don't." Then Neil's anarchistic temperament kicked in. "Tell him to F**K OFF." Then, as if to make sure that the controller got the message Neil added, "Tell him to F**K OFF in French." He didn't need telling in French. He understood perfectly well in English. His face reddened as he pulled a notebook out from his black leather satchel. "Une amende!" he growled. "You're about to be fined Neil," I advised him. "Cinquante francs!" the controller began to write in his notebook. "Fifty francs Neil." "I don't have fifty francs," Neil complained. The controller was having none of it. He said that if Neil didn't get his hands on fifty francs within one minute the train would stop at the next station and Neil would be kicked off. That did the trick. We didn't want to risk that the next stop wouldn't be Calais. In any event I expect the train could have stopped anywhere and Neil would have found himself turned out onto the platform of a one horse town in the middle of nowhere. Slowly Neil put his legs over the side of the luggage rack and lowered himself onto the seat. He sat down and pulled off his shoe before reaching inside. He pulled out the fifty franc note, that by now resembled a slice of Gorgonzola cheese, before climbing back into the rack. Neil waved the holey note in the Controller's face. He didn't rise to the bait. He took it, put it in his wallet then wrote Neil out a receipt for his payment. Neil hesitated in taking it. "What is your problem?" the controller asked in English. "You give me fifty Francs, I give you receipt. What do you vant? You vant me to make some 'oles in it?" Then he left and Neil climbed back down.

Swiss Alps

A summer hike across Switzerland.

Having spent a few winter ski holidays in Switzerland I always thought it would be fun to return in the summer when the snow had melted and the grass had reappeared. The chance came during one of the summer windows of being able to travel during the Covid pandemic. In England we had been told to stay inside whenever possible whereas the Swiss were being told to get out. I knew where I was heading! However, I would not be able to hunker down in a hotel somewhere so decided to go for a hike. I soon found one of serious length and a friend to go with. I was in the middle of a university degree so had plenty of time on my hands.

The Via Alpina National Route 1 is an eighteen stage hiking route across Switzerland from Sargans to Montreux. This journey is three hundred and seventy kilometres, takes in fourteen Alpine passes and in places reaches in excess of two thousand eight hundred metres above sea level. It is part of a much longer route through Alpine regions of Slovenia, Austria, Germany, Liechtenstein, Switzerland, Italy and France. However, as my previous hiking journeys had been one or two day trips in the UK when I was in scouts I didn't want to bite off more than I could chew.

The Via Alpina National Route 1 is a must for keen hikers and relative, but well-prepared, novices alike although it was fairly challenging in places so a head for heights is advised; it can be tackled in one trip as we chose to do or can be completed in sections over several shorter excursions. Whichever way you decide to do it, you will not be short of spectacular views each time you venture out. We experienced the beautiful Engstlensee Lake at the top of the Jochpass, we hiked close to the daunting Eiger and Jungfrau and we were almost blinded by the glaciers glistening near the Hohtürli pass (the highest section of the route). It wasn't scrambles up and down mountains the whole time though - along the way we passed through several major towns where you might choose to spend a couple of days to catch up with a shower and a comfortable bed. One place we stopped off at was Adelboden, a village near the Wildstrubel mountain that hosts the FIS Ski World Cup for one weekend every year. High above Adelboden on the hike route at Tschentenalp, itself a small ski resort in winter, there is a giant swing for the young at heart to have a go on. It's quite an expensive country so we were pleased to discover that the swing is free and is a bigger thrill than many theme park rides. Apparently there are people who take a detour just so that they can have a go.

One major plus of the Via Alpina is that it is suitable for the more comfort-orientated individuals since each stage finishes where there is accommodation of some sort. This can include hostels, guesthouses or hotels. For those like us two poor undergraduates on a budget - and a low one at that - who were crazy enough to choose the most expensive nation on earth (according to CEOWORLD magazine) to visit, fortunately most towns also had campsites which is where we ended up more often than not. Although we camped most of the way along the route, having alternative accommodation options was very useful, especially when we needed a day off or when our tent unexpectedly broke. We had borrowed a two-man tunnel tent that weighed only around two kilos but when one of the fibreglass poles snapped we spent several days trying to find a camping shop that sold replacements. Whilst there were plenty of shops no one had any pole repair or replacement kits which we felt was a bit odd, a bit like going to a newsagent's and finding that it had no newspapers. We soldiered on with our flabby tent roof until another camper gave us a spare pole that was miraculously the same length as our broken one so we were able to effect the necessary repair. We eventually found a camping shop where we discovered what the problem was. Whereas back in England at the height of lockdown everyone was being implored to stay inside and so took to DIY, in Switzerland it seemed that everyone was being encouraged to stay out, so once summer arrived the Swiss took to the hills and mountains en masse, having made a trip to the *Campingladen*.

There were many amazing places that we visited on the hike, but one that I would definitely recommend staying at is the Kandersteg International Scout Centre. It's open every day of the year. You could take a much-needed rest day after climbing over the Hohtürli pass, and whilst you're there enjoy the array of activities they have to offer.

Kandersteg is where Great Britain ski jumper Eddie 'The Eagle' Edwards did much of his jumping practice. He tells a story that he used very old equipment that included a helmet that was only attached to him by a piece of string. One day he was on a ninety metre jumping hill. When he launched himself into the air such was the force that the string snapped and his helmet flew off. He says that not holding onto the helmet was one of the biggest mistakes of his life because, although he jumped thirty-six metres, his helmet jumped eighty-six and with better style!

What makes this route particularly amazing is the friendliness and hospitality of the locals. So much so, everyone you pass will say, "Gruße" (pronounced "Gru-say") which means "greetings". We were fortunate enough to meet some very welcoming and helpful people. There was the family in Adelboden that helped fix our tent, and there was also another family in Gstaad that we chatted to and who gave us loads of their cake to eat. However, the icing on the cake, so to speak, was the guy who stuck his hand in his pocket. Ordinarily it would fall into the category of a random act of kindness - a small nonpremeditated action by one human being towards another who would normally not be known to each other. This was no small deed though, more something of such huge significance that we were talking to each other about it for the rest of our trip and beyond. The man's name was René and we came across him at a campsite in another tiny winter ski resort called Château-d'Œx. We had spent the evening chatting to him, not least of all because he was on his own but also as he offered us food and beer. In the morning he told us that he was so impressed with our trip he had paid our campsite fees. Naturally we were very surprised but also extremely grateful. It wasn't as if we could refuse. It wasn't as if he was offering to pay and we were replying, "No it's fine thank you." Like someone who leaves your table in a restaurant and goes up to the waiter and settles the whole bill, or, better than that, someone who gets up from another table he had, without any discussion or an attempt to sound magnanimous but not really meaning it, simply paid our bill. What a generous man! It's acts like that that one remembers for the rest of one's life. It didn't finish there however, there was more to the matter. He explained to us that sadly his wife had died a year ago. As part of the healing process he had taken it upon himself not to do just one good deed a day but several. And so, not only did he pay for our campsite that night, he also gave us fifty Swiss Francs to spend on our day out in Geneva. So generous.

With enough adventures on our three week trip to fill a book all by ourselves, I shall confine myself here to the first incident and one of the more bizarre incidents - to us at least if not the Swiss mountain residents. It was something that, should it ever happen over a winter piste, would probably make the front page of *The Sun*. The first was on the first day when we were already high up on a mountain pass. We came across what looked like a small, rectangular, wooden post box. The only problem was there wasn't a house nearby. We decided to open it seeing as there was no lock and have a peep just to be nosey. Inside we found a bottle of gin, a bottle of a local liqueur, a quantity of disposable glasses and an honesty box. "Help yourself," was written on a piece of paper inside the box. So we did. "I can't imagine this in the UK," my friend suggested. He was right. My parents have some friends who live in Headcorn in Kent. One morning they walked to the end of the field at the back of their house that borders a small but well-used country lane. They put out a table, a chair, a basketful of freshly-laid eggs, an honesty box and a sign that read something along the lines of, "Eggs, so much each, put the money in the box." When they returned at the end of the day they were more than a little surprised to find the eggs all gone, the honesty box gone, the sign gone, the table gone and the chair gone. We put some money for our drinks in the box and continued on our way.

The bizarre incident happened on day six whilst we were having lunch. We had grown quite used to the sight and sound of low flying aircraft with roped-up cargo dangling beneath the fuselage. Many of the farms are not conveniently situated alongside any main road and so rely heavily on helicopters to transport equipment and provisions. As we looked up at one particularly low-flying helicopter we saw what we thought was a fibreglass cow being transported in its rope sling. As the helicopter flew by, far too close for our comfort, we realised that the cow was a real one, albeit dead. Then there was another helicopter with another cow, then yet another. As the third flew past it was just as well that I wasn't literally open-mouthed because the decomposition process of number three was much further advanced than the other two. The helicopter swept past in the direction of the others that were already far down the valley and we were treated to a perversely imagined rendition of the "gastric" Red Arrows, with a rather noxious substance being spewed across, over and down, landing very near to where we were seated and then onwards down the mountain. We later discovered, for we had to ask, that the airlifting of dead cows down the mountain is not a particularly rare occurrence in Switzerland. They cannot simply be left on the mountain to decompose as they would pollute the water table. They need to be transported off the mountain, have the cause of death established then be incinerated. We imagined them being whisked off to the bovine coroner's for an inquest. He would have been busy that afternoon.

All in all a great trip and one that I will have to do again sometime. Hopefully I will bump into René. I wonder if he skis?

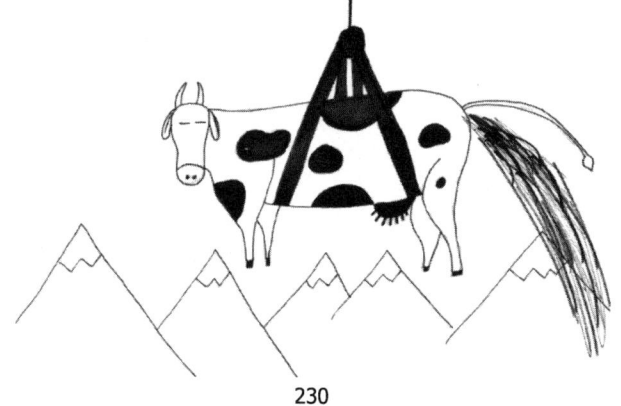

Tignes

Double trouble on the Bollin and Fresse chair lifts.

There is a chair lift in Tignes that is there for no other reason than simply to strike fear into every uninitiated skier's heart. What madness befell someone that they could construct such a farcical system that looks to all intents and purposes like a single normal chair lift but is nothing of the sort? The two lift queues for Bollin and Fresse six-man lifts in Val Claret are side by side. You join one queue or the other. The gates alternate opening and so every second chair has, say, Bollin passengers. Both lifts appear to use the same cable and this is where the comedy starts. Bollin travels a mere six hundred metres before coming off and turning sharp left ready for you to alight for a short ski back down or traverse to a linked lift, whereas Fresse is one thousand, eight hundred and eighty-five metres and takes you right to the top of Tovière from where you can ski back down to La Daille in the other valley. There's plenty of information on the boards at the front of the lift queues that everyone shuffles under but who ever reads those?

We knew we wanted to go to the top so we got in the Fresse queue. Simple. The six of us shuffled forward, through the gates, plonked ourselves down on the chair, put down the restraining bar and put our feet on it. We chatted away quite happily until one of my friends said, "That chair up there, three up, has just turned left." "No way," said another, "they all go to the top." "Then why were there two different names?" "I don't know." "And two queues?" "Just to spread us out a bit, to stop too much pushing and shoving." "Look, the next one's gone straight on." "So where are we going?" "I don't know." Then the passengers on the chair in front lifted up their restraining bar and this is when we began to panic. "We've got to lift up the bar otherwise we'll hit the platform!" (We wouldn't have done but it goes remarkably close.) "We need to get off!" The chair in front did a sharp left. "Lift up the bar!" A couple of my friends had already taken their feet off but instead of waiting for the rest of us they had started to lift up the hand rail. At least they tried to. All that did was bring the knees of those who hadn't removed their feet up to their heads, a position from where it was almost impossible to slide one's feet off, but one of our number managed it and then got one ski jammed. "We're going straight on! Put the bar down!" Now the bar's being pulled down and my skis are *under* the foot rest. Maggie was screaming, Mike looked like he was adopting an aeroplane crash position, Sam had shut his eyes, Duncan was trying to climb out and Sarah had fainted. And that is how we went straight on through the lift building and onwards up to the top. My skis actually skimmed the platform as we went up. "Anyone having a heart attack?" I asked as we continued on our journey. No one spoke for a while. They were all totally traumatised by the anticipation of an accident that they were mostly convinced was just about to happen - but then didn't.

I had to laugh. This year we were back in Tignes and we skied over to La Daille. We approached Fresse and I gave my friends a quick rundown. However, when we arrived at the lift Fresse was closed and it was only possible to go up Bollin, alight, ski over and go up Tufs which is what we did. At the top of the Bollin there was the most enormous arrow pointing left and ALIGHT - only in English* - on a huge banner across the place that was the site of so much comedy all those years ago. If I had my choice this lift would be alight alright - up in flames.

*I wonder why.

Troyes

Culinary carnage, alcohol angst and parapet prancing all in one evening on the way down to the Alps.

Anyone who has ever driven to the Alps will probably have come across Troyes (pronounced Twah), a cathedral town positioned at the end of A26 motorway, also known as the *Autoroute des Anglais,* that starts at Calais. It is a very convenient stopping-off point for the night when breaking the long drive into two days. My wife and I and another couple with a small child, on our way to somewhere in the Alps, had arrived late afternoon and decided to have a quick look around the old town with its well-known half-timbered houses before having a bite to eat.

Being a Friday evening we should have booked in advance but we hadn't and we were struggling to find somewhere to eat. Eventually we went into what described itself as a pizzeria although there was much steak in evidence, my friend Dave's favourite food. I popped inside and found that it was almost full, despite only being about 7pm. No, they didn't have space but if we came back in an hour they would be able to accommodate us. In the meantime they suggested we went to a small bar just a few doors away. I mention this only because it was in there that we discovered *sirop* which is quite a big thing in France. It's a sweet, sickly liquid, a bit like English squash only concentrated. The French have it in water, lemonade, beer, white wine; they pour it over ice cream and use it in cooking. By law it has to be a minimum of 55% sugar. When we were trying to decide what to give the youngest member of our party to drink the waitress suggested a dash of strawberry *sirop* in water. It went down a treat.

After an hour we wandered back to the steak house pizzeria where we were shown to a table. We ordered more drinks and a steak each.

Now Dave is one of those people who believes that French chefs always undercook meat and he's sort of right. In Britain we tend to go for rare, medium or well done. In France they have four / five options:
Bleu - Cooked under a very hot grill for about a minute on each side.
Saignant - This is French rare but as *Saignant* means bloody you should not be surprised when you're served very rare. It has slightly longer under the grill on one side than a bleu.
À point - Medium-rare. It means "perfectly cooked" and medium-rare is what French chefs consider perfectly cooked. Still rare by most British standards though.
Bien cuit - "Well cooked" but still not quite British medium.
The only way you're going to get a steak that is completely cooked through in France is to use the very untechnical "Très [Very] bien cuit." Good luck with that though; Dave came a cropper just with "bien cuit."

Our waitress asked us how we would like our steaks cooked. I translated. Dave was the only one to order fillet steak. He asked our French waitress for "bien cuit" and off she went. A couple of minutes later she was back. "Monsieur te chef a dit que..." etc. etc. I smiled and turned to Dave. "Your fault!" I said. "What's the problem?" he asked. "Our waitress here has just been told by her chef to say to whoever has ordered *le filet* bien cuit that he is not prepared to *incinérer* (incinerate) the meat. Either the customer has *le filet* à point at most or order, "...une coupe inférieure de viande." (A lower cut of meat). Dave looked at the waitress then at me with a frazzled expression. "She didn't say that!" he scoffed. "Oh yez, I did," the waitress replied.

On the way back to the hotel I spied a bar with a band inside on a small stage playing as if there was no tomorrow. We didn't need anything more to drink (we had been drinking for England - and France), it was getting late and we had a bit of a drive in the morning. Nevertheless Dave and I popped in for a nightcap whilst our wives went home with the little one.

Once inside Dave went off in search of a toilet and I went up to the bar. "Deux bières s'il vous plait." Cue much twirling of glasses and ice. "Deux bières," I said to myself. "Deux bières." The waiter had half filled two tumblers with ice and was now pouring large measures of Baileys into them. "Bières, Bai-lezz, Bai-layyys," I said to myself. The waiter came over and put the two glasses down on the bar. "Et deux b-i-ère-s s'il vous plait," I asked slowly and methodically. Fortunately I didn't get two more Baileys on ice but what I thought I had originally asked for - two beers. I told the returning Dave (who was looking incredulously at the beige concoctions) that the barman was giving all English customers a free drink. "How nice of him," Dave said very unenthusiastically. He drank his slowly before touching the beer. He gave the barman a big smile and a nod and received a long grin in return. He was watched all the time until he had drunk the whole Baileys drink. It was a great bar with a fantastic atmosphere. Everyone was very friendly and we managed a few stilted conversations.

We stayed in a Best Western hotel that was nearby. Our rooms were next to each other but on either side of a corner, several floors up. This was very useful when I found that my wife had locked me out (unintentionally?) of our room. Knowing that she always slept with the window at least slightly open I realised that I could go into Dave's room, climb out of his window onto a very narrow parapet, crawl round to my window, goodness knows how high up I was, and tap on my window. It wasn't until I had executed this act of bravado that I then found that our window was firmly shut. I shimmied back to Dave's and climbed back in. I slept on his floor that night.

In the morning over breakfast I explained to Dave what had happened. "'Bières,' after a few beers, must sound like 'Baileys' in French." "You sod," replied Dave. "I hate Baileys. I only drank it to be polite and what do you think the waiter thought of me? I was standing there nodding and raising my glass at him for a good five minutes. At least he was smiling at me." "Dave," I said. "Did you realise that there were no women in that bar?"

Val d'Isère

Beware of overweight middle-aged men coming down the piste out of control.

I love Val d'Isère. It's a great place for intermediates plus it also has some blues and greens up the top so good for the family although you may have to get the lift down in places. The long blue back into town, Santons, is now a red! Some say it should be a black.

I had been here several times and it's where my children learnt to ski. I love to impress friends when they comment on the attractive old church with its dominant spire in the centre of town. I tell them that it was built in 1664. (Before that worshippers had to make a rather tricky journey to Tignes.) What I don't tell them but they probably guess is that I only remember this because it also happens to be the name of a certain beer!

One major change since I learnt to ski in the 1980s is that now 99% of adult skiers wear helmets whereas in 1985 it was about 1%. Children, on the other hand, have always worn helmets as far as I can recall. So when, around 2010, my children started to ski and it wasn't just hiring skis and boots but helmets as well but only for the children I began to wonder why I shouldn't be wearing a helmet. However I had never bashed my head or come near it so I was in no hurry until a friend of mine said that it's like wearing seatbelts in your car: it's not necessarily you that is going to do the damage. "Beware of overweight middle-aged men coming down the piste out of control," my friend said.

I was with two of my friends, Jack and Dan, in Val d'Isère a few years ago in January and on the first day I met the lads at rond-point. "What are you wearing?!" I exclaimed. They looked like they had Nazi helmets on their heads. They were the distinctive "coal scuttle" shape - high front, low back and grey. Jack explained that the previous year they wondered why the children had to wear them in ski school but not the grown-ups so they bought one each for themselves. I said that I had been thinking along the same lines recently and quoted, "Beware of middle-aged men..." at them.

We went up to Solaise then skied back down to Le Laisinant. There's nothing there so, although we were in need of a coffee, especially because there was light snow, we decided to get the six man TSD Laisinant Express back up the mountain.

Many of the larger chair lifts in France are TSD which describes those that detach from the main cable thus enabling one to experience a more sedate boarding and alighting. The older and smaller ones are TSF. These have chairs that stay on the main cable and give you a whack on the back of the legs if you're not careful. I've learnt over the years that if you're going to get a TSF the best thing to do if you're with someone is move a foot or so further forward when waiting for the brute to swing round and attack you. That way the other passengers' legs soak up the impact for you and whilst the seat is temporarily (i.e. for a second at most) at a standstill you can sit down in a calm and controlled manner instead of with a screech and "Ouch!" If you're on your own then stand at one side and grab the large pole that hangs down on either side to hold the seats in place. Your arm will be able to soak up the impact much better than a static leg.

We shuffled through the barriers and lined up with a couple of young French ladies who were on one side. As the chair came round the two girls demurely, sophisticatedly, gently, lightly and in a very French way - I'm sure you get the picture - turned slightly and flicked the snow off their seats before sitting down. "What a great idea!" I thought and did the same, shuffling forward to give myself a bit more time. However, timing is all on these beasts and you have to be quick. I wasn't and I was in the wrong place. Before I knew it I could feel my seat rising up behind my bum and there was no way I was going to get on so I bailed out to the right as the chair turned and went on its merry way. I glanced up and was surprised to see only Jack on the chair along with the French girls. Where was Dan? I looked around and saw him in a heap to the left. "I saw the French girls wipe their seats so decided to do the same!" he shouted. "Just like me!" I said. "I won't try that again! Are you okay?" Dan had one ski off and one ski on. "I'm fine," he replied as he tried to get up. "I...just...need...to...." "NON! Arrêtez vous!" (NO! Stop!) the lift attendant shouted. Too late, Dan was standing up, but not for long. As he stood facing me, smiling I saw what was coming. OUCH! His head took a direct hit from the chair coming down and he collapsed once more to the ground.

Eventually we sorted ourselves out and got back on the lift. At the top we met up with Jack. "What happened?" he asked. "Blame the girlies," I said as we gave him a blow by blow account.

"Beware of overweight middle-aged men getting on the lift out of control," he replied. "At least you know now why we've bought helmets."

I went and bought one for myself that lunchtime.

Val d'Isère

The lads go lingerie shopping for their wives back home and get a little less than they bargained for.

I was in Val d'Isère skiing with some male friends and as my wife said that I didn't need to bring her home a gift I decided to buy her something special. I think that was the correct response. I asked one of the girls on reception at our hotel what would make a good present and she said, "K-nickers." So that was that.

On the last evening I went, accompanied by my friend Alan, to Caresse, a small lingerie shop in the middle of the main shopping area. It was full of men. The sales assistant and probably the owner was waiting. Short, middle aged, well-dressed, manicured, made up, perfumed, professional - she was in charge and she knew exactly what I needed. "Can I 'elp you?" "Yes!" "You vant zumzing for your vife?" "Yes!" "Sophisticated wiz a little, um..." "Yes!" "What size?" "Um..." "Like me?" "Same height, a bit..." "Zinner?" "Yes, thinner. Sorry." "No problem." She brought out a burgundy silk negligee. It was stunning. "How much?" "Or zis one?" Zis one was shorter. Which is cheaper? The longer one was cheaper. "You know. Less negligee, more fun, more money!" she exclaimed. "I'll have the longer one." Madame took my card and placed it on the till, probably in case I changed my mind, while she wrapped up my purchase. I didn't look at the price once I was told that contactless wouldn't work. She stuck my card in the machine and handed it to me. I didn't look at the amount; I just entered the PIN. I walked out with my purchase beautifully wrapped in tissue paper and gift wrapped and placed in a fabulous, branded, designer bag.

"Come on Alan," I said. He was dragging his heels. "Perhaps I ought to buy Janice something other than a t-shirt," he said. "That's a good idea. Back we go."

Once inside again we went through the same routine to begin with. Then Alan explained that he didn't want a negligee but maybe some underwear. "Do you have, um, knickers?" Of course she did; loads of them. "You want to zee my knockers?" Alan's face was pink. "Er, yes please." I smiled. "What size?" "Um..." "Like me?" "A bit..." "Zinner?" "Yes, thinner. Sorry." "No problem." Madame was very thorough, even though she was quick and to the point. Plenty of open questions. She knew what she was doing. She produced a pair of red lacy knickers. There wasn't very much of them at all. Alan frowned ever so slightly. "Imagine your vife in zees!" Madame's eyes opened like saucepans and she smiled, a large conspiratorial grin. She waited a moment while Alan presumably was imagining. Finally Alan asked, "Do you have something...." "Smaller? Yes, of course." Madame produced something that looked like a piece of tangled string. "Er, a little bigger actually." "Oh, no! Surely not!" Madame tried another tack. "Does your vife, does she like zee tong?" "The what?" "The tongue Alan," I interjected. "Does Janice like the tongue?" "Well, um..." Now Alan was bright red. "I'm not sure what she's going to bring out but maybe it's going to be something from the Anne Summers department," I suggested. Madame held back for a moment whilst Alan and presumably all the other male shoppers were imagining Janice in the act of liking the tongue. Then she produced another pair of red knickers with ever-so-slightly more material and which at least to my mind resembled something that you put your legs into. "Zee tong?" she said, waving them in front of Alan's nose. "I think she means the thong Alan," I said in a sudden moment of understanding. "Yes, zee tong," Madame repeated. Alan bought them and slowly his face returned to its normal colour.

My wife loved her negligee but Alan wasn't so fortunate. When I next saw him I asked him how well Janice had received her gift. "Not at all well," he replied. "She said, 'Who do you think I am? I am not wearing those,' and chucked them in the bin."

The following year he bought her a t-shirt. I told him what he should have made sure was on the front of it.

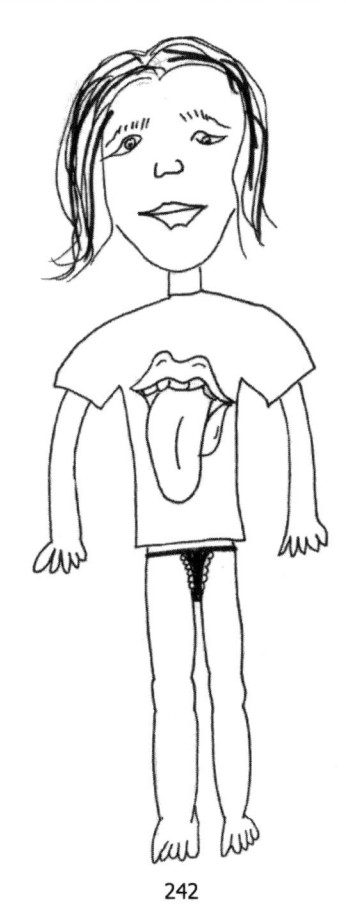

Val d'Isère

French bistro dining v. Karen and nachos.

Le Petit Danois is the après ski bar of choice in Val d'Isère if live music is your thing. Actually it's a great place even if live music isn't your thing. It has tasty, reasonably priced burgers and a load of pool tables. It's an excellent place for making new friends. Nowadays it's about the only venue in Val d'Isère that has live music most evenings. No wonder my friends and I were drawn to it, and to continue to be so. It's an archetypal après with a happy hour, free shots, audience participation. Then there's Fax Red Erik 6.5% imported Danish beer. And Karen.

The first time I went into Le Petit Danois I was in a group of four male friends. We were actually on a mission to sample the finest dining that Val d'Isère had to offer and it didn't disappoint. On this particular evening we were booked in to 1789, the year of the storming of the Bastille, a very French bistro serving some really cool gourmet food such as foie gras and snails and so on. We were looking for a quiet pub for a drink or two and found the Danois tucked away up a side street. It looked very welcoming from the outside so we popped inside for a pint. Whoop, whoop! Live music! Karen Ystén and her guitar were in full swing and it was sounding great. So we had two pints, then a couple of shots, then Karen took a break so we said, "Hello," like you do. Well, like we do. But we can chat, and so can Karen, so we had another pint and another shot, then decided to stay for the second half even though it meant running to 1789.

We hadn't factored in an encore. I looked at my watch. Just one more pint and another shot. Then Karen came over and had a drink with us. "WE NEED TO GO!" I exclaimed.

There was no sign of movement. We were now going to be late. I asked Karen how late could one be for a table in Val d'Isère before it's given to someone else. "Not very," she replied. "1789 is very popular." I managed to extract one of my friends and left the other two behind sitting at a table with our new favourite singer and the two of us charged down the road.

Le patron at 1789 wasn't too impressed with our being twenty minutes late, neither was he too enamoured that we were two and not four as booked. We said that the other two would probably turn up shortly but he replied with a rude French word that means something like "tough" if we're being polite and separated our table into two doubles. The other was soon occupied but not by our friends. We ordered aperitifs, a bottle of St Emilion and the Frenchest menu items we could find.

We dined on *os à moelle et ses toasts* that translated as marrow but the *os* bit wasn't so my friend was surprised to find a hunk of hollowed out bone turn up on his plate. I had *les cuisses de grenouilles* (frogs' legs). We feasted on *la potée Savoyard* which is a Savoyard speciality that includes pork knuckle, bacon, sausage, cabbage, carrots, turnip, potatoes and chestnuts. We then had a cheese platter washed down with a couple of *digestifs*. We were surprised to find vegetarians and vegans were catered for, sort of. They had one dish (unnamed) - *selon l'humeur du chef* (according to the chef's mood). Probably a lettuce leaf, ha, ha, and that's if his mood is good. As for a bad mood...

We had had a fantastic meal! We paid the bill and crawled back to the Danois to find our friends. They weren't difficult to find. They were at the same table, still with Karen, having not moved an inch. There was a bottle of toffee vodka in front of them. It was empty. "We've just had an amazing meal!" I told them. "And you two have been black-listed. We had marrow, frogs' legs, Savoyard specialities, cheese and biscuits, apéritifs, digestifs and a bottle of St Emilion. What have you had to eat?"

A few plates of nachos? So much for a week of fine dining! But we had made a new friend and every year we go back to Val d'Isère and we meet up with Karen and her husband, Uffe. As for 1789, we haven't been back. But we will go again, just not the night that Karen's playing Le Petit Danois.

Vercland

If gondolas could talk.

My boyfriend and I had been going out for a few years when I finally managed to get him to go skiing. I had skied every year with my parents when I was younger but since meeting Pete we tended to go somewhere hot for our holidays - I was missing the Alps.

Pete was a non-skier. He said that he didn't fancy snow for a holiday and that was that but I didn't give up. I told him that the Alps could be very warm; plenty of people go to ski resorts without skiing and it was very romantic up in the mountains. Finally he relented. He said that he would pay his way but that I could organise the trip and there was no way he was going to get into a lift of any description.

I settled on Vercland (Samoëns, 800m), part of le Grand Massif but very quiet in the evenings. Just right for Pete to maybe think about where he could take our relationship without being distracted by work and our always being out in the evenings back at home. Some amorous evenings were just the ticket I decided and who knows what might happen and what question might just be popped? I intended to make sure that something did, and something did indeed but not the way I could have imagined in my wildest dreams.

We stayed in a small boutique hotel near the lift. It was delightful. Everything was perfect. In the morning we would get the bus into Samoëns, then I would go off and do a bit of skiing then come back to meet Pete for a coffee then repeat for lunch before finding somewhere busy for après before a shower, a lovely meal and, um, whatever. However

I didn't seem to be getting too far in advancing the *amour* and was beginning to feel a little despondent. Pete was having a great time but that wasn't the main reason for the trip as far as I was concerned.

Halfway through the week Pete suddenly announced that he was feeling brave and would be happy to go up in a lift with me. I didn't need telling twice. At Vercland the lifts comprised some tiny gondolas that were referred to as "eggs" by some of the locals. (I have since found out that they had gained iconic status by skiers in the Grand Massif and were quite famous. When they were commissioned in the 1970s they were considered futuristic objects. They were last used in 2020 before being superseded by the Grand Massif Express.) There were supposed to seat four. The egg would open and in you jumped before it closed up again. There was no door as such - the sides would part. Once inside you would sit with knees touching the person opposite. I made sure that we were going to be the only two in our egg then we jumped in once I had put my skis in the outside rack. No sooner had we left the station than Pete was on his feet despite the, "No standing inside the gondola while in motion" sign. "I don't like it!" he whimpered. I stood up too and gave him a gentle kiss. "Mind your head and sit down, it'll soon be over," I reassured him gently as I remembered my first ski lift and my thinking that the cable was going to snap at any moment despite the fact that cables don't just snap due to the way that they're made. Pete sat down. I could see that he had gone quite white in the face and his hands that were gripping his knees were trembling. "I can't do it!" he muttered. "Pull the alarm! Speak to someone!" "There's no alarm and no one to speak to darling," I said. "If the lift stopped then what would we do?" "Jump!" he blubbed.

I sat quietly just wishing the ride would soon be over although I wasn't sure what was going to happen once we got off as there were only two ways down and one was on skis which he didn't have. Suddenly and without warning he stood straight up and very quickly. This was a big mistake on his part or was it intentional? His head hit the thick curly metal bar above us in the cabin. In its entirety it was the shape of an upside down question mark that held the gondola to the cable; he had head-butted the curling bit in the middle. He crumpled to the floor and I screamed. His eyes were shut and wouldn't respond to my calling his name. For some reason I now searched (in vain) for an alarm. "Oh gondola, what shall I do?" I sobbed. Then Pete opened his eyes and I had my answer and another one beside. "Oh hi Jackie," he said, sounding a little confused. "Where am I?" "On a ski lift in France," I replied. "Oh," he said, "Whereabouts in France? What happened?" I seized the moment. "You stood up a bit too quickly and knocked yourself out, but don't worry, it was for less than ten seconds but we will get you checked out as soon as possible. In the meantime the answer's, 'Yes!'" I bent down and gave him a kiss on the top of his head. Pete was frowning. "This may sound a bit odd, but what's the question?" "Oh darling," I replied, giving his hair a stroke and finding quite a big bump that was rapidly developing, "You had just asked me to marry you!" "Did I?" he replied. "I was, um, probably I think certainly thinking about asking you on this holiday but I don't remember..." "So are you retracting?" I asked. "Oh no, no, no!" he said, "No, not at all. That's lovely. Oh thank you. You have just made me the happiest man in the world!" "And you have made me the happiest woman!"

By now we had reached the top of the lift and the walls were about to part. "Sit up on the seat," I commanded, "or you'll fall through!" He wouldn't have done as the floor is a solid plate but it made him move. I jumped out and Pete dazedly followed. Sensing something may be a little awry, a lift attendant came over and took Pete's arm. He asked in French if everything was okay. I gabbled away in English that yes it was then told him that Pete had asked me to marry him whilst on the lift and I had accepted and then he had knocked himself out but he was okay now but he should be checked over as he was a bit concussed and so we would go back down in the lift and find a doctor. The lift attendant was having none of it. He told us to come and sit in the first aid cabin while he summoned help.

Two years later we were married and now, thirty-two years later, we are still married and we have two wonderful children. Pete has kept me the happiest woman on earth even though I had to put words into his mouth whilst he was temporarily unconscious. How despicable! How different things might have been if gondolas could talk. Fortunately they can't and neither will I, not to Pete anyway but I'm sure that if you do he will forgive me. I love you Pete with all my heart - don't be cross!

Wengen

A big stink in the gents' toilet.

Wengen, a beautiful car-free resort surrounded by the dramatic Jungfrau mountain, is a resort that my family will never be able to go to again - particularly one restaurant and specifically my husband.

I had chosen Wengen for my family as my two children weren't quite teenagers and although they were competent skiers I was attracted by all the family-orientated activities including skating and a trip to Top of Europe which is a high-altitude building that is reached via the Jungfraujoch railway. There's an even mix of all the various grades of run to keep everyone happy.

Day one of every ski holiday always involves my husband looking for some of the more out-of-the-way pistes as he's always going on about ski school getting in his way and reckons that, as they don't go very far from base to start with, we should be able to avoid them by doing the opposite. We went miles; for all I know we were in Grindelwald which is linked to Wengen to make a huge ski area. We ended up on a slope that was very quiet and for a while I thought we were the only people on it. The weather was atrocious and it took us ages to get anywhere because we couldn't see beyond the ends of our noses. We didn't know where we were and so had to rely on the marker poles on either sides of the piste and making sure that we were between them and not with both on the right or both on the left. My children were complaining that they were very cold. My son said that his goggles, "...aren't working properly," and my daughter just wanted to go back to the hotel, probably something to do with the fact that she had found that it had a swimming pool. My husband was complaining that he could really do with going to the toilet and when I said that he might as well have a pee at the side of the piste he curtly informed me, "It's more serious than that."

We inched our way down this piste with me complaining that if we didn't get to the bottom soon I would 'phone the piste attendants and request a rescue.

Finally a building through the snow storm hove into view. My husband's first words were, "It looks a bit posh," and we were on a bit of a budget however he had said just a few minutes earlier that we could stop at the first place we came to so that was that. In any case, he had some business to attend to and I told him that whatever we had to eat or drink it would be cheaper than a helicopter rescue.

Once inside this beautiful old building that turned out to be a restaurant I was surprised to find quite a few people milling around. I can only imagine that there was a lift or skidoo service as hardly anyone had passed us on the piste. It was a bit late for elevenses and a little early for lunch but I usually had a bit of spare capacity in my stomach and today was no exception. We sat down at a very welcoming table that was made up for lunch with cotton napkins, loads of glasses, decorations and a candle - you get the idea. My husband said that he wasn't at all hungry and had gone off in search of the toilet. Whilst he was absent a waiter came over and pressed a menu in my hand. I was more interested in the wine list and so flicked through that instead. I was pleased to discover that the restaurant boasted over one thousand wines. I was beginning to feel quite at home. A large log fire was burning away and over a very large gin and tonic I wondered if the other customers had been there since the day before and had simply decided not to go home. With my husband failing to reappear I ordered a bottle of wine and some nibbles.

Whilst we were waiting for them to be served my husband suddenly appeared but instead of coming over to our table he went straight up to our waiter and then there was a load of pointing and then another man went over to talk to them. My husband disappeared back towards the toilets with both the waiter and the other man. After a couple of minutes all three emerged and my husband came up to our table looking very flustered. He told us that we had to leave just as our wine and nibbles arrived. I said that I intended to finish my gin and tonic, then drink my wine and eat my nibbles first but my husband said that we all had to go "Now! And leave the drinks and food." I didn't move. When my husband repeated what he had just said I told him how much the wine had cost and then he looked very cross and asked me why I couldn't have picked a cheaper bottle. "Because that was the cheapest bottle," I explained whereupon my husband told me to put the cork back in and shove it in my rucksack along with the nibbles, "...because we have to go now!" he repeated.

We did eventually get down the piste and had a cheaper, but quite late, lunch that took up most of the afternoon. It wasn't until we had finally managed to get the children off to bed that I found out what had happened. My husband said that the reality was that he had been beyond desperate for a number two and that is what he delivered in the restaurant toilet. Quite a large number two, in fact. However, when he had tried to flush his business away he couldn't because the water pressure appeared to be very low. He said that he tried a couple of times but the cistern was taking ages to refill and there was no loo brush. His pipeline was very, very stuck. In the end, when he reappeared, it was to do the right thing and inform the waiter and then the owner that his business was stuck. The only problem was my husband speaks not much French / German, certainly no poo French / German, only food and drink, and so the waiter and owner couldn't work out what the problem was. In the end my husband led them both into the toilet. The three of them crammed into my husband's cubicle; he lifted the lid and pointed at his enormous poo. The waiter and owner looked at it and then each other. "Watch," my husband said pointing and he pressed the flush button whereupon a cascade of water came down the bowl and took my husband's torpedo off on its onward journey. The waiter and owner looked at each other and shrugged their shoulders. The owner, said, "Gut gemacht, Herr," [well done sir] before hurrying back out.

Zell am See

A pac-a-mac hood causes confusion and chaos.

With only six days skiing available to my wife and me every year we were always determined to be out on the slopes come fine weather or foul. We always used to go away in January, it being the cheapest month to go to the Alps, with another couple but it also meant that one ran the risk of spending a week skiing in near zero visibility.

One year we went with our friends to Zell am See, a beautiful, medieval lakeside town in Austria. Sunday had been gloriously sunny but by Monday morning the cloud had come over and it had started to snow. We were trying not to be discouraged though. We went down to breakfast but sat forlornly at our table looking out of the window praying for the snow to stop. It didn't. In fact, every time we looked it seemed to be getting heavier.

"Come on!" I said. "We can do this."

We made sure that we were fully zipped and buttoned up before we left the boot room. My wife, for reasons best known to herself, wasn't wearing a woolly hat, she just had a furry hair band that would probably have kept her forehead warm but it didn't stop the hair on her scalp collecting snow so she spent much of the first part of the morning making a passable impersonation of a cartoon monk. We jumped on the TrassXpress gondola that made its way up the mountain. When we alighted we found a small complex of shops and bars. "Let's go and have a coffee and decide what we're going to do," my wife suggested. No one demurred.

We spent far too long over a single coffee in this packed establishment. The front door was shut and the windows were all steamed up. It was like an elevenses (more like tenses) après-ski. When we decided that we really were outstaying our welcome we zipped and buttoned up and headed out once more into the snow. I think we managed two bends in the piste before we sighted another café. No one said a word. We took off our skis and headed inside. It was equally rammed. It seemed that everyone had the same idea. Mostly English of course; everyone else was probably still tucked up in bed, shopping or in the spa. This time we had a coffee with a Danish on the side, so to speak. Again we all but outstayed our welcome before heading out once more into what was by now a blizzard.

Then my wife started to complain of a wet head. At the time it was very fashionable to wear one-piece ski suits and my wife had one of course. It made going to the loo even more of an effort than usual though as it meant, for females and men going for a number two, that one would have to unzip from neck to groin before emerging like an unpeeled banana in order to attend to the undergarments before finally getting down to business. However hers did have one advantage that she was just about to discover - a pac-a-mac hood: one of those flimsy plastic efforts that folds up into almost nothing and can be brought out in an emergency, as this indeed was. It was tucked away in her collar to which it was attached and held in place by a couple of poppers. It looked slightly incongruous; a beautiful violent pink ski suit with a skimpy plastic hood but it did the job.

After a few more corners and, being Austria, a couple more cafés / bars it was getting very close to what could just about be legitimately described as "lunchtime." We hadn't even managed one piste in its entirety but decided that if we went for lunch at that point then the weather might clear; otherwise we would possibly be skiing further down in the rain. We found a large piste-side restaurant and went inside. It was fairly quiet and I reckoned that not many skiers had yet made it this far down the slope. My wife, whose small bladder had been bombarded with coffee, coffee, coffee and a small beer that was anything but, headed down the steps in the middle of the restaurant to the subterranean toilets whilst my friends and I sat down at a table and began to look at the menu.

During a break in the conversation I suddenly had one of those uncomfortable feelings that something wasn't quite right. My wife had been gone rather a long time. Too long in fact. I knew that the all-in-one plus hood may have added a few extra seconds to the ablutions but not a full ten minutes. A man in a bright blue ski suit had followed my wife down the stairs shortly after her and had just emerged with a smile on his face. I noted where he was sitting in case I was suddenly called upon to provide a witness statement for the police over an alleged sexual malfeasance or worse.

When my friend suggested out loud that Susie had been gone rather a long time that was my cue to act. "Keep an eye on that guy," I said, pointing at the perpetrator on the other table, "whilst I go and find out whether she's still breathing." But as I stood up Susie appeared, slowly and methodically, up the stairs from her sunken convenience looking very sheepish. Evidently she had not been engaged in any untoward activity; at least if she had it was consensual. She sat down, unzipped her ski suit, wrapped the arms around her waist and sat down. I put an arm around her. "Why were you so long?" I asked. "And why's your hood all warm?" "Can we sit round the corner please?" she asked as she immediately got up and walked to the other side of the restaurant. The rest of us followed like lapdogs. There was the hint of gossip in the air.

"It's like this," she said, once we were tucking into our gulaschsuppe, "and it's all a bit embarrassing. But ho-hum. I was dying for a pee as you know. I went downstairs and there's a communal washing area. I went through into the ladies and into a cubical. You know how it is when you're desperate. I was literally jumping up and down whilst trying to unzip. I couldn't stop jumping because I knew that I would wet myself but I had to stop moving so that I could get hold of the zip. I was seconds away from a ski suit being soaked inside as well as out. I timed it to perfection. My urethra opened whilst I was still in the process of sitting down and goodness did I pee. I peed and peed and peed. Oh my goodness I'm surprised you didn't hear my scream of ecstasy. It was like..." "What happened?" I interrupted.

"I stood up with a huge grin on my face. When I say 'stood up' I was only partially successful because something was holding me down from behind." "That bright blue ski suit guy?" I suggested. "No, you idiot, listen. I craned my neck around and I couldn't believe it! My stupid friggin' pac-a-mac hood had managed to wrap itself over the toilet bowl like a demented Dutch cap and I had basically filled it up completely with my pee. Not a drop had gone into where it was supposed to go. I had to very slowly lift up one side of the hood and poke it carefully into the bowl whereupon the tsunami continued into its rightful place. I was then left with a stinking wet hood. I tied my ski arms round my waist and limped out into the washroom holding my piddling pac-a-mac by my fingertips away from my ski suit as much as I was able. I then sort of twisted it round to my front, shoved it under the soap dispenser, squeezed at least five shots of alpine meadow onto it and rubbed it well in. Next I turned the hot tap on it. Then, as I was holding it down in the Dyson thing and jigging up and down lest it melted, blue ski suit appeared. 'I don't know vhy you are bozzering doing zat,' he said with a puzzled look on his face. 'Az soon as you get outside it will be wet again.' 'Not with what I have just had in it,' I told him."

Somewhere in the world I like to think that there is a Dutchman who met an English woman in a communal washroom in a restaurant in Zell am See who was drying her hood and probably to this day is wondering what she had in it. I'm hoping he now knows the answer!

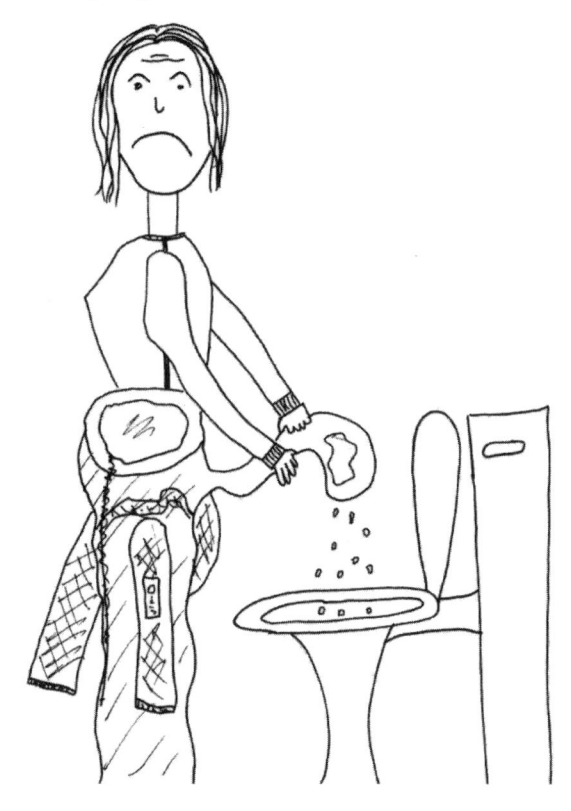

Zell am See

Pussy flugels hit the high notes.

One January, towards the end of the nineteen eighties, I went to Zell am See with my wife and best friend - that's two different people. My best friend's wife was in the advanced stages of pregnancy and so couldn't fly. She sent her husband, Charlie, along with my wife and me with her blessing. She thought that Charlie's usual approach to skiing with his own personal timetable of up by noon, ski for an hour, lunch, ski down to après, dinner, more après, would be severely curtailed and that he would be doing more skiing and less partying than ever before on a snow holiday. I was determined to show Charlie the error of his ways and that the comment, "There's some snow here somewhere," would not need to be uttered because he would be on it all morning and afternoon for at least seven hours each day.

As we sat on the transfer bus our rep., Ali, came round and introduced herself to us. "What's new?" Charlie asked. "Have you skied before?" "Yes." "Then the answer is nothing, that is apart from Red Bull." "And what is 'Red Bull?'" enquired Charlie. "You don't want to know. It's a so-called energy drink that's just been born in Austria and it's disgusting. Full of caffeine and sugar. It's the equivalent of goodness knows how many cups of coffee. Take it in the evening and you'll be up all night and then down all the following day and maybe even the day after. It gets worse though. Some bright spark has started throwing in a shot or two of vodka. Vodka Red Bull. You'll be up all night then both up and down all the following day and the day after. Don't touch it." I looked at Charlie. "Point taken," he said and nodded sagely. "That's my boy," I thought. He really had turned over a new leaf, however temporarily.

The first day we were on the slopes at a fairly reasonable ten o'clock. Charlie had been up for about half-an-hour and had grabbed a croissant as we left the hotel. Settled on the chair lift I asked him if he had had an early night. "Nope not all," he replied. "I went for a little walk and ended up in quite a lively bar. You should come along. What d'you think Helen?" "He can have one night out with you alone Charlie; why don't you save it up until the end of the week? We could all go out together somewhere more normal tonight." But Helen excelled herself at après ski and so had an early night on her own while Charlie dragged me off to his bar.

It was very quiet when we entered. It was that sort of dead time between après ski and party time when most ordinary people are having their dinner. We had eaten but the verb would more accurately be "scoffed." Charlie had already made his mark. "Hi Charlie," said the barman. "Who's your friend?" "James," I replied. We plonked ourselves down on a couple of bar stools. "Fancy a flugel?" asked Charlie. "You're going to have to list the ingredients first," I demanded gently. "Shot of vodka, shot of crème de cassis, couple of shots of Red Bull." "I'll have a beer please," I replied. "And so will I," said Charlie. "And a flugel." It was going to be a long night and it was - for Charlie. I left him around ten o'clock talking nineteen to the dozen like a wind-up chattering doll whose spring had jammed.

Fast forward several years. Charlie was now a father as was I. We had a lad's trip to Val d'Isère and flugels were back on the menu. We had the lowly Charlie and three of my friends, all international investment bankers who were working at very high levels within their individual departments. We started off at The Underground, a bar that is, well, underground on the main drag. It was the dead time of the evening again. "Get them in please James," Charlie demanded. "The guy here's French. We'll have flugels." I walked up to the bar and ordered five of the disgusting concoctions. Yes, I am a weak man. "C'est quoi - 'flugel'?" "C'est un shot de vodka, un shot de crème de cassis et un shot de Red Bull" I replied. "Ici pas de Red Bull, mais nous avons Pussy." Charlie's eye's lit up. (He doesn't speak French.) Seems like in France it's called Pussy. As an aside it's not only the French that have problems with drink names. Germany now has a beer that is named F*****g Hell, ostensibly named after a village in Austria that subsequently changed its name to Fugging, and Hell which is a German word for pale.

We consumed our French flugels, plus some more plus some beers then staggered up the stairs and into the main street. We crossed the road and sauntered up a side street to Dick's Tea Bar named after the eponymous Dick Yates-Smith who opened the jet-setting bar in the late nineteen seventies. We piled through the heavily sound-proofed door and into the presence of Mullit, one of the greatest contemporary alpine rock covers' bands who were just about to launch into something, well, loud. They took me straight back to the days of my youth when you could stand no more than a few feet away from the musicians, separated, in this instance, by a line of beer barrels across the front of the stage.

It was my round. I went up to the bar and in my best French ordered five flugels. "C'est quoi, 'flugel?'" This time I had it right. "C'est un shot de vodka, un shot de crème de cassis et un shot de, um, Pussy." The bartender shrugged her shoulders and went about her business with glasses, ice and the necessary ingredients. Ask for a shot in France and it more than likely won't be measured like they are nearly always done in the stingy UK. Probably they'll be poured - straight from the bottle into which has been inserted a long stainless-steel spout.

And that's how the evening progressed: flugels, more flugels and even more flugels. The music was intense and the place was packed. Marianne now knew the ingredients if not the measures. International investment bankers, more used to claret and gin and tonics, lost their keys, their coats and very nearly their minds as Mullit pounded their instruments playing such classics such as, "I Fought the Law." "I'm not fighting anyone," said international investment banker number one in a whisper; he found a quiet corner and gently collapsed.

No one made breakfast. Nor lunch. Surfacing began about four o'clock in the afternoon with Charlie appearing at the bar and ordering a flugel, "but one with no alcohol in it." "So, just Pussy?" suggested the barman. Charlie managed the faintest of smiles. When we were all finally together again, having been back to Dick's to retrieve lost property, Charlie said that he had an announcement to make.

"I would just like to make it clear that something went very wrong last night. I told you the ingredients of a flugel but not the measures. I thought that would be self-evident. Obviously not. Once we got into Dicks we were no longer drinking three shot short drinks. Instead each drink was HALF A FRIGGING PINT!" "That's a lot of Pussy," I groaned but it wasn't very funny then and it's not funny now. Still, it put me off energy drinks for life so some good came of it. Thanks Ali.

Zermatt

The bar that's not what it first appears to be.

From the moment I arrived in Zermatt I knew that I was going to love it! A charming, car free resort with loads of skiing. It's also possible to ski over into Cervinia in Italy by taking Trockener Steg cable car and then a couple of drags.

I was on holiday with my husband, Brian, and another couple, Michelle and Peter. Peter was having lessons so the three of us were left to our own devices each morning. One day we got up early and took the first lift to pop over to Cervinia. The run on the other side was wide and steep (red). We stopped at the first café for a couple of coffees by which time we had to start our return to meet Peter for lunch. We skied down to a cable car, went back to the ridge where we had started our descent and began our long return back to Zermatt on mostly reds.

We hadn't been going long when Michelle said that she needed to go for a wee and it was quite urgent. Brian said he was still thirsty and I was always ready for a bite to eat. Every time we reached a bend in the piste we thought that round the corner there would be a restaurant or bar. No such luck. On we skied, down and down until we came across a hamlet with probably no more than five or six buildings right on the edge of the piste. There were no garish signs or large groups of people but there was a drawing of a wine goblet on a sign that was stuck on a pole protruding up from the snow. "This'll do!" I shouted. Michelle jumped out of her skis and headed for the building with my husband and me following on behind. She opened the large wooden door, ornately carved and decorated with several wreaths, trinkets and bells. We found ourselves in a carpeted hallway. There was wallpaper on the walls and a number of pictures hanging. It felt ever-so-slightly different to the usual Alpine eatery with none of the hustle and bustle of people rushing to and fro with plates of food and drinks. I went off in search of food whilst my husband headed for another closed wooden door with BAR on it. At the end of the corridor I found a door with a glass window in it. I pushed it open and stuck my head inside. There were several people in what was a largish kitchen but not a load of food being prepared. "Excuse me," I asked, "but where is the restaurant please?" "No restaurant," came the unexpected reply. I turned and walked back along the hallway where I met my husband. "Weird bar," he said. "It was like a sitting room with children playing on the floor, doing puzzles and a load of women chatting. I asked them if I could have three beers but someone said, 'No drinks.' Most peculiar."

Then Michelle appeared, smiling and frowning in equal measure. Smiling because she had managed to satisfy her call of nature that had been on the verge of becoming a scream but frowning because the toilet was not what she had expected. "One loo with a stained glass window and a Bible on a small table. Most odd."

As we stood in the hallway wondering whether to walk or run out a lady appeared from nowhere. She was dressed simply and spoke softly. "May I help you?" she enquired in perfect English. "Yes, thank you," I replied. "We were just looking for a loo and something to eat and drink." "My child," she replied, clasping my hand in hers, "We can offer these items to pilgrims but they are not usually available to skiers." "And may I ask why that is?" I asked. "Yes," she said. "It is because we are a religious order. But you can join us for sext if you like." We declined her offer and ran.

We had a story for Peter that lunchtime. Michelle finished with a flourish, "...but then she wanted sex with us!" "'Sext,'" said Peter who had read Theology at university. "Sext: it's one of the ancient monastic Daily Offices like Matins and Evensong." "I still would have run," said Michelle.

The following day the three of us did the same piste again. When we reached the wine goblet there was a large group of skiers that had stopped and were gathered round it. As we skied past Brian shouted out, "It's a great bar, you should try it!"

Zürs

Helicopter accident above this fashionable resort.

My family came out here last Christmas when we rented a wonderful ski chalet with another family who are friends, in this high-end resort. Not only is it reassuringly expensive, it has its own biomass district heating. This means that the whole of the resort is fossil fuel free. Amazing.

We wanted to take our presents with us and as we were driving this meant that we could. It also meant we could buy what the children wanted rather than get them new clothes or equipment whilst we were out there. That said, our son, Jacob, had no idea what he wanted for a change so my husband suggested to me that we buy him a remote control helicopter. What I thought this meant was that my husband fancied having one but as I had no idea where to start I just said that that would probably be fine.

We had a superb morning's skiing on Christmas Day and then we came off the slopes early to open our presents. That's when I lost my husband. He had done well with his choices for me (a pearl necklace) and our daughter (she did want a new ski suit) but when it came to Jacob I wasn't too sure. However, all my worries melted away when he opened his gift to reveal a huge and reassuringly expensive (my husband told me later) remote control helicopter. My son's eyes lit up and I smiled inwardly as my husband's friend looked approvingly at his purchase. "I can't wait to get my hands on that!" he exclaimed so I had to remind him that it was Jacob's present and not his. I then had to stop both of them from helping Jacob put it together. It wasn't very difficult though; all he had to do was clip in the rotor blades and charge it up. Then there were a few minor things plus reading the instruction manual. My husband read all of it which must have been a first. Then he tried to read it in French. Goodness knows why. After that he decided to have a quiz with his friend based on the instructions. My friend and I went to bed.

We were staying in a large open-plan chalet so Jacob and the two fathers had great fun flying the helicopter around the sitting / dining room during breakfast. Then they had it going up and down the stairs. I had given my husband a new 'phone, a beautiful Samsung that was one 'phone with two screens; it was not at all cheap. However, although he likes a bit of tech, two items at once was obviously too much for him even though one wasn't his and he spent most of Boxing Day evening with his friend flying the stupid helicopter around some more. They finally put it to bed when it ran out of juice and needed a long charge. Only then did he turn his attention not to me but to the 'phone. He does like a bit of photography also so, with five cameras, he wasn't going to be disappointed. When he finally came to bed he found me dressed in no more than my pearl necklace. He jumped into bed and was soon fast asleep. Sigh.

We all went out skiing together the next day and my husband started really getting into the camera on his new 'phone. He took some great photos and videos that were so clear. In the evening in between loading up his 'phone with apps and whatever, with input from Jacob who was asked to more or less sort the 'phone out, he and his friend took it in turns to pretend they were drone operators scanning foreign lands (i.e. the coffee table) from thousands of miles away, playing with the helicopter that, quite frankly, was beginning to annoy me quite a bit. Then my husband said, "I have a brainwave!" This is always a bad sign. He said,

"How about if I attach my new 'phone to the runners on the bottom of the helicopter and start the video? Then we can power up the chopper and send it on a mission. It can film the magnificent view from on high." "The coffee table, the dining table and us," I reminded him. "It's a start," he replied. I yawned and so did my friend.

Once he had wrestled his 'phone back from Jacob the two men constructed a sort of wire basket shaped like those you get on hot air balloons and suspended it from the runners as my husband held the helicopter and his friend took the controls. Soon they were buzzing it around the chalet once more. When the helicopter finally landed the two men were beside themselves with excitement. My husband released his 'phone from the basket and they eagerly played back what had been recorded. It was actually quite impressive. They were talking animatedly about how they had got up close to the olive in my vodka martini when my husband's friend's eyes suddenly lit up. "What is it?" hubby asked. "Suppose we took the helicopter up the mountain tomorrow?" he suggested. I was having none of it. "It says in red letters on the box, 'indoor use only.'" "That's nothing," said my husband. "They just put that there to stop people being irresponsible with them outside near power lines and the like. But there aren't any power lines at the top of the Muggengrat [chair lift] so let's do it - tomorrow." "Don't lose it dad," said Jacob but he received no reply; the two men were already discussing how they were going to get the helicopter safely on the chair lift. In the end they just stuck it, poking out, in my husband's rucksack having taken the propellers off. My friend and I stood up and announced that we were going to bed. No response, they were too busy discussing which ski lift to take it on. "TOGETHER!" my friend added. Still no response. Oh dear. "Maybe we should go and find ourselves a couple of ski instructors," my friend suggested. I don't think she was entirely kidding.

The next day our group took the long chair out of Zürs and then onto the Muggengrat. At the top we all met at the side of the piste where it was relatively quiet. "This'll do," said my husband and out came the stupid helicopter, propellers and remote. He attached his 'phone to the wire basket, put the propellers back on and everything was checked over. Then he started the video recording. "We need to get a move on," said my husband, "as I'm expecting a call from work soon as my boss has gone back in to focus on the new financing for [large Plc] and I don't want to miss him just because we're flying a helicopter and filming some great videos." "Can I have the remote dad please?" asked Jacob. "No," said my husband and with that he pressed on the start button. The helicopter rose off his friend's hands. It was hovering about twenty feet in the air when my husband said, "Let's try a little forward direction." He pushed on the joystick and the helicopter rose some more and then started to move forward. "That's odd," he said, "it's supposed to be going forward only but it's going up as well." He pulled back on the joystick but the helicopter continued to move forward and up. "We'll be getting some good film," said his friend but my husband didn't respond. By now he was flicking the joystick forward and back, forward and back, then side to side, side to side, then round in a large circle but the helicopter was still moving forward and up at a forty-five degree angle. "Turn it off!" my husband's friend commanded. "It will crash but we can get it back and repair it." My husband looked at the helicopter and then down in a vain attempt to work out where it might land. "It looks like off piste," he said rather pathetically. "I would rather that than the head of someone who's on piste or walking round town," said his friend. "Good point, here goes." I noticed sweat pouring down my husband's face even though it was below freezing. He pressed on the off button. Nothing. The helicopter took no notice, forward and up it went, on and on and on. By now it was probably about a mile away and was but a small blob in the sky. "My new helicopter!" wailed Jacob. "My new 'phone and my career!" wailed my husband as the anarchic blob continued on its journey south towards St Anton.

That afternoon our two husbands and Jacob disappeared off into town whilst my friend and I did some more skiing with the other children. I was beyond annoyed when we arrived back at the chalet to find that my husband had been and bought another helicopter. This one was even bigger! "It's Chinese but just as good if not better than the other one. And we worked out what the problem was," he said. "The guy in the shop is an expert." After dinner he told me something along the lines of the radio signals in the first one were designed to bounce off walls and ceilings and therefore control the device. With no surfaces to bounce off, such as outside, it had no way of responding to controls. "So what's the point of buying a new one instead of just reimbursing Jacob?" I asked. "This new one's just going to do the same thing." "Oh no," he replied. "This one works by GPS. This also means that if the signal goes down it returns to home. I can programme it to return to outside the chalet. It will then return there if the GPS fails or I can preset it to override the controls once it's up in the air. All I have to do is input the co-ordinates. Look, I'll show you."

I think my husband was probably pleased that I then started to take an interest and let him show me how to set co-ordinates. He droned on and on about it but I was a model student. Finally he stood up and announced that he was going to bed as it had been a long and stressful day. Off he went and so did my friend's husband. "We'll be along in a minute," I said. "I'm just going to finish my wine." Once they were out of the room my friend and I looked at each other and smiled. We knew just what we had to do. We powered up the control box and pressed RESET before making a few adjustments. Then we went to find our snoring / boring husbands.

The following day was very much the same as before: we got on the same chair lift, went up the same mountain, found the same launch spot. The only difference was that this helicopter didn't have a camera. "Can I borrow your 'phone darling?" my husband asked. "No way!" I replied. I knew what was coming and I wanted to film the action.

Jacob asked if he could have a go this time. I think he was a little surprised when I said, "No!" He gave me a very strange look and rightly so.

The helicopter went up, up in the air. My husband jabbed at the controls just as before as it went south and then suddenly veered east. "What the..." my husband shrieked. "It's not responding!"

"Don't panic," said my husband's friend. "There's obviously a signal problem on this mountain. Remember it will work its way back to our chalet. We can ski back down and find it waiting for us there. Clever thing. Let's race it!"

I glanced over at my friend, she was smiling. She caught my eye and winked. They wouldn't be getting another one I calculated and we would soon be getting our husbands back once they realised that the second helicopter would not be returning to the chalet but was heading back towards - China.

***

Do you have a favourite ski story? Do let me know! Write to johnhemmingclark@gmail.com or dictate it on WhatsApp 07968 525692.

If you've enjoyed *If Gondolas Could Talk* please also leave an Amazon review. I would be very grateful. Find *If Gondolas Could Talk* at www.amazon.co.uk and scroll down to and click on "Write a customer review" then "Submit". Thank you.

Register to receive advance notification of the publication of the follow up book - and check out my other efforts - at

www.johnhemmingclark.com